VOLUME 6

THE COLLECTED WORKS OF ARTHUR SELDON

The Welfare State: Pensions, Health, and Education

THE COLLECTED WORKS OF ARTHUR SELDON

VOLUME 1	The Virtues of Capitalism
VOLUME 2	The State Is Rolling Back
VOLUME 3	Everyman's Dictionary of Economics
VOLUME 4	Introducing Market Forces into "Public" Services
VOLUME 5	Government Failure and Over-Government
VOLUME 6	The Welfare State: Pensions, Health, and Education
VOLUME 7	The IEA, the LSE, and the Influence of Ideas (includes an index to the series)

Arthur Seldon

VOLUME 6

THE COLLECTED WORKS OF ARTHUR SELDON

The Welfare State: Pensions, Health, and Education

ARTHUR SELDON

Edited and with a New Introduction
by Colin Robinson

LIBERTY FUND, Indianapolis

This book is published by Liberty Fund, Inc., a foundation established to encourage study of the ideal of a society of free and responsible individuals.

The cuneiform inscription that serves as our logo and as the design motif for our endpapers is the earliest-known written appearance of the word "freedom" (*amagi*), or "liberty." It is taken from a clay document written about 2300 B.C. in the Sumerian city-state of Lagash.

Printed in the United States of America

09 08 07 06 05 C 5 4 3 2 1
09 08 07 06 05 P 5 4 3 2 1

Library of Congress Cataloging-in-Publication Data

Seldon, Arthur.
The welfare state: pensions, health, and education / Arthur Seldon; edited and with a new introd. by Colin Robinson.
p. cm.—(Collected works of Arthur Seldon; v. 6)
Includes bibliographical references and index.
ISBN 0-86597-547-7 (alk. paper)—ISBN 0-86597-555-8 (pbk.: alk. paper)
1. Human services—Great Britain. 2. Welfare state—Great Britain. 3. Great Britain—Social Policy—1979– . I. Robinson, Colin, 1932– . II. Title.

HV248 .S45 2005
361.6'5'0941—dc22

2004063301

LIBERTY FUND, INC.
8335 Allison Pointe Trail, Suite 300
Indianapolis, Indiana 46250-1684

CONTENTS

INTRODUCTION

Volume six of The Collected Works of Arthur Seldon consists of eight articles and one book that set out Seldon's critique of state-provided welfare. They span a period of almost forty years, from 1959 to 1998. From the earliest article, the general lines of the critique become plain, and they are maintained consistently throughout Seldon's work, as he explains the development of the "welfare state."

The welfare state, says Seldon, cannot in the long run be the solution to the problem of poverty. It is driven by misguided egalitarian views that make it universalist, providing "benefits" for the middle classes as well as for the needy instead of concentrating on those who genuinely require help. State-provided welfare suffers from the same problems as do other state activities. Because it finances welfare through the tax system, it damages incentives to work; it also diminishes incentives to save for the future, to provide for medical and other emergencies, to educate, and generally to provide for one's family, as the state appears to take over such responsibilities. Moreover, the administrative costs associated with the accompanying bureaucracy are invariably excessive compared with the competing costs of private provision.

Another significant argument that Seldon stresses throughout his work is that, once the state begins to provide "free" welfare services, such provision becomes very difficult to stop. State welfare may appear to be justified as a temporary expedient but, as people's incomes rise, Seldon says that most people should be capable of providing for their family needs. The welfare state should decline relative to incomes, and perhaps absolutely, as those incomes increase. But state welfare provision is, by its nature, self-perpetuating: governments are invariably reluctant to let go. Seldon quotes, with approval, in several articles the prophetic words of the famous British economist, Alfred Marshall, who told the 1893 Royal Commission on the Aged Poor that he disapproved of universal pensions schemes because "they do not contain, in themselves, the seeds of their own disappearance. I am afraid that, if started, they would tend to become perpetual."[1] Seldon argues that, had people known early in the twentieth century when the British welfare state was conceived that incomes would rise so much, they might have found a better way of dealing with poverty than supplying the "crutch" of the welfare state. A crutch, Seldon says, is a useful device for helping those with broken limbs, but it is a hindrance once that limb becomes healthy. The crutch of the welfare state, which leads to unnecessarily high taxes, poor incentives for savers, and damage to the family, is not easily removed.

The first article in this volume was written in 1959 for the journal *Time and Tide,* which had a section titled "Notes on the Way" in which guest authors were encouraged to express radical ideas. An editor hoping for such views must have been pleased with Seldon's contribution, which contends that the welfare state must be removed as "wealth grows and spreads" or it will "impair the abilities it helped to nurse." The article, titled "The Reluctant Crutch: Replace the Repressive State by the Liberating Market," is the first publication in which Seldon uses the crutch as a simple analogy to reveal the essence of the problem of state welfare. He puts it as follows: "A crutch helps a broken leg to heal, but once the leg is healed the crutch gets in the way; and if it is kept too long, the leg will never learn to walk again." Keeping the welfare state too long means that it becomes "a vast, wasteful, futile machine for taking money out of people's pockets and putting it back into their purses, with a large slice for administrative drones sucked up on the way." The aim should be to replace state provision by markets, gradually withdrawing state assistance.

Seldon points to the expense of state welfare provision and the scope for cutting taxes if the role of the state were reduced. He proposes no communal provision of new services that people could provide for themselves: in particular, the proposals being put forward (at the time he wrote, in 1959) for a new compulsory pension scheme should be scrapped, because most people are increasingly able to save for themselves. People deserve to hear that, as state subsidy is lost, taxes can be reduced. Thus, "people will gain for they will be exchanging a crutch for a healthy limb." The politicians ought to be preparing the way.

1. Alfred Marshall, *Official Papers,* Macmillan, 1926, quoted in Arthur Seldon, *Pensions for Prosperity,* IEA, 1960 (the second paper in this volume).

Article two in this volume, *Pensions for Prosperity* (IEA Hobart Paper 4), written in 1960, concentrates specifically on pensions. In his foreword to the paper, Oscar Hobson, arguably the foremost financial journalist of his day, writes that Seldon "throws down a challenge to all the old-fashioned dogmas of welfare statism" (p. 9).

Seldon begins from the comment by Alfred Marshall, quoted above, about how state pension schemes are likely to become perpetual. He points out that, in Britain, private provision preceded state provision, and he goes back to first principles to show that private provision is inherently superior. For example, investment managers in private companies are likely to be more effective in pursuit of the interests of pensioners than "the directors, managers and professionally trained advisers of a State Investment Authority, exposed to political pressures and departmental jostling and without the stimulus, the discipline or the measuring rod of competition" (p. 23–24). In practice, argues Seldon, the British state pension scheme has been characterized by "uncertainty, unpredictability and capriciousness" (p. 24). It has discriminated against the needy: it "distributes bread to people with cake and denies a second loaf to those with only one" (p. 11). It has piled up deficits as politicians have succumbed to pressures to make general increases in payments. These problems will not be solved, he says, by introducing the "graduated" pension schemes (second state pensions, with contributions varying with income), which both the Conservative and Labour Parties favored at the time he wrote.

According to Seldon, a new approach is required that moves away from the prevailing philosophy of state dependence but that gives help to those (and only those) who genuinely require it, recognizing that the number of needy will decline over time as affluence spreads. The purpose should be to allow "every man and woman to live *without* assistance from others; and the role of assistance should be not to replace but to fertilise, nurture and hasten independence" (p. 41). He then sets out a detailed program for a gradual transition from dependence to independence in place of the government's scheme, which was "conceived in fear, composed in haste, adopted in ignorance" (p. 47). Seldon's fundamental reform plan would start by repealing the latest legislation, the 1959 National Insurance Act; it would encourage private provision for retirement in place of the state scheme; and it would wind up national insurance over a period.

Article three is a very explicit and penetrating attack on the "universalist" principle that underlies the welfare state. "The Future of the Welfare State" was first published in *Encounter* in 1967 and twice reprinted elsewhere.[2] The views of the universalists who want "social benefits to be equal and shared by all" are "inhumane," writes Seldon, because "equal treatment of people in unequal circumstances is not equality" (p. 59). He asserts that the state will not be able to raise sufficient revenues to satisfy the universalist principle and that, in any case, it is "foolishly wasteful" to hand state aid to the whole population when only "10%, or 15%, or 20% . . . need it" (p. 54).

The role of the state in welfare, says Seldon, is "not to organise and provide welfare but give the purchasing power to people without it, and perhaps to lay down minimum requirements for buyers and minimum standards for sellers" (p. 53). He sets out a program of reform, in stages, that would give more to people in need, provide everyone with choice, increase welfare, and reduce taxation. The longer this fundamental reform is delayed, he emphasizes, "the more convulsive the upheavals when change is enforced by rising incomes, growing social aspirations, and overseas example" (p. 63).

In the fourth article, Seldon turns his attention to one of the most distinctive features of the British welfare state, the National Health Service (NHS). *After the NHS* is IEA Occasional Paper 21, published in 1968, and subtitled *Reflections on the Development of Private Health Insurance in Britain in the 1970s.* It started life as a paper prepared for a conference in Australia on voluntary health insurance, but there are some additional thoughts, in an epilogue, about international experience of state and private medicine. In his foreword to the paper, Ralph Harris notes Seldon's isolation in his crusade against state welfare: "[he] has fought at times almost single-handed against political complacency and all-party conservatism to compel reconsideration of the assumptions on which universalist welfare policies were perched" (p. 68).

Published on the twentieth anniversary of the founding of the NHS, the article starts by reviewing the state of the NHS, pointing out "its major emerging disadvantage, that the state has been unable to raise enough tax revenue to provide medical care at rising standards" (p. 72). British politicians have been out of touch with public preferences for health care, says Seldon. "The method of the polling booth does not suffice" (p. 79): a market is indispensable if preferences are to be revealed. He goes on to explain how a market in health care could and should be established, with private insur-

2. In Robert Schuettinger, ed., *The Conservative Tradition in European Thought,* Putnam, 1970, and in Hardy Bouillon, ed., *Do Ideas Matter? Essays in Honour of Gerard Radnitzky,* The Centre for the New Europe, 2001.

ers having the primary role but with the state acting "as a long-stop for the exceptionally chronic, the exceptionally costly, and the exceptionally poor" (p. 95). He ends on a note that has echoes in his later writings about welfare: "People in countries with widely differing but rising incomes seem to want more *individuality* in medical care (and in other welfare services) to go with their expanding choices in ordinary everyday or household consumption. . . . The days of a 'free,' tax-financed NHS are numbered" (p. 103).

The fifth work in this volume is a short book, *The Great Pensions "Swindle,"* published in 1970[3] with a very specific purpose—to draw attention to and to explain the implications of "the massive inflation of state pensions" (p. 115) proposed in the 1969 National Superannuation and Social Insurance Bill. The word "swindle" was not Seldon's: it had been used by politicians of both major parties when referring to each other's pension proposals. As Seldon points out, "the very practice of presenting 'national insurance' as insurance rather than as a form of taxation . . . is objectionable because it is deceitful. That is the source of the national insurance 'swindle'" (p. 128).

The book begins with an open letter to Richard Crossman, then minister for social services, who is criticized for not consulting the public about his scheme and for not explaining to the public its implications—for instance, that it is a means of "reshaping the social, economic, political and moral framework of society" (pp. 113–14) and that it is likely to ensure that, instead of people having occupational schemes,[4] they will become wholly dependent on the state on retirement. There is, says Seldon in chapter one, something wrong with a political system that legislates for "a universally compulsory method of saving for retirement which few except several score actuaries, civil servants and politicians understand, which would be rejected on principle by the mass of the citizenry, and which is unsuited to the social order for which it is framed" (p. 118).

In the rest of the book Seldon explains in detail why the origin of the proposed new scheme is the government's need for more money that it can raise openly through general taxation and why the scheme has nothing to do with normal principles of "insurance." He goes back to the origins of the welfare state to reveal the errors that were made, and he exposes the fallacies in the

3. Seldon summarized the conclusions of the book in an article in the *Daily Telegraph* that is reprinted as "The Great Pensions Swindle," in *The State Is Rolling Back* (volume 2 of these Collected Works).

4. Occupational schemes are private schemes provided by an employer to which both employee and employer contribute.

Crossman scheme, which is just "one more effort to pass the buck to the future" (p. 214). Returning to the arguments he used in *Pensions for Prosperity* (article two in this volume), Seldon argues that, instead of Crossman's dangerous move toward centralization and government control, fundamental reforms are required to encourage voluntary provision for retirement, with the gradual winding up of compulsory national insurance.

Article six returns to general arguments against state provision of welfare services. *Wither the Welfare State,* originally a lecture, was published by the IEA in 1981 as Occasional Paper 60, its title indicating Seldon's view that in the long run the welfare state will wither away: the only way it could be maintained would be by a degree of government coercion the electorate would not tolerate.

In this paper, Seldon looks back at a century of the welfare state—a "wrong turning." He marshals the latest statistics to demonstrate how it has gone awry and the extent to which people are escaping from the uniformity it imposes as it attempts to create "equality by coercion" (p. 237). Welfare services would have developed in a better fashion, he claims, if the government had not intervened to provide compulsory state education, medicine, housing, and pensions. The welfare state is supported both by false ideas and by vested interests. It embodies not seven but eight deadly sins, which Seldon identifies. Eventually, it will wither away because "it will be increasingly difficult to attempt equality when supply and demand facilitate diversity" (p. 261). "We cannot depend on a government of any party to liquidate the welfare state as an act of patriotism or in response to public preferences. In the end it will be market forces that will make the welfare state yield to private choice and technical advance" (p. 263).

Articles seven and eight had their origins in a symposium in the October 1994 issue of the IEA's journal *Economic Affairs,* for which Seldon was guest editor. The articles in the symposium were turned into a book, IEA Readings 45, published in 1996, titled *Re-privatising Welfare: After the Lost Century,* which Seldon edited and introduced with a preface. "The lost century" refers to a phrase of Michael Beenstock's that indicates that private markets in health, unemployment, and other benefits were developing late in the nineteenth century, before the state crowded them out by imposing its own form of "social" insurance. This idea—that a whole century was lost because of misguided and damaging government intervention—neatly encompasses Seldon's views on the subject of social insurance.

In addition to his preface, Seldon made two contributions to the book, both of which are reprinted in this volume. The first is his chapter on pensions, "Pensions Without the State," and the second is his final, summary chapter, "The Verdict of History."

"Pensions Without the State" starts by reviewing Seldon's earlier work on the subject, showing how voluntary saving by all income groups began in the nineteenth century and continued through the twentieth century. The extension of the state pension in 1948 began a "damaging conflict" between the "growing savings habits of the people" and the political process and forced people to pay the fraudulently described "National Insurance contributions" (p. 272). It would have been better if markets had been allowed to discover "new methods of preparing for comfortable retirement" (p. 274). Seldon points out that he had for forty years been urging fundamental reform, with a move to mainly private provision, but governments of both major political parties had failed to take notice. The lesson of history is that "pensions cannot be left to the political process with its short-time horizons and its temptation to tax or borrow to disguise its inability to create the welfare services the people would prefer" (p. 275).

"The Verdict of History" is not just a summary of *Re-privatising Welfare;* it is an excellent, succinct account of Seldon's views on the deficiencies and dangers of the welfare state after decades of consideration and argument. The welfare state, he says, is a "political artefact [with] its origins . . . in the party politics of the Victorian era" (p. 279). It may seem to have some achievements to its credit but the opportunity cost has been huge. Any benefits have come about through the application of massive resources that could have been used in other ways: the true cost has been the "better welfare it suppressed" (p. 280). The probability is that, without the welfare state, markets would have continued to evolve to provide, inter alia, education, health care, pensions, housing, and unemployment insurance, tailored to meet the demands of individuals. State welfare has suppressed experimentation by monopolizing welfare services. Furthermore, it has been socially divisive for the middle and the working classes, the latter having to "content themselves with what they are given by the state" (p. 282).

The obstacles to change, says Seldon, are fundamentally political. Governments are unwilling to reveal the imperfections of state-provided welfare by opening it up to competing private "methods of production" (p. 284). But consumers will nevertheless find means of escape as they become increasingly unwilling to tolerate second-class services: "If the political process cannot produce modernised welfare services because it is prevented by ideological faith in the state, by bureaucracy, and by vested interests, the market process will replace it" (p. 285).

The ninth, final work in this volume is a contribution to a book, *The Retreat of the State* (Canterbury Press, 1998), which reprinted the 1998 Launcelot Fleming Lectures,[5] sponsored by Norwich Cathedral and the University of East Anglia. The lectures addressed the issue of whether the state had become too big and should retreat. There were four distinguished lecturers: Lord (Nigel) Lawson, former chancellor of the exchequer; Rev. Michael Taylor, former director of Christian Aid; Lord (David) Owen, former foreign and commonwealth secretary and leader of the Social Democratic Party; and Arthur Seldon.

Seldon's chapter in the book, "The Retreat of the State in Social Welfare," begins by emphasizing the "excesses of the democratic state" (p. 290). Governments are not all-seeing, impartial, and efficient: they tend to yield to those who importune most, not to the most deserving. Seldon argues that governments should return purchasing power to people and free prices so that genuine consumer preferences will be revealed. But the state has advanced so far into people's lives that it finds retreat difficult.

Even if the government does not retreat voluntarily, says Seldon, state welfare will be rejected (and, indeed, already is being rejected) by individuals and families. State services will always be short of the tax funds required to raise their standards. People will rebel against mediocre services. Rising incomes will permit them to pay for private services by fees or insurance; advances in technology are providing tailor-made services to replace the standardized state variety; resistance to higher taxes is increasing; and various means of escape from state services are opening up (for example, the revival of barter).

As in all his writings, Seldon sees hope in the prospect of a consumer revolt that will restore the market. A government may imagine it is immovable, but it can be bypassed by consumers and will eventually have to retreat from social welfare and other "superfluous functions." He ends the article:

> But it is retreating too slowly. The subjects are rebelling. And they will continue to rebel until government retreats sufficiently to liberate the freedoms created by economic advance. (p. 303)

5. Launcelot Fleming was Bishop of Norwich in the 1960s.

THE RELUCTANT CRUTCH

REPLACE THE REPRESSIVE STATE
BY THE LIBERATING MARKET

The Reluctant Crutch

Difficult as it was fifty years ago to construct the Welfare State as we know it, it looks like being even more difficult to dismantle. The case for dismantlement hardly needs restatement. In the perspective of social history the Welfare State is a temporary expedient designed to accelerate the transition from poverty to self-support. It must, therefore, be removed as wealth grows and spreads. If not, it will impair the abilities it helped to nurse.

Moreover, since the cost is borne increasingly by those who benefit, it becomes a vast, wasteful, futile machine for taking money out of people's pockets and putting it back into their purses, with a large slice for administrative drones sucked up on the way.

Although the case is clear enough, the reasoning behind it will need to be employed assiduously if it is to be seen for the common sense in it. The metaphor of the crutch is perhaps the easiest way to drive it home. A crutch helps a broken leg to heal, but once the leg is healed the crutch gets in the way; and if it is kept too long, the leg will never learn to walk [again]—(at all).

This does not mean that the need for all forms of State assistance or paternalism will gradually shrink; some will continue for decades, and there may be new ones. But they will be outnumbered by those which become superfluous. The *content* of State welfare will change, but its *size* will shrink, certainly in relation to the rising national income, but also perhaps absolutely.

In terms of economic machinery, the aim must be to replace the State by the open market. Instead of paying for doctors and medicines, for schools and universities, for unemployment insurance and for pensions by taxes, we shall get them in the open market and pay as we buy, or anticipate payment by insurance.

Of course, the process must be performed slowly in order to minimise disturbance and hardship. As the need for help falls away, State assistance can gradually be withdrawn; some people will still need help or guidance by 1980. But the process cannot wait until everyone can dispense with help. Patients with broken legs that have healed do not have to carry crutches until the last leg in that ward has healed. We cannot wait until every man can afford to buy medicines and education and life assurance out of income before all the rest are allowed to do so.

It is not sensible to wait until every parent is a paragon before permitting any parent more freedom in education. Social welfare and good government do not require that the best shall be judged and treated as the worst.

Politicians may shrink from such a reversal in the attitude to social reform that has dominated English political thought. But those who do have forgotten that the Welfare State is becoming a system of double entry bookkeeping. For every communal service enlarged or added, a tax has to be raised or begun.

Conversely, for every free or subsidised service that is reduced or withdrawn, a tax could be removed or cut. If, say, every parent whose income was high was required to begin the de-crutching process in education by paying 2s. 6d. per week for each child in a State school or 2s. 6d. for each visit to a National Health Service doctor, a cut could be made in a tax that, as nearly as possible, benefits them—perhaps a reduction in the income tax, or purchase tax, or in the tobacco or beer taxes.

The more the two sides of the account are seen to be intimately linked, the faster the public understanding of the process and the greater the welcome for it.

There is a long way to go. As taxpayers we paid in 1957 £2,200 million in income tax, £710 million on tobacco, £480 million in purchase tax, £420 million on beer, wines and spirits, £330 million on petrol and oils, and £660 million in National Insurance and Health contributions. Out of these and lesser taxes we recovered £1,140 million in National Insurance, pensions and assistance, £890 million in education, child care, school meals, milk and welfare foods, £690 million in health services, £400 million in housing, and other amounts in the lesser services.

In all, the social services cost about fifteen per cent of the national income (over £3,000 million—out of some £19,000 million). In perhaps twenty-five years, when personal incomes are doubled, the proportion may need to be no higher than five per cent, and it might be possible to reduce the proportion of the national income taken in taxation from its present thirty per cent to fifteen per cent.

One thing is quite clear: it would be wrong to plan the communal provision of *new* services which people are increasingly able to provide for themselves. The outstanding example here is retirement income. By personal saving, by life assurance and annuities, and by contributions to occupational pension schemes, people are providing out of income for retirement. We should rejoice at the urge to independence after a life of work.

Yet we are now proposing to embark on a new compulsory State pension scheme that must impair the ability and the willingness of many, especially wage earners, to save voluntarily. The pretext that it is necessary in order to plug the gap in the existing pension scheme is too flimsy to be taken seriously. Democracy is taking a wrong turning.

The most stubborn problems may be the political one of giving the people a lead, the administrative one of arranging the changes so that the disturbance and hardship will be minimised (they will not be entirely prevented), and the public relations tasks of showing that for every loss of subsidy there will be a gain in tax, that on balance the people will gain for they will be exchanging a crutch for a healthy limb.

Above all, the need is to reorientate thinking on the social services. Nassau Senior and Alfred Marshall laid down the right line many years ago. It is now being taken up by liberal economists in this and other countries. The gains in personal and civic dignity, political stability, and economic prosperity that would accompany the transition from dependence to independence are clear.

Economists, actuaries, administrators and social workers have yet to work out ways and means. It is for the politicians to prepare the way.

PENSIONS FOR PROSPERITY

FOREWORD

The common assumption underlying the *Hobart Papers* is that rising incomes are creating greater scope for policies that permit wider freedom of choice in personal life. They do not automatically solve all social or economic problems; they require to be accompanied by changes in the legal and institutional framework of society in order that the *opportunities* they present may be translated into reality.

Fifty years ago poverty among old people led to state pensions, which have now grown into the vast system of cross-payments from some groups of people to others that has become known as "social insurance" although it has little resemblance to insurance as that word is usually understood. Now that real incomes have more than doubled, it is high time discussion moved out of the old grooves. Yet in 1961 a Conservative Government is planning another enormous instalment of "social insurance" for a second state pension varying with earnings to go on top of the basic National Insurance benefit.

What does it all mean? Where would it lead us? What would it do to the pensions which people are building up for themselves through their places of employment or personally? Is this new political scheme well-adapted to our present and future needs?

In this *Hobart Paper* Mr. Arthur Seldon answers these questions and throws down a challenge to all the old-fashioned dogmas of welfare statism. Not only does he argue that the new state scheme is unnecessary and undesirable: he also shows how the paraphernalia of public subsidies and benefits inherited from the past might be discarded as private arrangements make them unnecessary.

And he couples this with a plea that we be more generous to the dwindling minority of people who remain in need.

When Mr. Seldon's earlier pamphlet, *Pensions in a Free Society,* was published in 1957 I said in the *News Chronicle* that it was "a penetrating, stimulating, controversial examination of fundamental principles . . ." During the last two years a vast amount of propaganda has been poured out on Labour's plan for National Superannuation and the Conservative reply to it; and the life assurance companies have made their contribution in a series of pamphlets. Yet the public does not appear very impressed by the rival policies.

One of the dangers in matters of this kind is that principles become submerged in (often unavoidable) technical complexity. The author has, however, taken up the challenge of the Cambridge economist, Mr. Walter Hagenbuch, who said of his earlier proposals that if they had been more detailed they would be "a serious competitor, on paper, to the Labour party scheme." Accordingly, in this study, which is concerned directly with the Conservative scheme but more generally with the principles underlying the role of the state in provision for retirement, Mr. Seldon goes some way to filling out the proposals made in his earlier paper. They are sure to provoke wide discussion, and they will do much good if they cause us to question notions that have been entertained uncritically for too long.

Oscar Hobson

I. First Principles

When the 1893 Royal Commission on the Aged Poor asked Alfred Marshall what he thought of a "universal scheme of pensions," he argued against them because, he said:

> they do not contain, in themselves, the seeds of their own disappearance. I am afraid that, if started, they would tend to become perpetual.[1]

Politicians concerned with the pressures of public life may be forgiven for taking a shorter view: state pensions were introduced in 1908. Fifty years later we must make respectful obeisance to Marshall for his political insight.

If it had been known around 1900 that incomes would treble in half a century, other arrangements might have been devised for helping people who had not been able to save for their old age. It is now debatable whether state pensions were the best way of helping needy old people, or whether they are suited to a system of representative institutions. Some of the opposition to them was silly or obscurantist; but their history shows that while state pensions may have been the most practicable or expedient means of helping needy old people they have brought disadvantages that were not foreseen when they were introduced. These defects require urgent scrutiny before we embark on another 50 years of pensioneering.

State pensions provided wholly by the taxpayer were followed in 1925 by the system that began as subsidised compulsory national insurance for retirement but has degenerated into another system of universal state benefit financed almost wholly by the taxpayer. That because of rising incomes he is increasingly subsidising himself is an added irony. For political reasons, but also possibly because of administrative convenience inseparable from large-scale administration, the principle of equal, compulsory and universal benefits has become deeply rooted in the system. But equal benefits for people with unequal need is a mockery of equality; it is discrimination against the needy. It distributes bread to people with cake and denies a second loaf to those with only one.

The discussion of pensions in Britain has been overlaid by political prop-

1. *Official Papers,* Macmillan, 1926. Marshall wanted to help old people in more selective ways.

aganda, sociological subtlety and actuarial expertise. It is time to go back to first principles. In a society which values personal liberty, which increasingly yields incomes high enough to permit saving for retirement, and in which people are capable of apportioning income between working life and retirement, arrangements will as far as possible be left to individuals. A man will be free to decide whether to spend most of his income on himself or his family while young enough to enjoy it and leave the future to take care of itself, or to live modestly while he earns and look forward to years of carefree ease when he retires. This is an intimate, elemental, personal decision, and a free society will not lightly tamper with it.

What pension arrangements are best likely to fulfil this philosophy?

II. Private Pensions in Practice

Private pensions came to Britain before state pensions. Their publicity or public relations have not been as good, but their achievement has been greater, for they are the product of voluntary agreement; one man in a private scheme is a greater testimony to the free society than ten in a state scheme.

Pensions are not the only form of saving for retirement. Individuals own about £40,000 million in national savings, building societies, industrial and provident societies, friendly societies, banks, stocks and shares, government securities, life assurance policies, houses, household goods, business assets, and other property. Personal saving ranges from the old sock to the old master.

In a nation of 15 million households, this is some £2,600 a household. Some persons own less than £500, and many less than £1,000—largely the older generation of workpeople who did not have much chance to save, or, if they did, had their savings whittled away by inflation. The rest of us, who have been earning in the more prosperous post-war years, owe them more than the beggarly £2 10s. a week we give a man or woman pensioner or the £4 we give a man and wife, supplemented though these benefits may be by National Assistance. But in devising pension schemes we are concerned with ownership and income in 20 or 30 years time, when they may have doubled or trebled. In any event, such retirement income is additional to private pensions, which nearly 10 million are accumulating. This leaves out of account both the basic national insurance benefit, which it is suggested below be reduced to its actuarial value or liquidated, and the proposed state graduated pension which it is argued is unnecessary and should be abandoned.

Origins and Growth

In the early days the attitude of the employer to pensions was paternalistic. They were regarded as a gift that was within his authority to grant or withhold. Since the worker had given "the best years of his life" to his employment, the employer incurred an obligation to support his old age. Accordingly pensions took the form of sums decided by the employer and paid out of current profits. In this way employers built up large liabilities; for, although the pension was within their discretion, a fund of *expectations* was accumulated that could not lightly be dishonoured.

The newer attitude is that a pension is part of the employee's remuneration that is deferred. The distinction is fundamental. For if the employee was building rights during his working life, they had to be embodied in some recognisable, tangible form. Hence the beginnings of formal pension schemes, based on funds built up from employees' and/or employers' contributions.

These funded schemes spread slowly after the 1914–18 war. The first large scheme insured with a life (assurance) office was installed by the Gramophone Co. (now Electrical & Musical Industries) in 1930: it was administered by the Legal and General Assurance Society. Yet by 1936 only 1.8 million people had been covered. After the war high taxation of profits, the tax concessions on contributions to pension schemes,[2] and high labour turnover combined to produce much faster growth.

By 1951 6.3 million and by 1958 8.75 million people were covered. The figure now is probably not far short of 10 million, comprising about 8 million men (out of 16 million employed) and 2 million women (out of 8 million), more than half in life office schemes.

The 1958 estimate is that of the Government Actuary.[3] He put the number covered in private industry at 5 million, in the nationalised industries at 1.5 million and in the public services (including the armed forces) at 2.3 million.

Moreover, the total is growing steadily—at an annual rate of about 350,000. All of these are in funded schemes, most insured with life offices, the balance in self-administered (i.e., internally-administered and self-insured)

2. The tax treatment is a vast subject in itself. Readers interested in details should consult works listed on page 48.

3. *Occupational Pension Schemes*, HMSO, 1958.

schemes. Funded pension schemes mostly began among the larger firms, which for reasons of large-scale economies tend to run their schemes themselves. Most of the subsequent growth has therefore been among the medium-sized and smaller firms, and because their schemes are generally too small to provide a wide spread of risk or to support the services of the legal and actuarial specialists required, they tend to be administered by pension consultants or life offices.

The Government Actuary's survey confirmed this position. He found that 76 per cent of "large" schemes (with some 500 or more members) were self-insured and 24 per cent insured with life offices. The percentages for smaller schemes were 34 and 66.

Pensions for Wage-Earners

It had been claimed by Professor R. M. Titmuss, Dr. Brian Abel-Smith, Mr. Peter Townsend and the Labour Party that occupational schemes were generally impracticable for small firms or manual workers, particularly in building, engineering, distribution, agriculture. It is not clear how this view was reached. Before the Government Actuary's report there was little published information on the number of private schemes installed by small firms or for manual workers. Early in 1958 a pilot survey, conducted with the help of a small number of life offices and pension consultants, showed[4] that from 1948 to the end of 1957 they had installed and were administering 400 schemes covering nearly a quarter of a million wage-earners. 170 schemes had fewer than 50 members, i.e., they were in the smaller firms. These figures seemed to throw some doubt on the Titmuss-Labour claim.

This impression was later confirmed by the Government Actuary's findings. He estimated that there were in 1956 37,500 schemes, 28,200 with fewer than 50 members. He also found that three-quarters of salaried men, a third of salaried women, two-fifths of wage-paid men and a quarter of wage-paid women were building up occupational pensions in firms with schemes.

Pensions, Pay and Fringe Benefits

There are many kinds of pension schemes, varying from generous to meagre. In a competitive labour market there is a tendency for the meagre to be made more generous, just as there is a tendency for firms without schemes

4. *Manchester Guardian,* 26th June, 1958.

to instal them in order to keep and attract employees. But it is a mistake to look for uniformity. Pensions are part of a "package deal" which includes canteens, sports facilities, holidays with pay and all the other non-monetary advantages described as "fringe benefits." Collective bargains covering large numbers of employees and firms may restrict the scope for flexibility, but there is no reason to suppose that all firms or all employees will want to divide total remuneration into exactly equal components. Where employers are free to offer and employees to accept remuneration in a form that fits local circumstances and personal preferences, a good pension scheme may be preferred to other benefits, or *vice versa.*

This attitude is well understood by trade unions in America. The general counsel of the Committee of Industrial Organisations (now amalgamated with the American Federation of Labour) put it clearly:[5]

> The union and management come to the bargaining table with some appraisal of how much money there is in the "kitty" for an increase . . . but it is the *total* cost of improvements which provides the framework within which the union and management bargain. If the 5 cents, for example, does not go into a health and welfare fund, it can go into a wage increase or extra holidays or double time for overtime on Saturdays. This is what collective bargaining is all about.

The flexibility of such arrangements—their scope for experimentation and education—is one of the advantages that a régime of private pensions can claim over a standardised system of state pensions.

The varying combination of fringe benefits and pensions is a measure of the degree to which they are integrated into the structure of labour remuneration, and illustrates the economic theory of "net advantages" that monetary and non-monetary rewards tend to compensate for each other.

An examination of the fringe benefits in 117 large companies[6] showed that pensions accounted for 53 per cent of the total expenditure on fringe benefits in 1958. The remainder comprised canteens (13 per cent), education (9 per cent), *ex gratia* payment, sports facilities, medical services, hostels, life assurance, and others. The total weekly expenditure on fringe benefits varied from less than 2s. to more than £2 per head.

5. State of New York Insurance Department, *Welfare and Pension Funds,* Public Hearing, 1955. Quoted in Paul P. Harbrecht, *Pension Funds and Economic Power,* Twentieth Century Fund, 1959.

6. Ralph Harris and Michael Solly, *A Survey of Large Companies,* Institute of Economic Affairs, 1959.

Variety and Flexibility

In contrast to the British unions, which are usually suspicious or obstructive, the American unions play an increasing role in the negotiation, and sometimes the administration, of occupational pension schemes. Two-thirds of American workers covered by occupational pensions are in schemes arranged under collective bargaining.

In both countries there is wide and still growing variety. This is the response to the variety in the circumstances, preferences, and needs of different industries, firms and people. Firms differ in size, in the markets they serve, in the grade, skill and size of the labour they require. People differ in the intensity, regularity or duration of work they want. Since occupational pensions are only one constituent in the assortment that constitutes the employee's remuneration, there are good reasons why they should vary.

In Britain there are contributory and non-contributory schemes. In contributory schemes the employee's contribution can be adjusted to suit late joiners. In all schemes the benefits can be adjusted to the growing and changing needs of families. Part of the pension may be surrendered for the benefit of widow or children. The pension may be based on average earnings, on final earnings, on the last five or ten years' earnings, on the best five in the last years; it need have no connection with earnings at all. It can be arranged to participate in the profits of fruitful investment or (at a lower premium) not. The rate at which the fund is built up may be adjusted to suit those who wish to build rapidly in the early years or leave the build-up until earnings are higher. Not least, the age at which the pension is drawn may be varied to suit people with varying capabilities or preferences. And so even in schemes designed for large firms the individual is not submerged.

Is the variety excessive? Pension schemes are often sold by professionals to amateurs. The market has been more or less imperfect; schemes may be adopted by personal recommendation or through chance acquaintance with directors or officials who have made little or no comparison of the alternatives available. This has probably encouraged some artificial and superfluous differentiation which discourages comparison. But a complex society may prefer the waste of too much variety to the constrictions, the inefficiency and the injustices of too little.

Moreover, it is at least equally arguable that the range of pension schemes offered by the insurance industry has not yet caught up with the desirable variety. The schemes are being more highly refined. One reason for this was the growing experience of the insurance companies as the demand for schemes increased after the war. Another is the breakdown of the rigid price structure of the companies that observed standardised "tariffs." A third is the increasing knowledge among buyers of schemes arising from the growing activity, especially in the last 12 years, of a new kind of pension consultant who advises on the most suitable scheme offered in the market and assists the insurance companies in devising modifications to suit particular firms or groups of firms. These consultants, including firms such as Noble Lowndes, Metropolitan Pensions, Bowring & Layborn, Leslie & Godwin, Hobbs Savill and others, have played a part in making the market for insured schemes more "perfect," both in the technical-economic sense of more competitive and in the everyday sense of more responsive to the varied needs of different firms and people. To this extent, the widening range of pension schemes has meant not excessive variety but increasing adaptability to complex modern industrial society.

Who Owns and Controls the Funds?

The funds built up by employees' and employers' contributions (or premiums) are invested in a range of assets designed to yield the pensions when they become payable. After exhaustive analysis of the growth of American pension funds,[7] an American lawyer and sociologist, Father Paul P. Harbrecht, has concluded that they are not owned in any significant sense by the intended beneficiaries, the potential pensioners. He argues that ownership has become virtually meaningless: it no longer carries power. This means a move towards a "paraproprietal" society in which power rests not on the ownership but on the management of investments. What is needed, he says, is a redefinition of the concept of property and property rights.

This analysis touches on the criticisms made by several British left-wing sociologists of the concentration of power and control over industry which the growing pension funds give their managers and trustees. Professor Titmuss has argued on these lines for some years,[8] and has returned to it in his latest Fabian Tract[9] in which he pillories the growing power of the life assurance companies.

> It is power concentrated in relatively few hands, working at the apex of a handful of giant bureaucracies, technically supported by a group of professional experts, and accountable, in practice, to virtually no-one.

7. *Pension Funds and Economic Power.*
8. "The Age of Pensions," *The Times,* 29th and 30th December, 1953, and other writings.
9. *The Irresponsible Society,* Fabian Society, March, 1960.

Father Harbrecht's demonstration of the divorce between ownership and control is a new version of the Berle and Means analysis of 30 years ago.[10] It remains an unresolved problem of the structure of company organisation: legislation on both sides of the Atlantic has been designed to strengthen the powers of the shareholders and to make the directors more accountable to them. The Jenkins Committee on company law may propose further improvements, but this problem cannot ever be solved finally. Delegation of authority cannot avoid the risk of misunderstanding or even abuse of power. We cannot run business enterprise by the direct consultative methods of the Greek city states. But if business bureaucrats can be brought to heel by making markets competitive, we have yet to find a way of making state bureaucrats in control of centralised organisations responsive and accountable.

The problem of the control by its owners (the prospective pensioners) of pension funds, whether accumulated in an assurance company or by the employing company, is comparable. Provided the employees are fully informed on the nature of the pension scheme they are offered as part of their terms of employment, there can be no complaint if the bargain is entered into freely in a competitive market for labour and in full employment. How far employees, or their representatives, should share in the day-to-day administration of the scheme and the investment of the funds is a matter for arrangement in each firm, and hardly calls for legal enactment of standardised procedures. What is clear is that the duty of pension fund managers is to administer the funds solely in the interests of the beneficiaries, and this normally means ensuring for them the largest possible pension. Is this achieved?

The Efficiency of Investment

The life and annuity funds of the British insurance companies now amount to about £5,000 million at book values, of which the pension funds probably exceed £1,000 million. The total grew in 1959 by £420 million, of which £350 million derived from pension schemes. Self-administered pension funds, of which there are about 2,500, have accumulated some £3,000 million, and are growing by about £250 million a year.[11] At the end of 1958, 19 per cent of the life funds of the companies were in ordinary shares and a further 21 per cent in other shares and loan stocks, making a total investment

10. *The Modern Corporation and Private Property,* New York, 1932.

11. *Report of the (Radcliffe) Committee on the Working of the Monetary System,* para. 827, HMSO, 1959.

in industry of 40 per cent; 25 per cent were in real estate, and most of the rest in public stocks. At the end of 1957, 21 per cent of the self-administered funds were in ordinary shares and a further 16 per cent in other shares and loan stocks, making a total investment in industry of 37 per cent; 5 per cent were in real estate and most of the rest in public stocks.

These percentages are averages for each group. The investment policies of insurance companies and self-administered funds differ: the Legal and General Assurance Society has much more than the average in real property; the Imperial Tobacco Company has invested almost the whole of its pension fund in ordinary shares. At the end of 1958 the spread in investment of 43 assurance companies was between 8 and 38 per cent in ordinary shares, between 9 and 40 per cent in British Government securities, between 4 and 45 per cent in mortgages and loans, and between 2 and 35 per cent in debentures.[12] They could not all be right; some must have been investing more wisely than others. But the errors tend to cancel one another, and the *net* error is less than it would be in a single state or private investment agency.

The general purpose is to invest the funds to yield income that will be secure, predictable and high. The task of the investment managers or committees is to achieve the best possible compromise between these often conflicting objectives. In the last few years (and even decades) investment policy has responded to changes in the fortunes of the various investments. Some idea of the change is seen by looking at the way in which the self-administered funds used their resources[13] in 1957: 37 per cent of the new money went into ordinary shares and 20 per cent into British Government and Government-guaranteed stock (at the end of 1956 the percentages were 21 and 34). This tendency to favour ordinary shares in industry rather than gilt-edged securities reflected the desire to offset inflation, avoid losses in the capital values of the misnamed "gilt-edged" Government stocks, and increase yields. More lately there has been a move in the reverse direction by some investment managers because the high prices and low yields of equities have increased the relative attractions of fixed interest stocks. Similar trends have been observable for some years in the life assurance investments; there the desire to improve yield has been sharpened by the competition to attract new policy-holders; hence the enterprising policies "with profits" or bonuses.

12. Quoted by Mr. G. W. Bridge, Deputy Chairman of the Legal and General Assurance Society, in an address, "The Investment of Insurance Funds," to the Royal Institution of Chartered Surveyors, 7th March, 1960.

13. These comprised not only new money from existing and new contributors but also the proceeds of earlier investments that matured or were sold.

The change in the distribution of the funds of the 43 largest insurance companies since before the war has been as follows:

	1939 %	1948 %	1958 %
Ordinary shares	10	11	20
Preference and debentures	30	19	21
Mortgages and loans	25	10	19
Property (including ground rents)	3	7	10
British, Commonwealth, foreign and municipal securities	31	52	29

Source: Bridge, *op. cit.*

The three main features are the fall in the gilt-edged securities from the record wartime level (which reflected the response to the request from the Government to support its securities), the doubling in the ordinary shares and the trebling in the property investments, which became more profitable as wartime building and other controls were relaxed.

The important point illustrated by these figures is that the investment of pension funds demands a sensitive response to changing market conditions. How well do the insurance companies and self-administered pension funds do their job *in the pensioners' interest*? Some companies and funds have responded more quickly than others. One reason for this must be that competition was not brisk enough to galvanise every company and fund into alert enterprise and opportunism. We have suggested above that competition among the companies has been increasing and may be expected to increase. The leading underwriter of pension schemes is the Legal and General, followed at some distance by the Norwich Union, the Prudential, the Standard, the Sun Life and the Eagle Star; but some of the medium-sized and smaller companies, such as the Guardian, the London and Manchester, the United Kingdom Provident, Scottish Widows, the General Life, the Northern and the London Assurance have helped to make the running with imaginative ideas, policies and publicity.

It is not clear how far the competitiveness among the underwriters and investors of pension funds has been impaired by the mergers of the last few years. Professor Titmuss argues that:

> as the power of the insurance interests (in combination with other financial and commercial interests) continues to grow they will . . . increasingly

> become the arbiters of welfare and amenity for larger sections of the community.

This judgement bears a family resemblance to Marxist predictions that private enterprise inevitably degenerates into business autocracy. The number of life offices underwriting and/or administering pension schemes has risen as industry has increased its interest in them; it is now about 45 out of a total of some 85 operating in Britain, although most of the business is done by about 20 offices. The beneficiaries are not helpless: like shareholders they can bestir themselves if they think their funds are not being employed competently, their rights can be strengthened at law, they can be protected by curbing restrictive practices and monopolistic tendencies, and, not least, they can change life offices if they can get better terms and service elsewhere. The reduction in the number of life offices is countered by the increasing competitiveness between them. There would appear to be no collusion among the offices on investment policy and decisions; the Investment Protection Committee of the British Insurance Association is concerned only with matters of general interest, such as the problem of voteless A shares. We do not yet know the competitive pull of the newer institutional investors: as incomes rise, other forms of retirement saving could rival pensions. And in the meantime, if the life offices become overweening or tyrannical, industry could run its pensions schemes itself, as of course many firms are doing.

What of the criticisms of undue control over industry? About 90 per cent of the £5,000 million is invested in Britain. The insurance industry claims[14] that far from exerting a wide and growing control over British industry through investment, they usually avoid buying large holdings of the equity of British companies and that on the contrary each office normally limits itself to 5 or 10 per cent in each firm. Since several offices may have holdings, the total insurance interest may be 40 or 50 per cent of the equity of some firms. But this is the upper limit. Over industry as a whole the insurance interest is much smaller. The amount of life office funds invested in equities at the end of 1958 was about £860 million at book values. The total market value of ordinary shares quoted on the Stock Exchange was approximately £12,200 million. The proportion of insurance holding was therefore at least 7 per cent; if the book values are translated into market values the proportion would rise to perhaps 15 per cent. Even if the mergers went much further, this

14. A good statement of the case was made by Mr. L. Ginsburg (Investment Manager of the Legal and General Assurance Society) in "The Insurance Stake in British Industry," in a Supplement, *Fund*, published with the *Policy-Holder*, 30th April, 1959.

proportion—between a sixth and a seventh—is not large enough to give the insurance companies domination over British industry.

It is common knowledge that some insurance companies own controlling interests in manufacturing and trading companies. The life offices' reply is that these exceptions are bound to be few, because to make the practice general would be to become involved in management, which would require staff and expertise they do not possess: the primary purpose, it is said, is investment, which dictates small holdings of shares in order to avoid involvement and to be able to abandon without major disturbance or publicity companies in whose managements confidence has been lost.

This position is feasible. Even so, it may be that holdings of only 10 per cent may occasionally require more than a passive role if the interests of the prospective pensioners are to be served. For while tacit control might be exercised by selling or indicating the intention to sell holdings, it may not always be easy to sell blocks of shares when the only likely buyers are other institutional investors. Sales in small lots may mean delay and capital loss. If a more active role becomes desirable to protect policy holders' interests, there need be no objection *so long as the insurance companies remain competitive.* This is the safeguard which Father Harbrecht and Professor Titmuss underestimate. What would be objectionable in three or four semi-monopolists (and certainly in a single, monolithic state investment authority) might be harmless in a score of competitors.

Furthermore, an active role may be desirable. An institutional investor, whether an insurance company, a pension fund, a unit or investment trust, is capable of bringing influence to bear on sluggish or reckless boards of directors that would not easily be exercised by individual shareholders. Again, investment without involvement—to hold voting rights and not to use them—may leave the management in a vacuum responsible to themselves or to small groups of shareholders who are able to exercise powers out of proportion to their holdings.

In any event, since pension funds are providing a very large proportion of new investment in industry, it may become difficult for the life offices in the next few years to avoid holding 20 or 30 per cent of the equity of a growing number of companies. Some method of keeping an eye on events may become imperative. Mr. Peter Drucker has described[15] the use by some American institutional investors of independent advisers as liaison officers with companies in which they invest to indicate when the passive role needs to be replaced by more active interest because trouble has been encountered or is

15. *America's Next Twenty Years,* 1957.

looming ahead. Whether this device is suitable in British conditions or not, some method of ensuring that the pensioners' interests are served may have to be evolved as the investment of pension funds in British industry grows. What is clear is that investment policies should be directed to serve the pensioners, not to mollify the political critics.

Father Harbrecht went too far in supposing that the growth of saving through pension schemes will upset the established system of property relationships. But there must be some method of ensuring that the managers and trustees are not diverting the funds from the primary purpose. Property ownership is spreading, but it looks like taking the form not so much of direct investment in industry as of indirect investment through pension schemes, unit trusts and other institutions. The owners must be given sovereign powers of control over their property.

The legal framework governing the responsibilities of the investment fund managers and trustees to the prospective pensioners may need to be redefined. But again it is clear from Professor Alan Peacock's study of the management of the National Insurance Fund,[16] from Lord Piercy's review of investment policies on the Continent[17] and from other sources that the solution is not to put investment into the hands of state officials and politicians—not because their abilities or intentions are necessarily questionable but because the pressures to which they are exposed are irresistible. The experience of the nationalised industries has by now weakened if not destroyed any belief in the efficiency, public-spiritedness or accountability of public authority.

> "[The] directors, managers and professionally trained advisers [of the insurance companies]" says Professor Titmuss "will not see—for it is not, after all, their purpose or business to see—that one of the most important problems of the future will centre round the socially effective use of rising national incomes . . ."

It is getting on for 200 years since Adam Smith explained that the market does not have to depend on men being saints or prophets. It takes people as they are and impels them to serve the general good by competition. The investment manager has his work cut out to do his daily job of watching prices, prospects and trends; we should cripple him if we also expected him *consciously* to bear in mind the "socially effective use" of his investments. But all

16. A. T. Peacock, *The Economics of National Insurance,* Hodge, 1952.

17. *The Supply of Capital Funds for Industrial Development in Europe,* Organisation for European Economic Co-operation, 1957.

the same "socially effective" *in the interests of policyholders and pensioners* he must make them, or lose his job. Can we expect that much from the directors, managers and professionally trained advisers of a State Investment Authority, exposed to political pressures and departmental jostling and without the stimulus, the discipline or the measuring rod of competition?

III. State Pensions in Practice

One might suppose that a standardised, compulsory, all-embracing system would have fewer and simpler problems than a patchwork of voluntary occupational pensions. The history of the system of state pensions in Britain suggests on the contrary that its outstanding features have been uncertainty, unpredictability and capriciousness. From the very start things did not go right. And it is now in such straits that a vast rescue operation, the new state graduated scheme, has had to be launched to save it from collapse. Its history is that of well-meaning but bewildered politicians, civil servants, administrators caught up in a Frankenstein that has put politicians to intolerable strain, shown up the quality of democratic leadership and public life, frustrated the efforts to bring aid and comfort to the needy, and played havoc with the careful calculations of actuaries, economists and sociologists.

The 1908 non-contributory pension was above board. It was to be paid for by the taxpayer, and as long as it went to those who needed it the taxpayer should have been happy to provide it. But the contributory pension of 1925 presents a different story. In name it was "national" (or "social") insurance. In fact it has resembled insurance as generally understood less and less until what remains of it is almost unrecognisable. The 1959 scheme finally dropped the pretence of insurance by abandoning the build-up of a fund. Like its predecessor it also does violence to another principle of insurance—the variation of premiums with risks. The 1959 Act, whatever else it may be, is not a plan for insurance as ordinary people understand the term.[18]

The Growing Deficit

But to begin from the beginning. The contributions required for the 1925 old age pension were calculated as the amounts that would have to be paid

18. State bureaucracies have little to learn from private practice:

> . . . adoption of the term "insurance" by the proponents of social security was a stroke of promotional genius. Thus social security has capitalized on the good will of private insurance . . .

American observer quoted by Professor Peacock in *The Economics of National Insurance.*

for 50 years from the age of 16 and invested to yield the pension at 65. But this scheme broke the rule of insurance from the outset. Instead of waiting until the contributions built up an adequate fund, the Government of the day paid the pension almost at once. Hence there was an immediate deficit, which was to be covered by a grant from the taxpayer of £4 million a year for 10 years. The intention was nevertheless to make the scheme self-supporting by raising the contributions three times every ten years until by 1956 (four years ago!) they were to be sufficient to pay for the whole pension. Likewise the contributions required for the 1946 pension were calculated actuarially: again the pension was paid almost at once (except that new contributors had to wait ten years); and the taxpayer's subsidy (the "Exchequer Supplement") was fixed at one-sixth of the contributions.

In both cases, a huge "deficit" was built up. The "capital" or fund required to pay the pensions soared to £8,500 million in 1948, £15,000 million in 1957 and is probably now approaching £20,000 million. Instead of this enormous sum there is only £1,500 million in the kitty.[19] Moreover, the fund is no longer growing. Starting from this year, annual payments for all National Insurance benefits would exceed income from contributions (largely because of the rising cost of "pensions") and the fund would *shrink* by amounts growing from £140 million in 1961–2 to £310 million in 1971–2 and to £420 million in 1981–2. By about 1970 (assuming no other changes) the fund would have been wiped out. And all this in spite of an "Exchequer Supplement" of around £125 million a year.

What Went Wrong?

What happened to upset these well-laid plans? First, inflation. The benefits had to be raised periodically to maintain their purchasing power. Secondly, as living standards rose, the benefit was raised to conform with the changing notions of what it should buy. Thirdly, the system was run not by economists, or sociologists, or actuaries but by politicians, who are concerned not so much with the technical aspects or consequences as with the pulls and pressures of opinion.

In 1926 Winston Churchill offered widows' pensions far in excess of the value of the contributions and despite warnings from the Government Actuary. In 1948 the Labour Government ignored the advice of Lord Beveridge that the new pension be built up gradually over 20 years as contributions ac-

19. This comprises mostly money taken from the Approved Societies and held for sickness benefits, and surplus unemployment contributions.

cumulated (those whose means were inadequate would have the difference made up by National Assistance). It began paying pensions far beyond the value of the contributions. Mr. Hugh Gaitskell[20] explained later that 20 years was a long time to wait and that the general public would not have accepted this "discrimination against pensioners" (other national benefits were raised at once).

Political philosophers may speculate on Mr. Gaitskell's explanation. Can a politician be forgiven for rejecting the right policy by passing the buck to "public opinion"? Was it logical to excuse an immediate increase in the old age benefit by reference to the (also unearned) increases in other benefits? Was it necessary to give the higher pensions to *everybody* in order to give it to those who needed it? Was the real purpose to protect old people against the "stigma" of National Assistance? Was it a chance grasped to further a political dogma? Was it vote-catching?

We cannot tell. But what we must see is that the system put into the politician's hand an instrument that exposed him to electoral pressure as is amply shown by the timing of pension increases in 1951, 1955 and perhaps 1958.

The Quality of Public Life

Quite apart from these increases, promises are continually being made by one political party or another. The debates in the House of Commons (but not in the Lords)[21] are more disfigured by accusation and counter-accusation of party political advantage than distinguished by demonstrations of compassion for our needy elders. The climax—so far—was reached in the General Election of Autumn 1959 when all three parties offered new or increased pensions. Labour and Conservatives offered new graduated pensions growing gradually over the next 40 to 50 years (did Mr. Gaitskell remember his objections to Lord Beveridge's 20 years?); Labour and Liberals offered an immediate increase in the basic National Insurance benefit. Where ideology, electioneering and policy are inextricably intermingled, no judgement is easy. Politicians who care for the quality of British public life may sometimes wish they were not exposed to persistent importunity and temptation where merit and vote-selling defy separation.

20. *Population Trends and Social Services.* Eleanor Rathbone Memorial Lecture, Liverpool University Press, 1954.

21. ". . . Whilst the debate [on the Government's White Paper on pensions] in the House of Lords showed real concern for the pensioners, the Commons seem to have been more concerned with the electors' votes." Article in the *Draughtsman,* journal of the Association of Engineering and Shipbuilding Draughtsmen, June, 1959.

In defence of the politician it may be added that pensions are one of the growing range of subjects in which the administrative "machine" has overwhelming advantages over the private Member of Parliament. He has no time or opportunity to assemble the material or the arguments capable of confronting the Government's "advisers." Election year was hardly the time in which to look for informed criticism of a complicated measure such as the 1959 Act. But more generally the inability of Parliament to scrutinise political compromises and expedients critically is one more reason for confining it to matters that it must undertake because no-one else can.

IV. Graduated State Pensions

By the mid-fifties there was thus a combination of occupational pensions, deficient in some respects, elaborate in others, but steadily growing, and of state pensions which inflation, rising living standards and political management had transformed from insurance to taxpayers' bounty and whose finances had been reduced to a sorry state. It was on this combination that the Labour and Conservative parties announced their intention to graft a second state pension that was to be worthy of its name. There were differences in the nature and extent of the schemes, but they had two basic common features: they would be based on contributions varying with income and they would "mature" slowly until the early years of the twenty-first century; thus they would produce in contribution revenue much more in the early years than would be required to pay the pensions. But while the Labour surplus was to be invested in industry, the Conservative surplus would be used to pay the older "basic" benefit.

The Conservative scheme is dignified with the actuarial name "assessmentism" (the cost of the pensions is assessed annually and the contributions to pay them arranged accordingly), or in common parlance "pay as you go"; the future pensioner is paying for existing pensions and will in turn have to trust to a future generation of taxpayers in his retirement.

Labour's National Superannuation has been much discussed in recent years. For the time being debate on it is stilled, and it may never be resumed.[22] For the Conservative scheme, the Government Actuary embarked

22. In so far as its purpose was to use the accumulated funds to acquire control over industry by buying vote-giving ordinary shares, it may be revived in the demand for the nationalisation of the insurance companies for which a member of the Labour Party Executive has called.

on the usual courageous estimates, covering the next forty years into the twenty-first century. He sees[23] the scheme yielding some £800 million in its first year, 1961–2, rising to £1,419 million in the year 2001–2 (when those of us of 45 or more will have passed on). This, he reckons, together with the annual "Exchequer Supplement" rising slowly from £170 million to £220 million, and the £50 million interest on the National Insurance Fund (invested in "gilt-edged" securities) will be about enough to pay the retirement benefit, which will soar from £680 million to £1,200 million, and the other National Insurance benefits and administrative costs, which will rise from £330 million to £360 million.

We must not take these figures too seriously: they bear an air of accuracy that is spurious. The Government Actuary's estimate of 1925 was some £18,000 million out 35 years later. That was not his fault; but are his successors likely to be more accurate? The only thing certain about the 1959 estimates is that they will be wide of the mark before 1969. But why was the new scheme introduced at all?

The Genesis of Conservative Graduation

The origins of the Conservative scheme are obscure. There have been references to Conservative discussions going back to 1954 or 1955, including a ministerial visit to Germany to see how national pensions were working there.

There was also the uneasiness in Conservative circles created by what was (wrongly) regarded as Labour's election-winning scheme. And there were some Conservatives who favoured graduated contributions to yield revenue but not graduated pensions.

Whatever the origins, the reasons for the new scheme given by diverse parties at various times were chiefly five. In roughly ascending order of plausibility they were as follows: First, pensions should vary with income earned before retirement. This pretext barely withstands examination. It is highly questionable on biological grounds whether a man earning £12 a week needs more (or less) coal or calories than one earning £13 or £11. After almost half a century of contributions the graduated pension would be 20s. a week for men earning £12 a week, 7s. less for one earning £11, and 7s. more for one earning £13 (the differences for women are 5s.). These would be additional

23. *National Insurance Bill, 1959: Report by the Government Actuary on the Financial Provisions of the Bill*, HMSO, 1959.

to the basic pension (£2 10s. for a man), so that the differences would be proportionately much less: £3 3s., £3 10s., £3 17s. Is it worth establishing the new system to yield—in 47 years' time—such results? Are we really expected to take this argument seriously?

A second argument was that occupational pensions were spreading too slowly. The excuse is flimsy. Why was progress not faster? The scale and rate of installation of the schemes have been very largely influenced by their taxation and administrative treatment, which have not always been designed to encourage the schemes but rather to ensure they were not used as a method of avoiding taxes. Although the 1956 Finance Act improved the tax treatment of insured schemes, it slowed progress down by diverting the life offices into redesigning existing schemes. The political debates since 1956 created uncertainty which discouraged the long-term planning that is the essence of a pension scheme. Finally, if occupational pensions are not spreading fast enough, the state graduated pensions will hardly move faster. What do they offer? 4s. a week in 1976 to a man earning £11 a week who joins the scheme in 1961 aged 50. 14s. a week in 1986 to a £13-a-week man who joins at 40. 34s. a week in 2008 to a £14-a-week man who joins at 18. How far can human credulity be strained?

Thirdly, the Government has argued that its new scheme is designed to assist the development of occupational schemes. It may do this if it leads firms to improve or instal private schemes in order to contract out. But the size of many existing private schemes is smaller than it otherwise would be precisely because there is a state scheme. And it must be supposed that the new graduated scheme would have a similar effect in the future.

A fourth argument was that the 1959 Act was a necessary reply to Labour's National Superannuation. This must be left to Conservative heart-searching. It is primarily a political matter, but it has an economic aspect in the older sense in which economists used to speak of political economy. As if in response to *The Times'* condemnation of "pensioneering," Lord Beveridge and others have asked that pensions be kept out of politics. If this means that pensions should be entrusted to technicians who will decide the problem "on its merits" it has no relevance for representative institutions. It suggests a confession of confusion, a wearisome wish to be rid of repugnant realities, a feeling that pensions are not best decided by party politics, and politicians. And there we can agree; but *the only way of taking pensions out of politics is to take them out of the state.*

There must remain doubt about the wisdom of the well-intentioned advertising effort by the life offices to influence the shape of the Government scheme. A paper by an insurance official on pension schemes and "the stewardship of the life offices"[24] says that the life offices:

> might have revealed the true value of some of the arguments so that no politician would have dared to advocate them.

This, he said, would have meant "being boldly partisan." But if the life offices considered the proposals of the Labour and Conservative politicians untenable,[25] it would have been more suited to their role as independent technical assessors to have confined themselves to judging the principles of the proposals than to have offered suggestions on how they should be carried out in the real world where decisions are ultimately political. Instead of condemning unequivocally the principle of state graduation, which could destroy private superannuation, they *appeared* to condone it.

A fifth reason was that the occupational schemes were hindering mobility of labour. This was a red herring. It is true that many employers in the post-war sellers' market for labour were offering pensions to cut down labour turnover.

But to bring in a state scheme to cure this disease was using a steam hammer to crack a groundnut. It would have been easy, for example, to reserve Inland Revenue approval to schemes that preserved pension rights either by paying a "transfer value" to the scheme of the new employer, or by creating a "frozen" pension which a departing employee would draw on retirement, or by some other method. The additional cost would gradually have fallen as pension schemes spread because pension rights brought in by new employees would have tended to offset those taken by departing employees.

The sixth reason was that graduation was desirable to put National Insurance "on a sound financial footing." This is the true reason. The old scheme was running rapidly into the red and money had to be found from somewhere to pay the old pensions. Broadly, there were two main ways. One was to say openly: "The old people must be given a tolerable income, as much as we can afford. The National Insurance method has broken down, so we'll do it by the straightforward method of a tax." The other was to call

24. A. S. Owen, *Pension Schemes at the Crossroads: The Stewardship of the Life Offices,* published in the Chartered Insurance Institute *Journal,* 1960.

25. The Institute of Actuaries and the (Scottish) Faculty of Actuaries said in May 1959: "The nature of the [Labour and Conservative] schemes precludes an effective internal discipline." *National Pensions: An Appeal to Statesmanship.* The Life Offices Association represents the life offices through their managers and/or actuaries. Because the actuarial is a key technique in life assurance, actuaries have graduated to administrative control as managers.

the tax a contribution and promise in return pensions thirty or forty or fifty years ahead. We may all still be paying much the same amounts[26] under the two methods, but under a straight tax the benefits could have been reduced as the generation of old people passed away, especially if, as is suggested below, the pension were confined to those in need and reduced to the amounts earned by contributions. Instead, state graduation would pile up pension rights far into the twenty-first century.

Will Contracting Out Save the Private Schemes?

This is not the end of the account. The new state scheme, unlike the old, is optional: employers may contract out and run private schemes. But the dice are loaded. The contributions are so arranged that the higher-paid employees subsidise the lower-paid and the younger subsidise the older. The tendency will therefore be for employers to contract out the higher-paid and younger and leave in the state scheme the lower paid and older. The Government Actuary was told to allow in his estimates for 2½ million employees contracted out, presumably on the assumption that they would be confined to those earning £11 (roughly the "break-even" point) or more.

Would contracting out on this scale save the private schemes? Far from it. In the first place the 2½ million would probably include many higher-paid people in the Civil Service, local government and nationalised undertakings, so that the number contracted out by private employers would be far fewer. Secondly, there would be a strong inducement for employers not only of women, but also of semi-skilled and unskilled men to contract in. These are precisely the people in whom the attitude of independence from the state and the habit of private saving stands in most need of encouragement. In 1958, the National Farmers Union, for example, had examined a scheme to be run centrally by the industry; it was held up by the political debate on pensions and will now probably not be adopted by farmers as widely as it might have been. Thirdly, some employers of the 7 million contracted in who continue their private schemes will cut them down.[27] Fourthly, where

26. Where taxation varies with income, the graduated scheme bears most heavily on those earning broadly £12 to £15 a week who are not contracted out.

27. A survey by the Association of Superannuation and Pension Funds shows, to date, that 26 funds with 39,000 employees out of 197 funds intend to contract in and cut down their schemes. 93 with 202,000 employees intend to contract in without change. 77 with 77,000 employees intend to contract out some employees. *National Insurance Act, 1959, Pamphlet No. 2*, May, 1960.

such occupational schemes are not altered, the additional cost of the graduated state pension will be carried at the expense of improvements that would otherwise have been made in the next few years. There is no cause for complacency here.

Fifthly, we have no experience of contracting out in this country. Nor has any other comparable industrial country. The reason is simple: it has been found impracticable. The British scheme is not merely one for "pay as you go" pensions; it is also a vehicle for the redistribution of income. Part of the contributions of the higher-paid would have been a gift to the lower-paid. The whole of their (graduated) contribution could then be used to buy a larger pension in the open market. A £12-a-week man of 30 would earn 5¼d. in state pension for a year's service; he could earn 9d. in a private scheme if the contributions earned 4 per cent interest, 1s. 2d. if 5 per cent, and 1s. 9d. if 6 per cent. A £15-a-week man of 40 would earn 10½d. in the state scheme, 1s. 9d. in a private scheme if the contributions earned 4 per cent, 2s. 4d. if 5 per cent and 3s. 3d. if 6 per cent. The higher paid would therefore be taken out, leaving the state scheme with the passengers, the subsidised lower-paid. In this sense the scheme is built on gimcrack foundations, and it takes no prophetic vision to foretell that it will need to be revised in a few years. In Sweden, where a state graduated scheme with redistributional effects was introduced in January, 1960, there have been similar doubts. This does not mean that it will not work in Britain, and many employers will undoubtedly follow the lead of Ind Coope and contract out. But it means that those who quote it in defence are depending not on experience but on unsupported conjecture.

Sixthly, if many more than 2½ million are contracted out, the Government Actuary's calculation will go awry. Some means will have to be found of finding the missing money. Apart from taxation, or raiding what is left of the National Insurance Fund (so long as unemployment remains below 4 per cent), the only way is to alter the graduation.[28] Raising the contributions from the higher-paid, or widening the income range would intensify the incentive to contract out. The purpose would be rather to discourage or stop contracting out; this would be done by making it more costly or administratively more difficult. And so the harm to occupational pensions would become still more glaring.[29]

28. Five-yearly increases in contributions in 1965, 1970, 1975 and 1980 would create a further buffer for a time.

29. Has the process started? The 1960 Budget proposes to allow £15 a year against income tax in respect of contributions whatever the contributions actually paid. This is a further re-

The Arithmetic of Contracting Out

Whether or not the Government's estimate is anywhere near the mark will not turn wholly on arithmetic: in an industrial community which rests on voluntary association between employers and employees, the degree of contracting out will depend also on how high a value is put on good relations between them. The arithmetic itself gives no clear guide.

The pension consultants and life offices are usually careful to add that their calculations, based on the contributions proposed, provide no more than a first step in the reckoning. An employer may calculate the saving or cost of contracting some or all of his employees in or out according to their earnings. But the ultimate financial cost cannot be decided from these figures. Three factors will affect the saving or cost: earnings, the contributions and benefits in the state scheme, and the pensions available in the open market. The differences in contributions for employees contracted in and those contracted out are quite small (roughly 1 per cent of the pay-roll higher for a firm with predominantly lower-paid employees contracted in and 1 per cent lower for one with mainly high-paid workers) so that changes in any of these figures could disturb the balance of advantage. But since it would be administratively impracticable or too costly to go into or come out of the state scheme every few years whenever the balance of advantage changed, the employer must make some judgement of the likely changes in the next few years.[30]

We may assume that earnings will go on rising. Contracting out would then be cheaper. This must affect the decision today. If the initial "break-even" point is, say £11, then if earnings rise by 5 per cent a year, an employer who looks forward two years would, on cost alone, contract out those earning about £10 or more; in expanding, prosperous firms the break-even point is still lower, in contracting or pessimistic firms that fear recession it may be higher. Secondly, if private pension costs continue to fall, as they have done over the years, then again it will be cheaper to contract out. On a long view it seems reasonable to suppose that private pension schemes will improve

distribution of income, an added inducement to contract out the higher-paid, and therefore a further reason for making contracting out more difficult.

30. It is possible to sympathise with the view that since the future is uncertain the only safe course is to be guided by what is known in the present. This does not avoid the need for judgement: it implies a judgement that there will be no change. But all three elements are continually changing.

and become cheaper, not least because increasing competition is stimulating the industry all round and waking-up the sleepier companies.

The third element—the Government scheme—is the most uncertain. The advice of some pension specialists has been to enter the state scheme but to keep the private scheme going in the hope that the weight of the state scheme would diminish as incomes, living standards and the private schemes grew. But "sitting on top" of the state scheme may not be a comfortable posture. If there has been extensive contracting out, either the state scheme must collapse or those who are in it must be prevented or dissuaded from contracting out and those who are outside it must be brought in.

Enlargement of the state scheme by the Government would conflict with its repeated declaration that it meant no harm to private schemes. Yet it may be forced to pursue it if the scheme is to raise enough money to pay the pensions. And inflation, rising living standards or political pressures may compel it to raise the benefits. We cannot tell how the Government would act until it is faced with the decision. We may not doubt its good intentions; but no ministers or Governments can foresee the future, stay in office for ever, or commit their successors.

The more this scheme is examined the greater the doubt whether it would be kept on a moderate scale, and the more pressing the reason for finding some means of avoiding the scheme altogether.

The Significance of Employer-Employee Relations

If each firm examines the effects on itself, it must reach this conclusion. Hurrying for shelter under the Government umbrella might appear to avoid the risk of having to run increasingly costly private schemes. But this would be a very myopic view. Employers would be incurring higher costs in the state scheme as contributors and/or taxpayers with little to show in better relations with employees. If they contract out, their private pension costs might be higher, but they would also get something worth paying for. Even on this domestic ground, and quite apart from the wider issue of the economic environment in which private enterprise lives, contracting out is the right decision.

Each employer is faced with two broad choices. He may contract into the state scheme and continue, cut down or close down his occupational scheme. Alternatively, he may contract out and improve his scheme (unless it is already better than the state scheme) or instal one that satisfies the requirements. We have seen that it would be cheaper to contract out the higher-paid employees. But why should he contract out the lower-paid? The short answer is the human factor; good relations with employees may be bought cheaply at the price. A pension is part of remuneration, one of the fringe benefits of a good job that should be negotiated between employer and employee: the state has no business here. Employers with a scheme may not wish to disrupt a nexus of fringe benefits in order to save 6d. or 1s. per head, and employers without one may not wish to provoke unfavourable comparisons with those who have. It may not be good for morale to introduce a form of segregation between employees who are in the company scheme and those on whom the employer is saving a few pence or shillings per week in the state scheme. An employer may earn more goodwill by establishing a private scheme tailored to the circumstances of his employees than by contributing compulsorily to a scheme they will see as yielding a pension from "the state."

Again, if he wishes to give pensions larger than those in the state graduated scheme, is he to contract in and instal a private scheme for the balance? It would be simpler to contract out and have one scheme to cover the whole[31] instead of two (in addition to the National Insurance basic benefit). Again, if he wishes to cover past service, he must (if he contracts in) establish a separate private scheme because the state scheme will take no account of service before April, 1961. Private schemes can allow for differences in departments or districts and for periodic review. Occupational pensions are a good way of keeping in touch with retired employees. Not least, employers who wish to generate a sense of loyalty to and identity with the firm as a continuing entity will prefer their employees to look to the firm rather than to the state for their retirement income.

There is also the employee's point of view. Which pension is likely to be more secure? A firm may go out of business; but if it does, it will (to qualify for "non-participation") have to satisfy the Registrar of Non-Participating Employments that it has accumulated funds adequate to meet its pension liabilities. What is the employee's security in a state scheme? It accumulates no fund; the money he pays in goes out almost at once to pensioners; when he retires he will have to rely on the contributors and taxpayers, on the value of money, on the Government, on the economic and social climate, and on

31. The administrative aspects need lengthy discussion to treat them in full. Mr. Gordon Pingstone has a good discussion in a paper, "State Pensions and their Impact on Occupational Pension Schemes," delivered to the Nottingham Insurance Institute, *Policy-Holder,* 21st January, 1960.

world conditions which the Government cannot control. If employees were told these things would there be an overwhelming vote for state pensions?[32] For "pay as you go" they might read "hope as you pay."

For all these reasons, employers may decide to contract out even at some cost. Even if there was no other reason, there is a good strategic reason for doing so: the more employees are contracted out, the less is this or any other Government likely to weight the scales against private schemes.[33]

The Government's estimate of the number who would be contracted out seems to have been based solely on arithmetic. If it proves about right, it would suggest that employers had acted or been advised on too narrowly financial grounds. The scheme could then begin in 1961 and the dilemma would be postponed for a year or two. But if employers take a longer view of the atmosphere in which private enterprise works best, the number contracted out will exceed 2½ million and the Government will be faced with the dilemma in the coming months.

V. Pensions Without Charity

Need the dilemma be faced at all? Is the Government scheme the only possible next step, or the best one?

Benjamin Disraeli spoke of two nations that lived side by side—the rich and the poor. Professor Titmuss and his friends have adapted the distinction to people in old age. A more significant contrast is between the people who are being made independent by rising incomes and those who remain dependent on "the state"—their neighbours in the bus, the pub, or over the garden wall. The failure or refusal to see the implications of rising incomes and the opportunity they offer for emancipation from dependence is a stubborn obstacle in the way of a progressive public policy.

The philosophy of dependence sees pensions as one of the "social services" that should be supplied to all citizens, freely, equally, compulsorily, *permanently.* They confer the protection of the state on every man, woman and child and give him and her a "badge of citizenship." The notion seems

32. The decision on contracting out is the employer's, but he must give a month's notice of his intentions and the Registrar may require more time for the views of the employees or their representatives to be considered. The implication that it is only private schemes that need to be watched is not supported by the history of national insurance.

33. Employers who wish to contract out must do so in good time, otherwise they will be in the state scheme. The parallel is with contracting out of the trade union political levy.

to have evolved from the development of the social services during the war. The emergencies of evacuation, makeshift schooling, improvised medical services and the rest could not be handled quickly enough by the more democratic process of the market. Public authorities with powers to override personal rights and liberties were able to build up an apparatus of social provision—orange juice for babies, rent tribunals for parents, pension adjustments, allowances for this, grants for that—which in the centrally-directed, singly-motivated siege economy of war assured everybody of basic requirements.

The error was to romanticise all this into the notion of a community working in selfless happy harmony for the good of all. This is a highly idealised over-simplification of the complex of social and human relationships with which the builders of institutions have to contend. In the war, the conflicts between private purpose and general advantage were not invariably effaced by the common danger. And in peacetime the badge of citizenship has become sadly tarnished. Even in this land of law-abiding, kindly, conscientious citizens it is producing attitudes and conduct that can in no sense be regarded as elements of a good society. The time of doctors is wasted by people with trifling ailments. Subsidised houses are occupied by people who can afford rents sufficient to cover their costs. Free state education is accepted by people who can pay for it. Children who can support their aged parents throw them on state assistance or, astonishingly, refuse to take them from hospital.[34] Young people who call for higher state grants in order to avoid dependence on their parents see nothing wrong in accepting dependence on other parents. Those who tell pensioners that a family means test is degrading because it implies dependence on their children are prepared to make them dependent on other people's children. All around us we see people who do not need help accepting money—pensions, family allowances, so-called "insurance" benefits—from their neighbours. There may be some rough justice in all this, if there is justice in equality of tax avoidance—or tax evasion. But a society in which parents allow neighbours to pay part of their milk bill, in which generals and dowagers draw a subsidised pension, in which women in costly cars draw up outside state schools, in which we are allowed or encouraged to get as much as we can for nothing, is hardly one for which we should be asked to crusade.

The philosophy of dependence starts out as a well-intentioned effort to

34. *News Chronicle*, 2nd May, 1960. See also *The Demand for Medical Care*, by Forsyth and Logan, OUP, 1960.

help the needy and create a spirit of community. It ends by undermining self-respect and endangering social cohesion. It fails to see that in order to help the needy, it is not necessary to seduce the self-reliant, that a harmonious society is built on individual independence as the basis of mutual respect.

In his latest thoughts on the subject,[35] Professor Titmuss, at one point, generously confesses error:

> Many of us must . . . now admit that we put too much faith in the 1940s in the concept of universality as applied to social security. Mistakenly, it was linked with economic egalitarianism. *Those who have benefited most are those who have needed it least.* (My italics.)

This would appear a significant shift in ground. Once we have replaced the futile straining after egalitarianism by the hopeful effort to give help selectively where it is needed, we should be able both to increase the scale of assistance to those who need it and to speed up the rate at which others can pass from dependence to independence. Yet later in his booklet Professor Titmuss goes back on his recantation:

> . . . services and social amenities . . . should be provided for everyone if they are provided for anyone.

So we are back to the "badge of citizenship," with indiscriminate aid to all and sundry at the cost of neglecting exceptional needs. But it is a pity to waste effort in this *cul de sac.* The real problem is how to help the needy more and how to replace dependence by independence as incomes rise and poverty disappears. How much poverty remains? How quickly is it being abolished?

The Abolition of Poverty

Poverty was first measured by Charles Booth and analysed by Seebohm Rowntree into "primary" (where income is inadequate) and "secondary" (where it is misspent). Primary poverty may be absolute or relative. Absolute poverty relates to inadequacy of the food, clothing and shelter required to sustain life. In this sense poverty in Britain has been abolished by rising incomes, supplemented where still inadequate by National Assistance: no-one in Britain today need go hungry, ragged or homeless. Relative poverty, how-

35. *The Irresponsible Society.*

ever, is implied wherever incomes are unequal. It is ineradicable from any society—free or state-directed, capitalist or communist—since state assistance could never make up the smallest incomes to the highest. But since what are regarded as *basic* or *minimum* standards rise with *general* living standards, some continuing measure of assistance to small numbers is probably inevitable.

It is difficult to estimate the remaining degree of poverty in these various senses. Professor Titmuss has spoken of "the submerged fifth"—the "seven to eight million people today living precariously closely to the margins of poverty," Mr. Gaitskell, more cautiously, of "the submerged tenth." Mr. Peter Townsend says "we should think in terms of the submerged fifth and not the submerged tenth" because the number "with special difficulties over a long period who cannot and could not be expected to overcome their problems on their own resources" is nearer ten than five million. He arrives at this approximation by listing the number of retirement and war pensioners, disabled, unemployed, sick, mental defectives, National Assistance beneficiaries, and several other categories, grossing up for size of family (e.g., the 450,000 unemployed yield "2 million men, women and children dependent on unemployment benefit") and allowing for the "overlap in some instances."

This form of estimating is open to several objections. In the first place, not all or even most recipients of one or more welfare benefits are wholly or mainly "dependent on" them. Mr. Hilary Marquand, a former Minister of Pensions, has suggested that at least half of the 5 million retirement pensioners have private sources and are not in need; even this estimate is probably too low.[36] Many war pensioners are prosperous and, like many receiving industrial injury or disablement pensions, are earning enough for independence. Probably the majority drawing sickness or unemployment benefit for short periods have other means, and in any event the average family has two or more earners.

Secondly, the overlapping would appear to be considerable. The 1,670,000 recipients of National Assistance in September, 1959, included almost 930,000 also receiving retirement pensions, 160,000 on unemployment or sickness

36. The Department of Applied Economics at Cambridge has found from a pilot survey into the means of retired people in Bedfordshire and Greenwich that "the more alarmist views about poverty in old-age are ill-founded." The main enquiry is expected to confirm broadly this finding: see *Economic Circumstances of Old People in Britain,* by Dorothy Cole and J. E. G. Utting, a research project assisted by the Nuffield Foundation.

benefits, and 170,000 receiving other non-contributory pensions or widows' benefits.

Finally, if we take as the most reliable index of primary poverty only those who receive National Assistance, we should take into account that there have been successive increases in scale rates, which have more than doubled since 1948, so that greater generosity, by extending the number eligible, inflates apparent poverty. Further, the assistance grants are made without debiting the recipients with a number of "disregards," including ownership of a house (150,000), 15s. a week in an occupational pension, in sick pay from a trade union or a club, in voluntary allowances from relatives, friends or charities (30s. in all), £375 in "war savings," a further £125 of other capital, and earnings of 30s. to 40s. Thus even those recorded as drawing National Assistance but no other benefit are not typically "dependent on" public funds alone. And, finally, the numbers qualifying for assistance do not indicate the extent of poverty in an absolute sense but only relatively to the standard which the community for the time being sets as the minimum. The level of assistance should be raised, and it could be the sooner we abandon the principle of universality. But since people who need it are being maintained at this level, is it helpful to describe them as "submerged"?

Certainly, whatever the number,[37] it should not excuse complacency but incite us to find means of transferring help from those who do not need it to those who could be given more. But we must fashion our institutions on the realistic assumption that the number in need will be lower in five, ten and twenty years. Apart from special cases—the mentally deficient or the chronically sick able to work but not to earn sufficient and who are unwilling or unable to claim assistance[38]—the largest category is that of the aged. Many people in their sixties, seventies and eighties are poor because they lived through times when their labour was not valued highly, or not valued at all in the depression of the 1930's, or because their savings were eroded by inflation. All these people should be given more assistance,[39] but by definition the

37. The most recent poverty survey, undertaken in York in 1950, showed well under 2 per cent in poverty by Rowntree's "human needs standard." Of these, two-thirds were old-age pensioners. *Poverty and the Welfare State,* Rowntree and Lavers, 1951.

38. Mrs. Audrey Harvey concludes from her study of *Casualties of the Welfare State* (Fabian Society, 1960) that a major need was to bring the social services to the notice of those for whom they were intended. A similar view was reached by Mrs. Barbara Shenfield in her work in the Midlands (*Social Policies for Old Age,* Kegan Paul, 1957).

39. If the family means anything in our social life, assistance from children or other relatives should not be excluded. Mr. Townsend's interesting surveys in Bethnal Green leave the impression that families are not doing all they can for their elders (*The Family Life of Old*

old *in need* are a dwindling minority. In ten or twenty years those who follow them will have earned sufficient to have saved for retirement. These younger people will not require assistance in their old age; and because they will know that as taxpayers they will be pulling themselves up by their own bootstraps, and because of growing self-respect, they will not want it. One of the depressing aspects of much social commentary, in all parties, is the static approach to a problem that is essentially one of change. Plans for pensions are laid for tomorrow with the mind steeped in the conditions of yesterday, or the day before.

People in the other categories will continue to need assistance for many years, but this hardly requires the vast apparatus of universal benefits. Even if we overlook the waste in clawing back by taxation superfluous largesse that should not have been distributed in the first place, or the implication that high rates of tax have come to stay for all time, we may note that this system regards everyone in an age of increasing affluence as poor unless all show that they are not. And it implies that we must continue with *universal* pensions until the last old spendthrift gaffer has died; he never will.

Selective assistance will eradicate primary poverty. Secondary poverty is subjective and therefore immeasurable. Mr. Walter Hagenbuch believes[40] "its root cause is deficiency of character and lack of education in the widest sense," and sees its cure mostly outside the economic and political fields in the moral influence and example of teachers and social and spiritual workers. One further solution may be added. People learn by trying. Broken limbs require a crutch while they knit together, but they are strengthened by putting them to the ground and letting them learn the job of walking themselves. People must be encouraged to be responsible by giving them responsibility.

Those who are ready for freedom and independence cannot be asked to wait until every parent has become a paragon, the last drunkard a teetotaler, and every weakness of human nature replaced by virtue. The over-riding purpose should be to enable every man and woman to live *without* assistance from others; and the role of assistance should be not to replace but to fertilise, nurture and hasten independence.

People, 1957). As a community of families we betray a blatant contrast between the penury of grand-parents and the relative riches of grand-children. When average male earnings are £13 a week, and many families have several earners, a gift of 2s. 6d. or 5s. a week to an aged parent is an eloquent indication that our family life lacks cohesion.

40. *Social Economics,* Nisbit and CUP, 1958.

The Transition to Independence

At some point we shall have to see that rising incomes make possible, desirable and necessary, a change in our attitude to social assistance. The transition from dependence to independence in saving for retirement will necessarily have to be slow in order to minimise dislocation, friction and hardship. That is all the more reason for beginning it without delay.

The main programme would be divided into three phases, immediate, medium-term, and long-term.

I. *Main Proposals*

A. *National Insurance Act, 1959*

1. The immediate step would be to repeal the Act and give employers without schemes three years in which to instal them or provide other facilities; promptitude could be encouraged by reducing tax concessions each year. Apart from requiring transferability, no rigid rules for schemes should be laid down because industry is too varied; the competition for labour in full employment should ensure that employees' interests are safe guarded.
2. Employees would not suffer because the schemes would be backdated to April, 1961.
3. A residual Government scheme for employees who are difficult to fit into an occupational scheme is discussed below.

B. *Encouragement of private provision for retirement*

1. The medium-term policy is the removal of obstacles and the encouragement of all forms of private provision for retirement—through schemes run not only by firms but also by friendly societies, trade unions, clubs, churches, by any other voluntary social units, or by individuals.
2. The tax treatment of persons in non-pensionable employment or in self-employment should be the same as of those in pensionable employment. If encouragement for saving is justified on the ground that individuals take too short a view of the future, the encouragement must be scrupulously equal for all individuals and for all forms of saving.
3. The approval procedure for the tax treatment of pension schemes should be simplified and accelerated. Individual approval should be replaced by automatic approval for schemes that observe stan-

dardised regulations. The Inland Revenue is primarily concerned with tax avoidance; the primary purpose should be the maximum rate of advance of freely-negotiated pension schemes, even at some risk to the revenue. The Inland Revenue may not be the best office to embody this approach.

4. Pension schemes for wage-earners could be encouraged by raising the amount that may be taken as a tax-free lump sum; the present limit is derisory. Encashment of contributions by employees changing jobs could be discouraged, perhaps by forfeiture of the tax concessions. These and other amendments in the law should be embodied in a Pensions Easement Act to hasten the spread of pensions.[41]

C. *Winding-up National Insurance*

This is the long-term objective.

1. The National Insurance benefit should be reduced, in stages, to the amount earned by the contributions of employee and employer. The *most* a married man with a wife five years younger could have contributed (and his employer for him) from 1926 to the end of 1959 was £250 for a pension whose capital value was £2,650 and whose weekly actuarial value was thus around 7s. 6d. This allows for compound interest on the contributions of 3 per cent. A private fund would probably have earned more; at 4 per cent compound the contributions would have amounted to around £275 and the actuarial value of the pension would be nearer 8s. 6d.
2. Contributors should be offered, as an alternative, over a period, a lump sum representing the value of their (and their employers') contributions at an agreed rate of interest. If the average repayment was £100, the National Insurance Fund would suffice for 10 million repayments. Requiring the sums to be invested for a minimum period at the discretion of the recipient (a proportion in Government stock) would have a beneficial educational value.
3. Old people in need would receive more generous grants in place of National Assistance to supplement their income from private saving or gifts from families; the grants would be determined by income codes calculated from returns of income as compiled for

41. The possible contents of this measure are discussed in an article by the author in the *Contemporary Review,* October, 1959.

income tax. Those whose income exceeded the current break-even point would pay tax, those whose income fell below the point would receive grants; the grants would thus form an inverse tax; they would be arranged to minimise the discouragement to private saving or family subvention.

4. Although the stigma of the old Poor Law has evaporated, it lingers in National Assistance; without exaggerating the psychological significance of names, we might describe the new grant by a name that conveys the spirit of an honorarium.
5. Income codes might also be used to indicate charges for state services now provided free or below cost: mainly educational, medical and housing, but also libraries and others that individuals can buy on the open market.
6. After raising the new grants, the balance from the savings in National Insurance benefits and from the new charges should be put to tax reduction.

II. *Ancillary Proposals*

1. *Publicity for private retirement saving*
   The life offices, pension consultants and consulting actuaries, jointly or severally, should familiarise the public with the advantages of pensions and other forms of saving for retirement (the taboo against professional advertising should be abandoned here, as it is being elsewhere).

2. *Supervision of pension funds*
   Life office and self-administered pension funds are virtually investment trusts and should be subject to similar regulation; in particular, self-financing from internally-administered funds should be limited.

3. *Needs of old people*
   More research, financed preferably from charitable foundations, is required into the needs of old people.

4. *Extension of dependents' allowances*
   The dependent relative allowance for income tax purposes should be greatly extended: it should be freed from proof of dependence, granted for any number of payments to persons of pensionable age in the family, and raised from £75 (shared where there is more than one donor) to £75 *for each donor* for as many relatives as he

cares to help. This would encourage nephews, nieces, grandchildren, sisters, brothers and other relatives to support or endow less-well-off elders.

This can now be done under Deed of Covenant, but some donors may not wish to be tied for 6 or more years. The possibility of extending the concession to non-relatives should be investigated.

The likelihood of these allowances being used for tax avoidance should not rule them out; as elsewhere, some avoidance (basically the result of excessive rates of taxation) is a price worth paying for the family endowment it might encourage; and it would make some state assistance superfluous.

5. *National Insurance (Reserve) Fund*

   To the extent that the National Insurance benefit is liquidated by repayment of contributions, the National Insurance Fund will be run down. In the meantime the investment of contributors' money in Government stock is in principle no less objectionable than the investment of a firm's pension fund in its own shares. At 31st March, 1959, the nominal value of the fund was £1,267 million but its market value £929 million. It is invested largely in Government securities and in the nationalised transport, electricity and gas undertakings, where it has lost heavily in capital value. The Fund should therefore be invested where it can earn the best return (not necessarily the highest in the short run) for the contributors. It should be taken out of the hands of the National Debt Commissioners and be administered commercially by a committee comprising nominees of the Treasury, the British Insurance Association and the Association of Superannuation and Pension Funds, and of the TUC.

6. *Pensionable ages*

   In view of the improvement in health and in the increase in the expectation of life, the ages at which the National Insurance benefit is payable should be raised, for men and women in good health, to 67 years.

Two possible courses have been rejected; a freezing of the basic benefit, and an increase in contributions to earn a higher pension. The first implies acceptance of the *status quo;* the second envisages an enlarged role for national insurance. Yet we must now see that the system cannot stand still: it has a built-in inflator that takes it from actuarial reality to political make-believe. The only way to stop it from growing is to cut it down. And the only way to do this is to place it, and the whole *corpus* of social services, in the realm of private decision as incomes rise.

The process might vary in tempo in the different services. Thus in pension benefits we might begin with a 10s. weekly reduction each year for several years. In education, there might be a nominal 5s. weekly charge for each child rising to something near the full cost. If all payments are based on individual income codes, these proposals would produce neither injustice nor hardship; but the assumption would be that all could pay unless they showed they could not.

In an appraisal of an earlier version of this proposal, Mr. Hagenbuch wondered[42] whether it might not be difficult to make the increase in the charge for social services politically acceptable unless they were "very closely linked" with successive reductions in taxation. Devising a link would be part of the process of dismantling the apparatus of dependence. Increased charges might not always easily be matched with lower taxes, but individual hardship would be avoided; and the transitionary frictions would be trifling compared with the injustices, distortions and wastes of the dependent state. Educating the electorate in the advantage of independence would require no more leadership than is devoted to policies of dependence. Nor would the political attractions be negligible. There is large scope for reduction in the taxes on the income, expenditure and saving of the growing body of taxpayers in a middle-class economy.

Too generous assistance scales might discourage the installation of pension schemes. This is a risk that must be taken. In time competition in the labour market, increasing pension-consciousness by employees, and rising social standards would compel employers to provide pensions or other advantages in their place. If private pensions are too slow, if people need to be urged to save for retirement, the way to encourage them is by tax arrangements. There would seem no need for a state pension organisation. Such a device might eventually be necessary only for casual or short-term workers, for whom formal pension schemes are difficult or costly to arrange. It would be easier to reach a final judgement after the three year deferment.

We ought to spend more on those whose needs are greatest because they are exceptional and do not fit easily into convenient administrative categories. Neglected children comprise one example. But these make a

42. "The Welfare State and Its Finances," *Lloyds Bank Review*, July, 1958.

winding-up of the superfluous services all the more desirable. The case is for a change in the content as well as for a reduction in the total weight of social assistance.

Conclusion

If we reject the philosophy of dependence, as all who value personal liberty and dignity must, we have to devise machinery that encourages independence.

If Labour's National Superannuation was unnecessary and undesirable, the Conservative graduated scheme is only one degree less so. It would perpetuate the device of national "insurance" that has failed beyond hope of rescue. It is unnecessary because people are increasingly providing for retirement in their own way. It would undermine the occupational schemes. It cannot be moulded to give individual industries, firms and people the pension schemes they want. It would discourage saving for retirement in all forms. It would weaken individual responsibility and, in the process, further strain and debase our public life and representative institutions. It would give a new lease of life to a state activity in which social accounting and tidy administrative arrangements frustrate human compassion and individual happiness. It would consume administrative talent and political sagacity, both scarce qualities that have become spread too thinly over the essential public services. Not least, even if it had the weight of economic, social and political argument on its side, it fails on moral and philosophical grounds because it would hold up progress from dependence to independence.

The Government scheme is an effort to patch up the consequences of 50 years of state pensions by foisting on the nation another 50 years of state pensions. It was conceived in fear, composed in haste, adopted in ignorance. It is a paper plan that could hardly last five years, much less fifty, in its present form; it had best not be begun.

FURTHER READING

Amulree, Lord, *Adding Life to Years,* National Council of Social Service (Incorporated), 1951.

Clark, Colin, *Welfare and Taxation,* Catholic Social Guild, 1954.

Crosland, C. A. R., "The Promotion of Welfare," Part III of *The Future of Socialism,* Cape, 1956.

Hagenbuch, Walter, "The Rationale of the Social Services," *Lloyds Bank Review,* 1953.

Harbrecht, P. P., *Pension Funds and Economic Power,* Twentieth Century Fund, 1959.

Hayek, F. A., "Freedom in the Welfare State," Part III in *The Constitution of Liberty,* Routledge & Kegan Paul, 1960.

Pilch, Michael, and Wood, Victor, *Pension Schemes,* Hutchinson, 1960.

Seldon, Arthur (Editor), *Fund: A Review of the Investment Policies of the British Insurance Industry,* by C. J. Baker, H. C. Cottrell, L. Ginsburg, R. G. Glenn; a supplement published by the *Policy-holder,* 30th April, 1959.

Titmuss, Richard M., *Essays on "The Welfare State,"* George Allen & Unwin, 1958.

Townsend, Peter, "A Society for People," in *Conviction,* a symposium edited by Norman Mackenzie, McGibbon & Kee, 1958.

THE FUTURE OF THE WELFARE STATE

The Future of the Welfare State

The theory and philosophy of the state services we collectively describe as "Welfare," mainly education, health, housing, and pensions, are based on the myth that they are or can be for free. The myth has been absorbed in the social sciences (except economics), in most journals of opinion, in all political parties. It is the essential reason why state welfare faces debilitation, disintegration, and decay. It persists because policy has for twenty years until the last few months been made with spare sparse hearing for the inconvenient sceptics who introduce doubts, provoke agonising reappraisals, and endanger intellectual conservatism.

State welfare services take a fifth, some £7,000 million, out of the national income of £34,000 million or about half of the public sector of £13,000 million. They invade every main facet of personal and public life. They evoke our humanity and compassion; and they reflect our ethics in the scale and aptness of the aid they give neglected children, the disabled, the long-term sick, penurious widows, bewildered families, the impecunious aged. They help to decide the cultural and physical conditions of life in the effectiveness with which they apply limited resources to education, to medical care, to housing, to pensions. They furnish the stuff of local and national politics. They closely affect and are affected by living standards, national finances, balance of payment crises, international wars and rumours of wars.

The education of politicians in office and stubborn economic realities are forcing the diagnosis of the critics of "free" welfare to the forefront of public debate. The sanguine hopes of the 1940s, aroused by Lord Beveridge's visions inflated by sociological wishful thinking and political ambition, have been fermenting into the bitter fruit of stringency for the "submerged," the "deprived," the "disadvantaged," frustration for parents and teachers, patients

Originally published in 1967 in the *Encounter* and reprinted in Robert Schuettinger, ed., *The Conservative Tradition in European Thought*, 1970.

and doctors, tenants and owner-occupiers, impoverishment for pensioners. In spite of unprecedentedly massive sums spent on state welfare there is *still* not enough; and there never will be. What there is *does not go to people who need it most.* "The language of priorities" bears the dreary accent of political calculation; and the dialogue on poverty between academics and the Labour politicians they once advised has become almost acrimonious.

There are "solutions" in plenty: *more money;* better administration; more centralised control; increased taxes; more doctors, nurses, teachers; higher pay for ditto; "education" of patients in the "proper" use of doctors and hospitals; "education" of administrators and consultants in the courteous treatment of family doctors and patients; discouragement of emigration, obligatory employment of state-financed in the National Health Service or state education; funds from armaments; prohibition or inhibition of independent education, higher charges for private beds in state hospitals; more rent restriction; state control of pension funds; *more money.*

These solutions are mostly pretexts or placebos. Even if they were all practicable they would not remove the central weakness: the pretence that education is "free" for all, that medical care is "free" for all, that housing is partly "free" for millions. Free services are advocated with fervour or resignation for reasons of compassion, administrative convenience, social philosophy, or political practicability . . . Yet the evil effects of the myth are the common currency of first-year economics: that if you depress a price you inflate the demand and choke off supply. This is the essential reason for shortages and waiting lists, for arrogance and arbitrariness from officials (who ration in the absence of price); for frustration and emigration; for concentration on electorally-sensitive medical services and postponement of hospital-building; not least, for the diversion of purchasing power to pleasurable consumption that moralising politicians can conveniently denounce as candy-floss.

The social policy emerging from the myth is deceptively simple. People must have education, medical care, housing, pensions; many people cannot, or will not, pay the price; *ergo,* supply them wholly or partly free; and, for administrative convenience, supply them to *everyone.* This is the solution of the Universalists and the Egalitarians in all three British political parties.

The pretence that the social services are "free" is one of the most deceptive that disfigure British public life. Sir Norman Angell condemned the claim that war really pays as the Great Illusion of the prewar years. The pretence that people do not pay for welfare is the great illusion of the post-war years. The offer of "free" plastic flowers or dish-cloths by business men advertising soap is derided by British sociologists and *literati* for misleading the housewife. The politician who offers "free" welfare magnifies the offence immeasurably. Even Professor J. K. Galbraith's risible caricature of the industrial corporation that can make the consumer buy what it chooses to produce did not attribute to its directors the altruistic motives professed by sanctimonious politicians.

The alternative solution to abolishing market prices for welfare is to restore them and enable everyone to pay them. The function of the state in a society that respects the individual is not to organise and provide welfare but give the purchasing power to people without it, and perhaps to lay down minimum requirements for buyers and minimum standards for sellers. This is the solution of the Selectivists and the Liberals; and again they are to be found in all three parties.

The role of pricing is generally misunderstood by Universalists. The *New Statesman* recently admonished the Minister of Health to maintain the National Health Service "free to all comers," but also to ensure that it continued in being. Astonishingly, there was no hint of recognition that pricing and supply might perhaps be linked. Was [the Minister of Health] being asked to run a press-gang in reverse and shanghai intending emigrants? Was he to organise indentured medical labour gangs from Asia?

Oddly enough [the editor of the *New Statesman*] has shown that he can see the purpose of pricing. He has welcomed the announcement by the Minister of Transport that she was considering road pricing because "it will embody a principle of justice—that people should pay for the trouble they cause and the benefits they receive." He also saw that the main alternative to rationing by price was "a permit system [which] would entail a vast bureaucracy, a probable black market and discrimination." "By what criteria," he properly asked, "would you decide which drivers were 'essential' and which not?" Mr. Mervyn Jones saw it even more clearly when he said in the *New Statesman:* "The alternative . . . to compulsion . . . is to exercise persuasion by price . . . to let the motorist decide for himself whether his use of the car is worthwhile *and to make sure that he thinks twice about it.*" (My italics.) Precisely: the "social purpose" of pricing is to make you think twice before using scarce resources and denying them to other uses that may be more urgent and productive. In principle this is as true of education, medical care, housing, pensions, as of roads, land for car-parking, water, or any other commodity or service hitherto supplied "free."

These are the two basic principles, Universal and Selective, on which British social services will be debated in the coming decade. Mr. Anthony

Crosland [the author of *The Future of Socialism*] has said, "The relief . . . of distress and the elimination . . . of squalor is the main object of social expenditure." This principle puts humanity before equality, selectivity before universalism. It is approved by "individualists," rejected by "socialisers." In practice the selective principle is the only one that will work in a period of rising incomes and growing aspirations. The main objections to it, that it requires identification of people whose incomes require topping up and that some will not ask for aid unless it is shared by all, is a smoke-screen in an intellectual rearguard withdrawal by the Universalists. They are also magnified for party political purposes. But the selective principle does not require the "Household Means Test" that broke up families in the 1930s: means can be identified by an impersonal periodic record of income. The objections lack cogency since a Means Test *is* applied in rate rebates, Council house rent rebates, students' grants, legal aid, the Option Mortgage scheme, and the "income guarantee" by Supplementary Pensions. It has been urged for nursery school fees by Professor A. J. Ayer, Professor D. V. Donnison, and Dr. Michael Young. It is to be applied to an increase in the price of school meals, and it will have to be used by the Government even more if increased help is to be given to families with low incomes because there will simply be not enough public money to give every social benefit to everyone. And by now it must be clear to even the most committed egalitarian that it is foolishly wasteful and inhumane to hand state funds to 100% of the populace in order to make sure that the 10%, or 15%, or 20%, who need it get it.

The argument on "social divisiveness" may, if it is not rebutted, become as stubborn of an obstacle to clear thinking and humane reform as the means test. It was put recently by a journalist with Universalist sympathies but an open mind, Mr. Rudolf Klein, in the *Observer:* The fundamental objection, he said, to allowing people to pay for welfare services privately was that it would introduce a double standard, one for the rich, one for the poor, because the middle classes who would leave the welfare state are those most anxious to raise standards.[1] On the contrary, it is state welfare services that would be "socially divisive" because they cannot, outside rigidly totalitarian societies, be made completely universal. No degree of comprehensivation of secondary schooling in Britain, or "integration" of private with state schools, would prevent some families from giving their children a better for-

1. The middle classes who use state services get what they can for themselves, often at the expense of the working classes. It is an illusion to suppose that there is one standard in state education or NHS (National Health Service).

mal education than the state provides, either because their income is higher or because they prefer to spend more on education and less on eating, clothing, smoking, drinking, motoring, or holidaying. No discouragement to private medical care will prevent some families from seeking more choice, convenience, privacy or comfort in sickness than is provided by the National Health Service. No encouragement to Council building or discouragement of Council house purchase by tenants, or inhibition of the building societies, will prevent some families from finding better homes than others think worth paying for. No degree of expansion in state pensions will ever prevent many people from accumulating more for their retirement than they are compelled to accumulate by (and through) the state.

If the Universalists believe otherwise, let them say that no man shall be able to buy better education, medical care housing or standard of life in retirement than the state can provide for all out of taxation. And then let them show that the Universalist welfare state is more than an egalitarian mirage by drafting the apparatus of controls required to create and enforce it at rising standards financed by increasing taxation: rules governing personal expenditure, inspected and policed; direction (and dilution) of labour for teachers, doctors, and nurses; the penalties of political displeasure and social disapproval of tax avoidance, even by restricting work in favour of leisure; increasingly savage penalties for tax evasion; control or prohibition of emigration.

It is difficult to believe that the Universalists accept or can practise the logic of their philosophy. They must find it especially difficult when rising incomes facilitate and encourage growing social aspirations; and even more difficult when they see communist countries resort to pricing in welfare: Russia charges for nursery schools, Czechoslovakia imposes health prescription charges, Poland changes from housing subsidies to housing allowances to families to enable them to pay market rents, Russian doctors advocate charges for hospitals. Do the Universalists really suppose that the notion of equality in state welfare, as a lowest common denominator, will be freely accepted by wage-earners accustomed to rising standards in everyday consumption?

Many Universalists earn middling or above-middling incomes of £2000 to £5000 or more as academics, writers, journalists, civil servants, lawyers, doctors, politicians. If they send their children to state schools, occupy state hospital beds when ill, live in subsidised Council or rent-restricted houses, and refrain from private saving for retirement in order to avoid privilege and share in parity of esteem, what do they do with their money? And if they buy books, records, go to concerts, the opera, live in spacious houses, entertain interesting people, holiday abroad, how do they prevent their children from deriving educational, social or cultural advantages denied the child of the plumber, the boilermaker, the railwayman? Do they really prevent their wives from seeing Harley Street doctors? Do they really buy the furniture and furnishings common in Council houses? Do they really avoid saving to supplement the state pension? Do they really reject scholarships or free places at public schools? How do they spend their money on goods and services that yield no privilege? And if they perform this feat in their lifetime, how do they avoid advantaging their children when they are dead?

The notion that state welfare can ever be completely universal is a chimera. At the best it will fight a gradually losing rearguard action against rising incomes, a man's natural wish to do better for his family than he had in his lifetime, the family's concern to subsidise its weaker members and shelter them from the competition of the meritocracy, and the foreign example of countries in Europe, Australasia and America that permit growing incomes to yield widening choice.

A system that sets out to provide state welfare universally will, in any society, capitalist or communist, have to permit growing "social divisiveness." But there is a method of creating social parity of esteem. It is to give purchasing power selectively to people who are in need in order to enable them to exert the authority of those who are not. State benefits in cash or coupon would enable everyone—wage-earner as well as salary-earner—to act as a buyer with enough purchasing power in the market to pay for education, medical care, housing or pensions from competing state, local authority, benevolent, charitable, "mutual" or commercial suppliers. Every man and woman would in time appear as a buyer, not a "beneficiary." Social origin and accent would become irrelevant. The market is tone-deaf. Such a system would remove the social divisiveness in the pseudo-Universalist system between the few who pay for a choice and the many who receive free state services with no option. The physically or mentally incapable who could not use cash or coupons would need services in kind or personal care; they are the helpless unavoidable in any society. Everyone else would be buying and paying for welfare with choice. Everyone would be a school fee-paying parent, a private patient, a tenant paying market rents, or an owner-occupier buying a home. In a market the discriminating, articulate, "middle-class" consumers (who subscribe to *Which?* and *Where?*) would keep up standards for the "working-class" consumers (who do not) in welfare as they now do in food, footwear and furniture.

And they would do so much more effectively than in Parent-Teacher or Patients' Associations because withdrawal of custom and loss of profits is more powerful sanction for the supplier in competition than political agitation by captive customers is for politicians, civil servants, Councillors, local education officers, regional hospital boards, headmasters, Council housing managers, or directors of hospitals.

The academic and the political Universalists have been rethinking welfare policy. The academics have come up with little new except more detailed evidence of poverty, a new emphasis on deprivation as relative rather than absolute, and no solutions to two dilemmas: the conflict between *equal* benefits and *humane* benefits, and the scope for choice in state welfare. At the 1966 Fabian Lectures, by what the *Guardian* has called "the poverty lobby," Professor Townsend combined a complaint that Labour had not done enough for people in need with a demand that it should give more aid to all and sundry. He has never explained how he reconciles humanity with equality, and his claim that there is general public rejection of Means Tests is wishful thinking. . . .

Professor Abel-Smith did much better in the third part of his lecture, as his 1965 Fabian Tract *Freedom in the Welfare State* suggested he might do. The first part was a complaint that Labour had slowed down the rate of increase in expenditure on the social services below its rate under the Conservatives. Even the increase of 28% for 1964 to 1970 in the National Plan, disembalmed for the evening, was lower than the Conservatives' 34.5% for 1958 to 1964. How to find the money for more state welfare? Easy: raise taxes. He does not see that choice in welfare might itself encourage effort and yield tax revenue. The second part was another complaint that Britain was spending proportionately less on social welfare than countries with smaller national incomes. He did not consider the reasons for these shortcomings: do they really lie in the mendacity of Conservative and Labour politicians? The third part contained, it seemed, a new note: the admission, at long last, that universal "free" benefits could not continue: perhaps the state might charge fees for some of its services and replace students' grants by loans.

But there was no effort to show how choice, the case for which he had recognised in *Freedom in the Welfare State*, could be ensured in state welfare. Recently he has conceded that in the end the solution is "to concentrate help where it is needed and to stop giving it where it is not." But this system requires Means Tests; there are "administrative snags" in Means Tests, so for a decade until they are solved higher benefits are given to all. The case for Universalism has thus toppled from the philosophic principle to a technical convenience. Now perhaps the debate can concentrate on how to devise the simplest, least inquisitive technique for identifying incomes and needs.

The political Universalists have shown more wisdom. First, Mr. Douglas Houghton, then Mr. Brian Walden and Mr. Desmond Donelly (and now Mr. Ray Gunter) [all leaders of the Labour Party] have virtually abandoned Universalism and embraced Selectivity though not without ambiguity and reluctant compromise that may prove impracticable. The academics are now in a quandary. Professor Titmuss' formula, "an infrastructure of Universalist services . . . within and around which can be developed socially acceptable selective services" is an attempt to save the academic argument but concedes its invalidity and impracticability. It is hardly tenable to argue that social benefits should be both equal and unequal. If selectivity is noxious or offensive, it should be avoided; if it is acceptable there is no argument for retaining universalism to avoid the social stigma.

His most recent formulation, in a forthcoming book, *Commitment to Welfare,* is ingenious but abortive. It is to combine universalist services with selective services based on "the *needs* of specific categories, groups and territorial areas and not dependent on *individual tests of means*" (his italics). But the composition of categories and groups changes: "Council house tenants" now includes people who are not in need of subsidy, and many who should have the subsidy are not Council house tenants. "Territorial areas" designated for state aid would contain people who do not need it, and others who do would live elsewhere. There is no escape: universal benefits must be replaced by benefits matched to the circumstances not of "groups" or "areas" but *individual people.*

Professor John Vaizey has demonstrated the dilemma of the Universalists in pointing (in a recent *Spectator*) to the "grave internal contradiction" in the "ideology of equality, an ideology to which I subscribe," of concentrating education on the able and on the deprived. The progressives and the egalitarians do not seem to be able to make up their minds whether they wish to open the world to the gifted child or to rescue the ungifted from his environment. Their dilemma is even worse than that: by wanting to make the comprehensive school a monopoly rather than an experiment, and by limiting the expenditure on education to the revenue that can be raised in taxes, they are putting equality before quality. The tragedy in their position is that there is no need for this unpalatable choice. It is possible to raise the minimum education that could be made available for *all* children by allowing parents who value it more to pay for more in the market. The egalitarians are not only inhibiting the gifted; they are also repressing the ungifted.

But the notion that people who value welfare and who can pay for it *should* pay is spreading. Mr. David Marquand, Dr. David Owen, and Professor John Mackintosh tentatively acknowledge ("Change Gear," *Socialist Commentary*) the relevance of selectivity for concentrating resources on people in most need and the case, in principle, for welfare charges. In their anxiety to recognise economic reality but not to abandon their philosophic moorings they strain after both but risk emerging with neither. They see that taxation is not always a better method of financing welfare than charges, and that users may be more willing to pay if they see a connection between payment and service, but they confuse the *purpose* and the *effect* of charging. They want charges but not if they "deter." But charges necessarily deter, and they should deter—that is how they husband resources and minimise waste. The solution is not to avoid charges but to enable people in need to pay them by supplements to income.

A decisive defect of the Universalist principle is that it is *inhumane.* It gives cake to people with cake and denies a second loaf to those with one. Some universal benefits, pensions, for example, are taxed: even so, much remains with the well-off and wealthy (pensions are taxed as earned income). But some benefits are not taxed at all. A state education is worth £280 a year to a family with two children at a secondary school, £560 if in a sixth form; medical care is worth perhaps £80–£100 a year to a family of four; Council housing £60 a year or more. Hundreds of millions of pounds remain in such pockets that could be distributed in larger family allowances, widows' grants, disablement benefit, retirement pensions to people in need.

Some universalists support the inhumane system because of a political fallacy: that social benefits must be equal and shared by all. For Professor Titmuss "the real argument is about equality." *But equal treatment of people in unequal circumstances is not equality.* It satisfies the yearning for equality less than a selective system which could relate aid to need.

Nor can the Universalist principle be maintained by higher tax yields out of rising incomes and faster economic growth. This was the doctrine propounded at the 1964 and 1966 elections; and it is implied by foreign example in writings from the National Institute of Economic and Social Research and from the Economics Correspondent of *The Times Business News.* There is no evidence that as incomes rise people will readily yield the increases to the state for enlarged welfare (or any other) services. Governments in political democracies may devise new taxes on employment, corporations or wealth; but they are yet to show that they can extract more than 40 to 45% of total incomes—even in wartime. And the contrast with European countries that spend more on state welfare despite lower national incomes demonstrates no more than that state welfare is desirable precisely where incomes are low—and provided they are unequal enough to furnish some large enough for redistributive taxation. State welfare should recede as living standards rise. It becomes increasingly superfluous.

British social policy since 1964 amply demonstrates the fiscal limits to state welfare when taxation is high. It is easy to ask for more state benefits but not to show how to raise the additional taxes. To his credit Professor Abel-Smith did not resort in his Fabian lecture to the too easy option of reduced armaments. The amount that could be saved by reduction in the £2.250 million defence bill would not provide the vast sums required to raise the amount and quality of the social services to the level required to the most needy, still less to satisfy rising expectations, so long as they must be provided for everyone. It is the universality and the "free"-dom of state welfare that remains the fundamental weakness of the British welfare state.

The latest effort to find tax revenue has passed from unchanged tax rates on rising incomes to higher taxation of static incomes. The Universalists would like higher family allowances (for all) to be financed by lower income tax allowances for children. This clumsy proposal confuses aid for the needy with the equity of the taxation system as a whole. But its significance is that it illustrates the dire straits of the Universalists. The politicians will have to recognise what the social administrators cannot see: that economic causes have political and fiscal consequences: Ossa cannot be piled on Pelion for all time. There is not much more room for adding taxes on personal incomes. Ingenuity in avoiding and evading taxes is not yet exhausted. . . .

Until recently, the common conclusions favoured universal state benefits. The appearance of a change in all three parties is therefore significant.

In Labour it seems to have begun in 1962 with the admonition by Young Fabians of their elders to reject the "utterly naïve" notion that the basic state pension could ever be raised sufficiently to take all pensioners off National Assistance and to see that some form of Means Test was unavoidable. . . .

The Liberal Party's spokesman on social security in the House of Commons, Mr. John Pardoe, has quickly seen the incongruity of universal social benefits and rising incomes. And at the 1966 Liberal Assembly he made no bones about the common sense of abandoning opposition to a Means Test.

In spite of one of the last unsordid acts in recent social policy, the 1961 graduated state pension (introduced to raise revenue without the unpopularity of a tax and to dish Labour), the Conservatives are also increasingly accepting the second half of the twentieth century and are promising to reconstruct the welfare state to give more aid to the needy. Younger Tories like Geoffrey Howe and John Biffen are streets ahead of their elders, and Sir Keith Joseph is revealing a subtle and sensitive mind.

The change from universal to selective benefits is impeded by a variant of the equality principle that ranges from a wholesome rebellion against privilege to a little-minded indulgence in envy. It ordains that no one shall have anything—better schooling, nursing, housing—unless and until everyone can have it. It is as potent a precept as any for postponing the day when all can have it. What is at stake is more than the blunting of incentives to individuals to earn more for their families, or indeed the role of the family in social life. It is even more than the logical dilemma of the egalitarian who is prepared to allow some inequality in income after taxation but no inequality in expenditure on education, medical care, even housing, and is content to see vast sums go to everyday consumption. The dilemma of the Egalitarian is that insistence on equality is insistence on *less than that possible for all.* Luton Council has told parents that a shortage of teachers prevents its schools from taking children at five; they must wait until they are six. Rebellious parents sought out local former teachers prepared to take their children for a year. The Council's Education Officer objected that no five-year-olds could have the teaching because not all could have it. If welfare services are to be organised by public authority on the principle "nobody until everybody," then everybody will have less than they could have and wait longer for more.

There is a further difficulty for the Egalitarians. If no one may move up in earning or spending income until all move up, there may be no movement at all. Example and demonstration are the *conditio sine qua non* of improvement. If no one may have something *different* which can be considered *better,* movement will be stultified. Equality is an idea reserved for a world without scarcity. Lenin saw it in *State and Revolution;* and John Strachey saw it in his Left Book Club era of the 1930s, although he was naïvely sanguine about the imminence of superabundance. But even if Utopia is still far off and differences in earnings are unavoidable and (in the Marxist phrase) socially necessary, we can top up the lower ones and make them *less unequal* bundles of purchasing power. To add to all of them in the name of equality, social cohesion, or parity of esteem, is to add champagne to the rich man's table and shin-bone to the pensioner's.

Sooner or later enough people in the Labour, Liberal, and Conservative parties will see that three basic aims in welfare are within our grasp: humanity, liberty and relative plenty. We could within a few years give much more help to the needy, create choice for all capable of using it, and secure much more expenditure on welfare out of the national income. But all three parties will have to abandon their conservatism and think more radically and adventurously. Labour will have to abandon its false egalitarianism, the Liberals their out-dated Beveridgism (which Beveridge himself might have abandoned), the Conservatives their propensity to ape anything that seems momentarily fashionable or expedient.

The notion that change in the welfare state is "politically impossible" has been blown sky-high by the field surveys of public attitudes and preferences in the last four years conducted by Mass Observation for the Institute of Economic Affairs, largely confirming or confirmed by surveys by Dr. Mark Abrams for *Socialist Commentary* in 1960, by Mr. W. G. Runciman in 1962 (discussed in *Relative Deprivation and Social Justice* in 1966), by *New Society* in 1963, by the National Opinion Polls in 1966, and by newspaper polls in the last few months. The findings of the IEA research is that there is no majority political preference for universal social benefits irrespective of needs. On the contrary, it has found that half or more of the varying samples of the population would favour social benefits related to need. The survey by Mass Observation (for the IEA) in June 1966 found that 53% of men and women thought that free health prescriptions should be confined to people in need, 57% family allowances, 73% subsidised Council houses, and 38% increases in state pensions.[2] A survey in April 1967 found that 65% of a national sample said that they would be more ready to pay more taxes if their money went to people in need than if it went to all and sundry.

There is no insurmountable political obstacle to a change in welfare policy that could give more to people in need, choice to everyone as soon as they could use it, and more welfare all round. It could, I believe, be achieved by reform in four stages.

Stage I, in which all social benefits, in kind as well as in cash, would be taxed. This gradual closing of the gap between "free" state services and full market fees for private services would ease:

Stage II, in which fees from people who could pay them would be charged for state services, the scope for charges widening in:

Stage III, in which cash (for coupons) would be distributed to enable everyone to pay for welfare, state or private:

Stage IV, in which taxation would be reduced and cash allowances or

2. The findings are detailed and alternative policies discussed in Seldon and Gray, *Social Benefits: Universal or Selective?* Research Monograph 8, Institute of Economic Affairs, 1967.

coupons gradually withdrawn. The stages would be reached at varying rates in different services, and some by-passed or telescoped.

The philosophy of "free" state welfare is based on jejune sentimentality about human affairs that does no credit to the common sense or practical judgement of academics, the *literati,* the doctors, teachers, lawyers, or the politicians who profess it. In the conduct of their private affairs they reject the assumption that human beings will not try to get as much as they can for nothing, or are not concerned about personal, private, family interests, or that to appoint a man a public official is to transform him into a selfless public benefactor.

Yet they persist in espousing a system of universal benefits because it satisfies their yearning for a pseudo-egalitarianism, because it assuages their guilty conscience about inherited or acquired wealth and social advantages, or because, contrariwise, it offers the prospect of political power in aggrandisement of the state. And all this in spite of its denial of help for the neglected, the sick, the suffering, the bewildered, and the aged, its denial of the liberty to choose, its incitement to spend on everyday consumption.

The USA is installing state welfare just when we are learning its defects, but Socialist and Communist countries are having second thoughts despite a political philosophy that requires universal benefits. Young men—and unclosed minds—avid for change should look East. The welfare state in Britain reached its present shape in the last twenty years. The longer it is left unchanged the more convulsive the upheavals when change is enforced by rising incomes, growing social aspirations, and overseas example.

AFTER THE NHS

REFLECTIONS ON THE DEVELOPMENT OF PRIVATE HEALTH INSURANCE IN BRITAIN IN THE 1970s

INTRODUCTION

As part of its educational purpose in explaining the light that economists and others concerned with the optimum use of scarce resources can throw on policy in industry or government, the Institute is reprinting, as Occasional Papers, essays or addresses judged of interest to wider audiences than those to which they were originally directed.

Occasional Paper 21 comprises material assembled for a Paper on "The Rôle of Voluntary Insurance in Social Welfare" prepared by Mr. Arthur Seldon for the Second Voluntary Health Insurance Conference in Sydney, Australia, in April–May 1968. A shorter version was distributed to 250 delegates and observers from a dozen countries. Except for several explanatory sentences and footnotes, the text remains largely as it was compiled in March 1968. In the interval the author has had the rare opportunity of discussing health services with specialist economists, Ministers, civil servants, doctors and insurance organisations in several countries on his way to and from Sydney and of studying documents on a wide variety of health services. In an Epilogue written since his return, Mr. Seldon explains his doubts about the continued existence of the NHS and draws lessons for Britain from all he learned about the strengths and weaknesses of state and private medicine in countries with differing social structures.

Mr. Seldon's review would be valuable at any time as an unusually constructive commentary on the British health services and the increasing strains they are exhibiting. It is made all the more significant by the twentieth anniversary of the establishment of the National Health Service on the 5 July, 1968, which we have chosen for publication of this *Paper*. No doubt the occasion will be marked by the customary quota of self-congratulation by party men claiming credit for their handiwork. So evident are the signs that all is not well with the crumbling edifice that we may expect at least passing reference to deficiencies, followed quickly by the verbal dexterity that equates every multiplying inadequacy in public services with a splendid "challenge" to still further exertion.

But what if Mr. Seldon is right in his diagnosis of weakness inseparable from an artifact which, however noble its inspiration, is foredoomed to failure by the absence of the discipline of pricing and the stimulus of competition? How otherwise can we account for the monumental scale of the acknowledged NHS deficiencies despite expenditure of £1,600 million compared with £170 million estimated by the wartime coalition government for 1975 (at 1945 prices). No amount of additional expenditure will bring nearer the unattainable goal of "the best medical care for everyone." More likely is it to widen the gap between the exceptional standard enjoyed by "important" patients with good political or medical connections and the crowded waiting-room and lengthening queue for the less fortunate. Since, leaving aside Britain's budgetary problems, there is no conceivable amount of additional public funds that can remove the scarcity of resources available for medical care (particularly in relation to ever more elaborate surgical and pharmaceutical therapy), it follows that rationing of supplies will always be necessary.

Mr. Seldon's discussion is reinforced by the evidence at home and overseas that private insurance provides a surer method of enlarging the supply of funds for medical care than exclusive reliance on over-strained public finance. In perhaps the most original part of his *Paper,* the author gives reasons for believing that, while the failure of the NHS is inseparable from its monolithic structure and method of finance, the shortcomings of private health insurance are capable of relief or removal through government action to enforce competition among suppliers by appropriate regulation of the legal and institutional framework and to enfranchise consumers by supplementing inadequate income by cash or vouchers.

Even for a colleague familiar with the exceptional qualities Arthur Seldon brings to his exposition of the economics of social welfare policies, this latest essay compels admiration for its clarity, cogency and not least its broad humanity untainted by condescending paternalism. Since he wrote the first edition of *Pensions in a Free Society* for the newly-formed Institute of Economic Affairs in 1957, Mr. Seldon has fought at times almost single-handed against political complacency and all-party conservatism to compel reconsideration of the assumptions on which universalist welfare policies were perched under the emotional impulse of wartime emergency, universal rationing, conscription and the surrender of freedom.

Now that his judgement has been shown to have been almost prophetic in pointing to the mounting crisis in financing public welfare services, his writing is assured of an ever widening and increasingly attentive audience throughout Britain and beyond. The Institute's constitution prevents it from endorsing or sharing the author's analysis or conclusions, but it offers them to public men no less than to teachers and students as an antidote to a faulty economic prescription that has too long obscured the damage to health and economy wrought by the state in persisting with its monopoly of medical care.

June 1968 *Ralph Harris*

I. Preamble — The British Situation

I approach the subject as an independent economist who sees the balance of advantage in economic systems designed to satisfy the consumer rather than the producer. The consumer may need guidance and advice, but in situations in which he can learn from experience of trial and error he must be empowered to make decisions. He may have to be guided away from error that itself impairs or destroys the power to make decisions; but tutelage and paternalism tend to outlive their day and prolong dependence. In medical care patients may be incapable of judging techniques, consultants and specialists, but they can employ advisers who can: the rôle of the family doctor as a medical broker is often under-rated. And in the non-technical "service" aspects of choice, timing, location, convenience, comfort and attention to individual preference, which may have decisive therapeutic value, the patient can learn to exercise the sovereignty of the consumer.

In the industrial economies of the West, and more gradually but also in the communist and developing countries,[1] rising incomes are reinforcing the power to make decisions and intensifying the expectation of rising standards, improved quality and more responsive personal services. So far these expectations have been increasingly satisfied in everyday, household consumption in the Western countries, but less so in medical care (and other welfare services) in countries where they are organised by the state. We may anticipate that rising living standards in all parts of the world—East and West, collectivist and capitalist—will strengthen the demand for medical services responsive to consumer preferences. The demand may be frustrated for a time by benevolent politicians who are anxious to use power "in the public interest" or who innocently mistake the rôle of the state in a developing society. Government may properly provide the "public health" environmental and preventive services or the developmental and research facilities that cannot, as efficiently or at all, be supplied in response to individual de-

1. Mr. Richard Sampson told us in Dublin that the African who adopted urban life in Zambia soon sensed the urge to pay for a doctor of his choice. A Paper to be published by the IEA in 1968 suggests similar developments in Ghana and other parts of West Africa, including crossing of frontiers from English-speaking to French-speaking areas and vice versa: the late Peter du Sautoy, *Choice: Lessons from the Third World,* Occasional Paper 22, IEA, 1968.

mands in the market. But it need not necessarily produce, organise, manage and provide personal medical services as a virtual monopoly financed by compulsory levies in taxation or social insurance.

The British National Health Service Act of 1946 did not require the state to *provide* health services. It prescribed the duty of the Minister of Health

> to promote the establishment of a comprehensive health service designed to secure improvement in the physical and mental health of the people and the prevention, diagnosis and treatment of illness, and for that purpose to provide *or secure the effective provision of* services. (My italics.)

In the last 20 years successive British governments have chosen to "provide" rather than "secure the effective provision of" health services.

They could have done so by providing purchasing power to enable individuals with low incomes to pay or insure for insurable medical services, and by specifying requirements if they considered that individuals would not insure or take medical advice and standards if they considered that suppliers would not provide acceptable or satisfactory services. The National Health Service provides not only "public health" but also personal hospital, consultant and family doctor services very largely in return for taxes and social insurance contributions: nominal charges for prescriptions, spectacles, dentures and other items provide some 5 per cent of the revenue; 95 per cent has been financed by compulsory levies.

In round numbers, the NHS disburses £1,600 million a year. Of the average of £30 annual expenditure per head of the population, it spends some £4 10s on "public health" services, £20 on hospitals, perhaps £2 5s on general practitioners, and £3 on prescriptions. "Public health" services thus account for about 15 per cent and "private" or "personal" services for some 85 per cent of total expenditures. An interesting debate has been renewed among economists on the theory of the "social" costs and benefits of private contracts. The division into "social" and "private" is not clear-cut. "Benefit" and "cost" cannot always be measured, or related to each other. The significant consideration for medical financing is the attitude of *individuals:* will they pay by "public" methods for services which they *regard* as personal or private to themselves, whatever the real or supposed "external" or "social" effects? The contrast between the ratio of 95: 5 in public to private proportions of financing and the 15: 85 in public to private proportions of services is the locale of the reconsideration by British economists and politicians of the financing of the NHS discussed in Section III.

The advantages and disadvantages of the NHS have been increasingly debated in recent years and months in Britain, by social scientists as well as by doctors; this is not the time or place to discuss the arguments and evidence.[2] My purpose is rather to indicate briefly the inferences that are being drawn from 20 years' experience of the NHS as it has been run—controlled by the Minister through centralised administration and financing and supplied largely "free" without direct payment—and to discuss more fully the implications for voluntary health assurance. The central apparent advantage of the NHS, that it ensures, on paper, equal access to medical care unrestricted by a cash nexus, is being weighed against its major emerging disadvantage, that the state has been unable to raise enough tax revenue to provide medical care at rising standards.

The Report for 1966 of the Ministry of Health indicates some of the issues for the academic and public debate. After some 17 years of a virtual absence of hospital building, the Report estimated that £75 million was spent in 1966–67, contrasted with some £46 million in 1938–39 (at 1967 prices). It referred to the annual average of £100 million in the 10-year Hospital Building Programme introduced in 1962, and observed: "the level of expenditure will be more than double pre-war." The independent observer may consider it

2. The order of magnitude of the deficiencies in manpower, equipment and buildings has been put by the Dean of the Faculty of Medicine at the University of Newcastle at a third of current and capital expenditure; he has argued that an additional £500 million a year is required from taxation for the NHS to give medicine the priority in Britain that it enjoys in the USA. In a House of Commons debate, a former Parliamentary Private Secretary to the last Chancellor of the Exchequer, Mr. James Callaghan, reacted to the statistic with incredulity: "Nobody in his right senses imagines that the Treasury will make that money available. There is not a hope . . ." (*Hansard*, 9 June, 1967, column 1554.) The inadequacy in public finance is, moreover, understated by this figure. To allot £500 million more to the NHS, large sums would also have to be found from taxation for education, housing, family allowances, pensions, and other welfare benefits and public services in order to maintain the comparability of the marginal productivity (or political necessity) of expenditure on all social benefits and public services. The total addition to taxation required to yield £500 million for the NHS would have to be considerably larger, almost certainly over £1,500 million and perhaps as much as £2,000 million.

The former PPS, Mr. Brian Walden, a Labour MP for Birmingham, commented further: ". . . health will get a low priority in this country. Why? Because the state cannot spend enough money on it, and it does not allow the individual to spend his money on it to anything like the same extent that he would if he were given a choice." Mr. Walden would like individuals to spend more on the NHS than they are doing through taxation, and the method he and other Labour politicians have in mind is that of charges for state health services. Their dilemma is that charges would lead to contracting out from the state system into voluntary insurance for private medical care. A former Labour Cabinet Minister has proposed a charge of £5 to £10 a week for state hospitals, a risk which could be insured for about 6d to 9d per head in families to cover 10 weeks of hospitalisation a year.

more significant to contrast the 1966–67 expenditure in the NHS with the expenditure *that probably would have been reached* in a more diversified system of government, municipal, voluntary and commercial hospital building. There can be little doubt that the trebling in living standards since the late 1930s, the growing contrast between abundance in everyday consumption and continuing deficiences in medical care, the growth in independent medical care and voluntary insurance that would have taken place *in the absence of the NHS,* and the example of other countries—Australia, the USA and in Europe—where private insurance has financed impressive advances, would have combined to accelerate the rate of hospital building, possibly to more than twice the pre-war rate. *And it is impossible to believe that there would have been virtually no new building from 1948 to 1962.*

Hospital staffing has also produced widespread public discussion and debate. The Report said: "The number of hospital medical staff has increased by over 60 per cent since 1949 . . ." Quality is more difficult to measure than quantity, and more easily omitted from political debate. The replacement of British-born by overseas-born doctors is not necessarily a sufficient indicator of diminished quality, but it creates non-medical origins of danger, not least language. The Report records that during 1966 home-born (UK and Eire) registrars rose by 18 to 2,217, overseas-born by 206 to 2,064. Home-born senior hospital officials fell by 49 to 1,320, overseas-born rose by 251 to 2,183. In all, home-born medical assistants, senior registrars, registrars, junior hospital medical officers, senior hospital officers and hospital officers post- and pre-registration rose by 144 to 6,806; overseas-born rose by 461 to 5,317. Emigration to North America, Australia and elsewhere and immigration from India and Pakistan continue. And waiting lists for non-acute surgery and other treatment do not shorten significantly.

The Report recorded an "upsurge in demand for health centres." There has been no upsurge in supply. Two were opened in 1965, eight in 1966. Re-

---

A further problem that confronts advocates of increased expenditure on health services as a whole beyond the 4½ per cent of national income in the UK is that, in most other Western countries, where the percentage is 5½ or 6 per cent or more, medical care financing is substantially through private, although sometimes compulsory, insurance. The reluctance in Western countries to pay for expanding health services through taxation as incomes rise is not yet adequately discussed in international comparisons of expenditure on medical care such as that of Professor Brian Abel-Smith, *Paying for Health Services,* World Health Organisation, 1967.

Health services in the USA are criticised as wasteful in "frills" and as encouraging hypochondria. It is not established that these faults are unavoidable in private financing; but, if the choice were between US excess and UK stringency, many in Britain—after 20 years of the NHS—would prefer excess.

ductions in public expenditure following devaluation of sterling may further postpone the response of supply.

The Report recorded "the first major review of the family doctor service since the start of the NHS in 1948." The new arrangements for pay and conditions incorporate government payment of some staffing and other costs that may impair the independence of family doctors in the direction of a system in which state guarantees may entail state influence or oversight. The report of a Committee on the production and marketing of drugs may also presage a further element of restriction on medical independence. How far family doctors are satisfied with the new and impending changes in remuneration and conditions may be seen in part from the statistics of emigration in 1967 and 1968. In the meantime overwork and overcrowding in doctors' consulting rooms continue.

Whatever the outlook in the coming years, it would seem that British doctors are showing more interest in other methods of organising and financing medical care. Although their views on the viability of the NHS differ widely, they asked the British Medical Association at their 1967 annual conference to create a Committee to prepare a report on "an alternative health service" for its Conference in 1969. An interim report to its 1968 Conference will indicate[3] its approach to diagnosis and cure. The Committee has discussed the scope for expanding voluntary health insurance, perhaps with a minimum laid down by the state, and made financially possible for the lower (as well as higher) income groups for most medical risks by state subvention. It is studying the lessons and warnings that can be drawn from the methods of organising and financing medical care developed in Europe, North America, Australia and New Zealand, including several countries from which there are delegates at this conference. They in turn may be interested to learn from a country with more experience of the achievements and disappointments of state medical care than any other industrial society this side of the Iron Curtain. International comparisons are often precarious; and transplants may be dangerous or premature. But exchange of information is a prelude to wisdom.

II. The Potential Demand for Private Insurance

For the first 12 years of the NHS public policy on medical care was conducted with little reference to "public" (private) opinion. In the absence

3. Now published: *Interim Report of the Advisory Planning Panel on the History and Financial Aspects of the Health Service*, BMA, 1968.

of a free market for medical care, satisfaction or dissatisfaction could be recorded only indistinctly through the muffled tones of infrequent political elections and the restricted reactions of patients unable to indicate approval or disapproval by moving freely between suppliers they favour or disfavour.

Two more reliable indicators were the growth of voluntary health insurance, discussed in Section III, and new attempts to identify attitudes towards the NHS in field studies that attempted to apply the techniques of opinion polling to market research. In 1963 and 1965 the Institute of Economic Affairs commissioned the research organisation, Mass-Observation, to conduct a wide-ranging survey among a national (quota) sample of male, married, heads of households aged 21 to 65, in order to discover attitudes and preferences on the NHS and to test the hypothesis, then widely accepted, that a change of public policy on medical care was "politically impossible."

To discover preferences between the NHS and private medicine, the survey employed the device of the voucher, a form of earmarked purchasing power proposed by Professor Milton Friedman of the University of Chicago as a means of creating choice in education in place of "free" state education provided without choice. Discussion with health insurers suggested that an annual subscription of £10 per head would cover the common range of risks at the average costs for hospitalisation, specialist consultation and treatment. The sample was asked whether it subscribed to:

> private health insurance which covers you for things like hospital treatment, specialists' fees and medicines.

Non-subscribers[4] (82 per cent of the sample) were then asked the advantages of a private scheme. Finally, they were prompted by being shown a card on which the advantages were listed as:

> able to choose your own surgeon
> earlier treatment
> privacy
> more personal treatment

and asked (in 1965):

> Suppose that, instead of a National Health Service the government offered you a voucher worth £5 a year for each member of your family (including

4. Subscribers were asked to which scheme they belonged and why they paid into it "as well as paying towards the National Health Service." Two per cent subscribed to BUPA, six per cent to the Hospital Saving Association, the remainder to other organisations broadly similar to BUPA and the HSA.

yourself) to help you pay for private health insurance. If you had to add another £5 for each member, do you think you would accept the offer?

The question was repeated for a voucher worth £7 to which £3 would have to be added. (The addition of £5 and £3 would roughly allow for the patient's fraction discussed below, p. 85–86). The findings are shown in Table I.

The response was thus obtained for two voucher values and in four socio-occupational groups. (Such methods might make possible a crude measure of the elasticity of the demand for private insurance and, indirectly, for private medical care in terms of price and, roughly, income.) The significant general finding was of considerable interest in private insurance and medical care even if they required out-of-pocket payment. The interest varied in the socio-occupational groups but was still nearly a fifth among the semi-skilled and unskilled for the £5 voucher and nearly a quarter for the £7 voucher. It would not be unreasonable to suppose that as knowledge of the private sec-

Table I. The Demand for Private Insurance

		Socio-Occupational Groups			
	Total	Upper Middle & Middle	Lower Middle	Skilled	Semi-Skilled & Unskilled
1. Total Sample	2,018	257	329	902	530
2. Voucher Sample	1,663	206	268	735	454
3. 2 as % of 1	82.4	80.0	81.5	81.5	85.7
% would accept £5 voucher	23	36	28	21	17
% would accept £7 voucher	30	47	35	27	23
Group as % of Total Voucher Sample		12.4	16.1	44.2	27.3
Approximate No. of Households:					
Total Households (million)	12.0	1.5	2.0	5.4	3.2
Voucher Sample (million)	9.9	1.2	1.6	4.4	2.7
Private Expenditure added to £5 voucher (£M.)	45.4	8.6	9.0	18.5	9.2
Private Expenditure added to £7 voucher (£M.)	35.6	6.8	6.7	14.3	7.5

Table II. Preferences Between State and Private Health Services

Alternative	Total Sample	Socio-economic Groups 1	2	3	4
	%	%	%	%	%
(a)	32	31	27	33	33
(b)	25	21	24	25	29
(c)	34	42	40	33	28

tor spread the market would grow. (Later research in 1966 by BUPA found that two-thirds of the sample had never heard of private health insurance.)

The second purpose of the 1963 and 1965 surveys was to test the assumption that reform in medical care away from centrally-directed, tax-financed "free" health services would not be countenanced. The total sample was asked:

> Suppose most incomes continue to rise in the next 10 or 20 years. Which of these three possible state policies would you prefer?
>
> (a) The State should take *more* in taxes, rates and contributions to pay for better or increased health services which everyone would have.
>
> (b) The State should take *less* in taxes, rates and contributions to provide a health service *only* for people in need and leave others to pay or insure privately.
>
> (c) The State should continue the present service but allow people to contract out, pay *less* contributions and use the money saved to pay for their own doctor, etc.

The findings are shown in Table II. These figures suggest that there was a substantial majority in favour of a change from the universal NHS.

Research conducted in 1966 for BUPA by the British Market Research Bureau confirmed the IEA/MO finding of a substantial (and hitherto largely unknown) interest in a choice in medical care. Like the IEA/MO surveys, the BUPA/BMRB research employed quantities in place of the qualitative attitude questions.[5] The BUPA survey asked its sample (1,729 men and women

5. The two approaches were analysed in Harris and Seldon, *Choice in Welfare*, 1965, and are contrasted in Seldon and Gray, *Universal or Selective Social Benefits?*, Research Monograph 8, IEA, 1967, and Seldon, *Taxation and Welfare*, Research Monograph 14, IEA, 1967. The view

aged 18 to 64) its view of tax reliefs, vouchers and government subsidies as means of easing the cost of private medical care. The findings of the two surveys can be compared by analysing the response to the voucher.

The value of the IEA/MO vouchers (£5 and £7 per head of the family) were named in the questions. If to the 23 and 30 per cent who said they would take the £5 and £7 vouchers respectively and use them to pay or insure for private medical care are added the 3–4 per cent then insured with BUPA-type insurers, and perhaps a further 2–3 per cent HSA-type contributors (many of whom are covered for a proportion of private consultants' fees as well as supplements to NHS benefits), the proportions rise to 28–30 per cent for the £5 voucher and 35–37 per cent for the £7 voucher, i.e., between a quarter and a third of the population for a half-cost voucher and between a third and two-fifths for a seven-tenths voucher. The BUPA voucher survey differed in several respects. It asked for opinion ratings on vouchers given to

> everybody . . . equivalent to their contributions to the National Health Service which they could use for the NHS or for a private treatment insurance scheme.[6]

Of the BUPA sample 23 per cent said they would obtain private treatment if they had a voucher with this value; the proportion rose to 27 per cent if the 4 per cent membership of private insurance schemes is added.

The prevailing low demand for private health insurance is in part the result of the legal, fiscal and institutional framework created by government. In the UK the subscriber to private insurance for private medical care, unlike the purchaser of an occupational pension, may not contract out of the state service. Unlike the purchaser of a life assurance policy geared to pay for private education, or a mortgagor, or a private health subscriber in the USA, Australia, Ireland and other countries, he is allowed no (income tax) rebate on the payment for the private service. The member of an occupational health insurance group may derive a tax advantage from the fringe benefit if

---

developed there is that "attitudes" to a specific medical service are of more doubtful value than *preferences* between *alternative* medical services or principles expressed in the knowledge of their comparative *prices.*

6. The sum was not named in the questionnaire, and it is not clear how many respondents know its magnitude. The sample comprised 1,437 men and women aged 16 to 64 among "the general public" (including some BUPA members) and 292 BUPA members. The NHS contribution in 1966 was 3s 4d a week (2s 8½d paid by the employee and 7½d by the employer), or £8 13s 4d a year to cover the employee and his dependants. Recently it was raised by 6d a week, paid by the employee, to £9 19s 4d a year.

his pay is below £2,000 a year. And private medical services that receive charitable payments under covenant may recoup the tax paid on them. Individuals who subscribe to private health insurance must pay for all or a large part of the state service they do not use, and there is no other form of state return of taxation paid by users of private health services.

Despite these financial loadings against health insurance there has been growing desire to pay for medical care in preference to accepting a standardised state service. The BUPA/BMRB study found that 18 per cent of the general public would pay for private treatment if there were "tax relief equivalent to their contributions to a provident scheme" (making 22 per cent in all) and 15 per cent if the cost of private treatment were "subsidised by the government to allow for contributions made to the NHS by private patients" (19 per cent in all). Thus, the present 2 million people covered by the eight provident associations might rise to 16 million with the IEA £7 voucher, 12 million with the BUPA-value voucher, 10 million with a tax rebate, and 9 million with a direct government subsidy.

These fiscal methods of removing the financial loading against or encouraging private insurance are common in many Western countries. Their effect on the numbers who would insure for private medical care can be no more than estimated by methods outlined here designed to ascertain the reaction in a hypothetical free market, both for private, competing systems of medical care and for methods of financing them. In the absence of such a market in practice, the observer concerned to study the comparative development of medical care in market and non-market institutions must employ hypotheses that are second best to market situations.

The conclusion that seems incontrovertible is that *preference in medical care organisation and financing cannot be measured without a market, actual or hypothetical, however qualified and imperfect.*[7] The method of the polling booth does not suffice, either because it elicits decisions on inseparable packages of policies of which medical care is one of many varying from civil liberties to foreign policy, or because opinion in a referendum confined to a single policy can be assembled only on general organisational structure and

7. The nature of the market for medical care has been debated by economic and sociological academics in Britain (and elsewhere). In countries such as the USA and Australia, where consumer choice, freedom for doctors, actuaries, insurance entrepreneurs and industry to organise and experiment in medical care financing and competition are common, there is awareness of the limitations of markets. In the UK, where markets are minimal, constricted and the subject of obloquy, we are increasingly sensitive to the consequences of their repression.

not on individual, personal service. The result has been that in the UK there has been a large gap between government policy and private preference. *British politicians of all parties have been out of touch with the public.* Government policy has not expressed individual preferences, and it has not used its agency, the Social Survey, to identify or measure them.

III. The Supply of Private Insurance

These are issues in public policy that cannot be ignored in a study of the organisation and financing of medical care. Our concern with them here is in their implications for the development of private health insurance.

The renewed public interest in health insurance in the UK derives essentially from the recognition in all political parties, increasingly among academics, and most recently among doctors, that taxation (including social insurance) does not appear able to raise enough finance to provide medical care to keep pace with living standards in the UK or with medical care in other countries. Proposals for augmenting the 4.5 per cent of the national income currently channelled to the NHS have been wide-ranging: a reduction in public expenditure on defence, higher taxes on income or expenditure, an earmarked Health Tax, a semi-independent Health Corporation, quinquennial rather than annual grants from the Exchequer, sweepstakes, more efficient administration. Few are free of defect. There is increasingly ready recognition of a basic truth in the payment for medical care that *public* financing is not the most fruitful method for what are experienced as *personal* health services. The dilemma was put simply by the former Cabinet Minister responsible between October 1964 and February 1967 for co-ordinating social policy in pensions, health and education, Mr. Douglas Houghton (now Chairman of the Parliamentary Labour Party):

> While people would be willing to pay for better health services for themselves, they may not be willing to pay more in taxes as a kind of insurance premium which may bear no relation to the services actually received.

His remedy is to raise direct charges for medical care in the NHS: "most of the charges would be for prescriptions and for treatment in hospitals."[8] Charges for prescriptions have now been re-introduced at 2s 6d per prescription after much debate within the government. Charges for hospital "board and lodging" and for treatment, for consultants and family doctors

8. *Paying for the Social Services,* Occasional Paper 16, IEA, 1967.

have also been considered, and fees likely to spread to a widening range of formerly "free" services.

The consequences for health insurance could be of three kinds. *First,* there would be increasing insurance to cover state medical charges. Mr. Houghton has spoken of a nominal hospital charge of £5 or £10 per week. The provident associations generally provide higher weekly charges for private beds in hospitals or nursing homes and they could adapt their scales of subscriptions and benefits to these lower figures. They could encounter competition from the 35 or so hospital contributory schemes that could cover some 15 million people through 4 million contributors with a £10 per week benefit (for 10 weeks) for a contribution of 6d to 9d a week per head of the average or larger family.

Second, if the membership of provident and hospital schemes grew to cover state medical charges, the tendency would develop for the members to subscribe and contribute for private medical services. The economics of a charge for state hospitals (or family doctors, or consultants) are self-evident. Small charges would not yield much revenue, which is their essential purpose. If the charges are raised, they will yield more revenue for the NHS but they may also induce a preference for private services. Mr. Houghton's proposal that hospital charges be based on an income coding, so that they increase with income, raises issues in economic theory, not least whether charges that vary with income acquire the characteristics of a proportional tax and lose the functions and effects of a price. If variable charges appear to be, or are regarded as, taxes, the resistance to paying taxes may re-appear. What seems clear is that charges for state medical care would stimulate private insurance; and it would probably also stimulate private medical services. Perhaps that is why some members of the Government are thought to oppose them; but their dilemma remains: they must risk either a deteriorating state service or growing private services.

Third, if private insurance and/or medical care expand, the growing number of subscribers and contributors may claim a more unloaded choice between state and private services in the form of tax rebates, grants or vouchers. If subscribers to provident associations had grown as fast as members of occupational pension schemes, which now number 12 million, income-tax rebates might by now have found their way into the programmes of one or more of the political parties. These new institutional possibilities, stimulated by academic debate, are being discussed in the three British political parties. Hence the significance of an acceleration in the rate of expension in British private health insurance.

What general principles should best underly a growing structure of *private* health insurance? How could it best channel into medical care funds that are evidently not accessible to taxation? How can it tap all possible sources of funds by *demonstrating* that medical care better than is available in a standardised state service can be provided by competing suppliers and methods of payment in the market place? These economic principles are submitted for the consideration of the experienced insurance administrators gathered here, not least to the pioneers who have built up health insurance despite adverse conditions in my country.

IV. Principles and Conditions of Development in (British) Health Insurance

I would emphasise that these general economic propositions are derived from experience of medical care in a country with a centrally-organised, largely tax-financed, health service provided (with few exceptions) at no charge at the time of service, and that they do not necessarily reflect development in, or, judgement or conclusions on, other countries or continents.

1. Market Price

The economist's characteristic point of departure is price. In the UK, a desire to remove the "barrier"[9] between the citizen-patient and medical service has led to the removal of price. Price is a reflection of the interplay between supply and demand: normally it varies inversely with supply and directly with demand.[10] It is a symptom of scarcity. The removal of the symptom has not destroyed its causes. The abolition of price has removed the "barrier" from people with incomes too low to pay it but, *first,* it has also removed or distorted the other functions or effects of price in measuring or disciplining demand and rationing or generating supply; *second,* it was not the only way to give people with low incomes access to medical care; *third,* only a small minority of UK citizen-patients have inadequate earnings out of which to pay or insure.

Delegates to the Conference, and students of the subject generally, may

9. Variously described as "economic" (the late Lord Beveridge), "price" (Professor R. M. Titmuss), or "financial" (Mr. Kenneth Robinson, Minister of Health).

10. The pivotal importance of price in regulating the supply and quality of services as different as refuse collecting and sea-side amenities is discussed in *Essays in the Theory and Practice of Pricing,* Readings in Political Economy 3, IEA, 1967.

know of the recent academic debate in the UK on the economics of the NHS in particular and medical care in general. As a participant, the view I have reached is that the abolition of price has been unnecessary and on balance undesirable:

First, it has depressed the supply of funds for medical care and inflated the demand for or strained human and material resources. The removal of price has created an unreal world in which resources that are scarce and should be husbanded have been made to appear plentiful because they are supplied "free." In my view this is the main lesson of the NHS since 1948. Removal of price, moreover, has not abolished rationing but changed its form from financial to administrative, that is, appointment systems, waiting lists, queuing, political wire-pulling, which can be more arbitrary than pricing.

Second, most people with low incomes could have been given access to medical care not by removing price but by enabling them to pay it. In the UK estimates of the population living below, at, or minimally above "the poverty line" vary mostly from 10 to 20 per cent. Some are mentally or physically incapacitated by age, illness or disability to the point at which they require personal care or services in kind, but most could be enabled by patient teaching, advice and guidance to learn independence, judgement and discrimination by giving them purchasing power to enable them to insure for insurable medical services.[11]

Third, to the 80 (or 90) per cent of the population whose incomes are adequate for insurance could be added perhaps 10 per cent or more who could be made financially able to insure. Together some 90 to 95 per cent of the population could pay the market price for a choice between state and private medical services and between competing methods of insuring for them. (The residual problems of failure to insure, uninsurable risks, etc., are discussed below.)[12]

11. The problem of the geriatrics, psychiatrics, chronics, and others often regarded as beyond the capacity of medical insurance is essentially economic rather than medical. The disabled or chronically incapacitated or aged are not singled out for exceptional assistance because they are disabled or chronically incapacitated or old, but because their disability or chronic incapacity or age prevents them from paying for medical care. In the UK opinion has been changing from "universal" to "selective" social benefits that take account of all causes of insufficient means or exceptionally high medical costs. If social benefits were redirected into supplementing relatively low income, private health insurers could use the market to provide cover for categories sometimes excluded by reference to physical characteristics.

12. The general objection to a price is that, like a regressive tax, its incidence varies inversely with income. This is not a decisive objection to pricing. It is rather a case for supplementing income. It is rarely argued that food, clothing or other necessaries of life should be free at purchase and financed by taxation. And communist countries that have tried such an

2. Functions of Government

Here lies one of the functions of government[13] in creating the environment in which the most effective and desirable forms of medical care can emerge: to supply the purchasing power that will enable all citizens, not only the wealthy, to pay for medical services; the only exceptions could be the incapacitated who need care in kind.

There is a choice of three methods of using public finance as long as, and where, it remains necessary or desirable:

(a) for capital expenditure, subsidies[14] may be best channelled direct to hospitals, health centres, doctors or other *suppliers* of medical services, at least in part and in the early stages of a reconstruction of British health services;

(b) for administrative convenience, subsidies might most cheaply be channelled to *insurers* for onward payment of suppliers; but

(c) for restoring a sense of reality to the market for medical care, knowledge of the costs of doctors' time, nurses' attention, hospi-

---

extension of nil pricing have found it does not work for long beyond periods of emergency or crisis in war or social disintegration.

13. The other main function, apart from providing "public health," is that of laying down requirements and standards referred to in other sections of this *Paper.* Research is not necessarily a function of government. Much is done in government-financed universities and hospitals, but some of the outstanding developments in antibiotics and other "drugs" has been the work of research by industry. In his celebrated Trueman Wood lecture in 1963 Professor Ernst Chain, who worked with Florey on penicillin, gave telling examples of the outstanding research in privately-financed industrial laboratories in the UK, USA, Germany, Switzerland, Canada and other countries. He concluded: "I, for one, prefer to have an active pharmaceutical industry and life-saving drugs, accepting in the bargain a few abuses, than to have a system in which theoretically no abuses are possible, but which produces no drugs." The more intractable danger comes from monopolistic charging by the state, particularly when it is tempted to use government services (or social insurance) as sources of revenue when taxation is proving difficult to raise. The opposite policy—government monopsonistic prices for established drugs fixed too low to cover long-run costs of research—may have other defects. In France it has incited the pharmaceutical industry to avoid the price regulations by marketing "new" drugs with minor chemical modifications. There may nevertheless be a case in the UK for modifying the excessive protection of patent laws.

14. It is seldom strictly accurate to describe purchasing power supplied by government in cash grants as "subsidy." In the UK in 1966 households comprising two adults and two children with original income between £676 and £1,195 paid in taxes 10 per cent more or less than they received in social benefits. A high percentage of UK social benefits represent a *return* of central government tax, local government rates or social insurance contributions.

tal equipment, subsidies should ideally be channelled to *citizen-consumers* so that they can pay.

Countries with varying social and economic conditions—industrial development, medical organisation, urban and rural complements, national and private income, household budgets and personal expenditure preferences—will employ these methods in varying combinations. The general direction of desirable reform, in my view, lies in channelling purchasing power to the ultimate consumer because it would enable a structure of market prices to be restored or created. Direct subvention to suppliers implies the provision of services below market prices. In some countries, and for a time, this procedure may be unavoidable or desirable. The argument remains that the fundamental requirement for restoring a sense of realism, knowledge, responsibility and economy in the use of scarce resources is to widen the area of market prices by channelling public financing to the consumer.

3. The Patient's "Fraction"

The patient should not only know the amount of the bill he is paying, which (unless there is monopoly, discussed below) is a measure of the value of the resources he has consumed, but also bear a part of it, unless his means are regarded as inadequate. Accordingly a contribution from the patient is a desirable secondary discouragement to over-use of medical services;[15] and a further form of public financing to carry part or all of the fraction or "deductible" could avoid the deterrent to seek early investigation of symptoms. Here again there may be a significant difference between countries. In those with widely-developed private insurance, in which the premium, paid as an identifiable bill by individuals and/or employers, acts as a reminder of medical costs, a small or nil deductible may be practicable. In the UK, after 20 years of distorted "social insurance" for a state medical service, most people cannot identify either the minor NHS component or, even less, the general taxation that pays the major part of its cost, and the absence of charges has removed any general public knowledge of medical costs. A deductible is therefore a desirable element in a reconstructed system of medical care financing.

The inferences are twofold. First, the patient should pay the bill in full,

15. The Germans (who do not pay by item of service) have a word for frivolous over-use: *Bagatellefälle.*

and claim reimbursement from the insurer and (where necessary) from the state for the patient's fraction. Expeditious reimbursement should become possible with mechanisation of claims, and if bills are rendered periodically (particularly by doctors who dislike cash payment) they can be paid by the insurance scheme before the patient meets the bill.[16]

Second, experimentation with a nil deductible is not necessarily undesirable; and no weekly limit is currently offered by an insurer, the Private Patient's Plan, for the cost of accommodation and nursing (although subject to an annual limit). It may teach valuable lessons; but if the experience of the NHS is valid, it may lead to over-use, at least until wider experience of paying premiums for private insurance restores sensitivity to costs. Few patients remain in hospital longer than they must, but if additional stay is cost-less, there may be a tendency for some to give themselves the benefit of the doubt in exaggerating symptoms.

4. Rating

The proportions of "experience" and "community" rating[17] in private insurance is again a reflection of social, economic and perhaps political circumstance. In a developing or paternalistic society private organisations may be deputed or permitted to operate community rating insurance. And where competition from the state, or between private insurers, is weak, community rating may be feasible or even desirable.

But in advanced societies, or where competition is vigorous, community rating (except in group schemes where risks can be averaged to yield economies) may have to give way to experience rating if specialist insurers are not to emerge and offer refined rates for particular categories of lower risk. This has been the experience in motor insurance in the UK; in occupational pension schemes the post-war emergence of cost-conscious and market-orientated brokers, stimulated by American and New Zealand en-

16. Reimbursement for the reasons outlined is preferable to exemptions (for children up to 15, expectant and nursing mothers, the chronic sick and the aged), the method used in the restoration of prescription charges in the UK.

17. In essence "experience rating" is the calculation of premiums to meet the health record and claims experience of the individual policy-holder, "community rating" is the calculation of premiums to cover the *average* records and experience of a *group* of policy-holders. In "experience rating" each individual meets his own costs in a strictly commercial contract; in "community rating" individuals with better-than-average experience pay more than and subsidise individuals with worse-than-average experience.

terprise, has caused the life assurance offices to refine their premium and benefit structures; and in fire insurance there has been an increasing tendency for accident offices to offer premium concessions to policy-holders who incur costs in fire prevention.

The combination of and trend in experience and community rating in the UK may be influenced by a further consideration. If independence from governmental (which in practice means political or party) control, or at least minimisation of control, is a desirable objective, private insurers who operate miniature "welfare states" with community rating and cross-subsidising of good and bad risks are less likely to resist governmental interest, regulation or control than if they operate commercially-calculated experience rating subject to competition and the discipline of the market. This does not mean they cannot insure people with high risks or low incomes. But it is the function of government to finance the loadings.

5. Non-profit Incentives and Enterprise

As experience in private health insurance expands in the UK the non-profit-making associations may expect more competition:

(a) between themselves: one of the "big three" and at least two of the "little five" are proposing to announce extended schemes of subscriptions and benefits in 1968;

(b) from new or expanding insurers: Independent Medical Services[18] is proposing to extend its insurance cover from general practitioners to consultants and hospitalisation;

(c) from the hospital contributory schemes: they have in recent years extended beyond NHS supplements (mostly cash benefits and part-payment for spectacles, dentures, etc.) to insuring for part of private consultants' fees. They have recently considered covering a possible charge for state hospital services (boarding and/or treatment). As their contributors become better-off they may also show interest in insurance to cover more responsive personal health services;

(d) from commercial profit-making insurers: several British companies, commercial or hybrid, offer cash benefits and medical costs; a British subsidiary of an American company has considered

18. Constituted as a company limited by guarantee without shareholders.

adding to its life policies cover for the cost of amenity beds in state hospitals.

This increasing competition in health insurance in the UK may be inevitable if, as I believe, the market continues to expand. Efficiently conducted non-profit-making insurers will not fear more competition from hybrid or profit-making insurers.[19] They may even welcome it as both a stimulus to improvement and an opportunity to demonstrate their superiority in providing a financial service that cannot be bettered in cost or quality. When I have discussed with several British insurance companies the scope for expansion in health insurance they have invariably replied that they could not hope to compete with the provident associations and keep costs down to 8 or 9 per cent of premium income or distribute 85 to 90 per cent in benefits.[20]

Nevertheless, the scope for expansion in the UK is so large that more commercial insurers may be expected. Even if it does not develop, more intensive competition may make it increasingly profitable for non-profit-

19. Health insurance in Britain is provided in some instances by non-profit-making organisations constituted as companies without shareholders, or by profit-making subsidiaries of non-profit-making societies.

20. The comparative costs of non-profit-making and profit-making, commercial insurers are a subject of debate in the USA. A Blue Cross spokesman has said that the cost of commercial insurers for group insurance schemes has ranged from 0.5 to 30 per cent and for individuals from 30 to 70 per cent. *Blue Cross: A Report to the Nation* (dated 30 June, 1967) has a table showing the operating expenses of "member plans" in 1966 as 4.9 per cent and "associate plans" as 9.4 per cent. On the other hand, J. F. Follman in *Public Health Insurance 1967*, published by the Health Insurance Associations of America, quotes the Social Security Administration as showing that in 1965 Blue Cross plans distributed 95.3 per cent of premium income in benefits and insurance companies' group schemes 93.1 per cent. (Blue Shield—doctor—plans distributed 90.1 per cent and insurance companies' individual policies 54.7 per cent.) Blue Cross insurance for hospital costs covers mostly people in group schemes. It is difficult to see how commercial insurers can compete with non-profit-making insurers for group schemes unless their costs and distributions are broadly comparable. The range of 0.5 to 30 per cent for commercial insurance costs must cover exceptional cases at the extremes and must include a high proportion of insurers with costs around 10 to 14 per cent and less. (It is easy to understand the much higher costs and the lower distributions in individual policies.) Far from the commercial companies seeking out the easiest business among the lower risks, it may be the non-profit-making insurers that find it easier to administer sizeable groups, leaving individuals and smaller groups in country towns and rural areas to the commercial companies. And until they adopt more refined experience rating it will be difficult for the non-profit-making insurers to compete with the more competitive costing of the commercial companies.

making insurers to adopt, or adapt, more "commercial" (in the sense of cost-conscious and consumer-sensitive) attitudes and techniques.[21]

In the long run, non-profit insurers must cover costs like commercial insurers: the term "non-profit" is indeed misleading and question-begging. But non-profit insurers, especially with ample reserves and the unique capacity to draw on local goodwill for private charitable funds, may be able to take a longer view as pace-setters. Not least I should like to see a spirit of adventure in taking risks to cover risks.[22]

The most stubborn criticism of private insurance in the UK is that it cannot cover the "exceptional" or "difficult" cases: hence, it is argued only the state can organise and finance a comprehensive structure of medical care, whatever its defects and shortcomings. Other countries, such as the USA, in which independent insurance covers large segments of the population, may understandably feel less urgency about employing all feasible incentives, motivators and prime movers. For us in the UK who increasingly value independence from political control for health services, training, research and scholarship, who see in private insurance the main hope of generating the

21. Among them are: (a) determined pruning of avoidable costs in administration, documentation, accounting and other "overhead" procedures; (b) a more systematic structure of rewards for efficiency and penalties for inefficiency among executives; (c) closer relationship between individual health risks and individual premiums, except in occupational or other group schemes; (d) the exercise of buying power to offset the market power of the relatively small number of suppliers (doctors, hospitals, medicine and appliance distributors and manufacturers, not least the state) who would otherwise confront a relatively large number of consumers; (e) frequent readings of public preferences by market research into the range, extent and condition of risks people would like to cover by insurance; (f) where desirable the construction of a nation-wide network of agents, brokers or other intermediaries adequately recompensed by brokerage or commission for their initiative, salesmanship or servicing; (g) more extensive and intensive publicity; (h) a pruning of reserves (as is now being undertaken by British building societies).

22. Among them I would include: (i) so-called uninsurable conditions, e.g. short-period psychiatric disturbance, normal but unpreventable conditions such as dental caries; (ii) inducements for avoidance of precipitate resort to doctors and hospitals, where forethought or "thinking twice" does not conflict with early diagnosis; (iii) insurance cover for medically approved first or other early consultation, possibly on a sliding scale; (iv) specialisation in separate policies for (a) hospital or nursing home treatment, (b) consultants, (c) family doctors (WPA permits separate subscription) at a wide range of premiums; (v) more refined loading for pre-existing (or even some "catastrophic") illness; (vi) variable deductibles so that subscribers can assure as much or as little of the "equity" as they prefer, with limits; (vii) renewable policies; (viii) multi-year policies as a means of reducing costs or stabilising premiums; (ix) guarantees of benefits to keep pace with rising costs at scheduled rates; (x) preventive diagnosis; (xi) premium waivers.

finances that seem beyond the reach of taxation, and who would like to see health services more sensitive to personal preferences, *the over-riding consideration is that insurance shall expand, voluntarily* or (if necessary for a time) *compulsorily, non-profit-making or* (if necessary for part of the task) *profit-making, as rapidly as human beings can devise.* The objection in Britain to the methods of commercial enterprise in health care—notably its high-pressure selling or its high-cost collection—could be mitigated or anticipated by expansion in the provident associations. Higher marketing costs may be acceptable if they reduce costs elsewhere, not least by economies of underwriting or computerisation; higher collection expenses from individual subscribers may be worth incurring if personal recruitment enrols subscribers who might not otherwise insure; and higher administrative cost may be worth paying for an item of service system than for a capitation, a case payment or salaried system that is less responsive to individual preferences and may raise costs elsewhere.

The decisive consideration for health insurance in the UK is to reinforce the sense of mission that has yielded impressive growth so far with a sense of urgency. If it is not to be commercial motivation, the non-profit-making insurers will have to draw on other inducements: a heightened sense of service in creating an alternative to a state monopoly, expansion as evidence of public acceptance, personal recognition for exertion, economy and excellence.

6. Competition and Monopoly

If the state is not to organise and finance medical care virtually as a monopoly, the alternative is an institutional framework within which the most satisfying and efficient scientific techniques and financing methods can be tried and tested, adopted or rejected in a competitive environment. Thus it should be possible to test payment of doctors by salary, capitation, case or unit of service. Competition is often imperfect, particularly where consumers cannot easily judge their purchases, where suppliers are few and large because of economies of scales, where entry is costly, and where the law permits tight organisation into strong bargaining units as buyers or sellers. But it is an indispensable technique for discovering the best methods. Competition in medical insurance subscriptions, benefits, and quality of service should be permitted, if not encouraged, within a framework of rules designed by government with the advice of insurers and doctors and sanctioned by the public. And it should be welcomed not only as a safeguard of the ultimate consumer, the citizen-patient, from monopoly, but also as the safeguard of medical care from avoidable government regulation.

In such a framework of laws and institutions, the criticisms of doctors in the USA,[23] Sweden, Australia, and other countries for restrictive practices, and the recent friction between insurers and doctors in several European countries, might have been avoided.

Competition can be international as well as intra-national. International exchange of ideas and experience might usefully be supplemented by their application in one country by methods found effective in others, to the benefit of the ultimate consumer through improved performance by insurers. It may be salutary for American insurers to develop in Britain, and British insurers to develop in other continents.

7. Voluntary or Compulsory?

In countries where citizen-patients have been allowed a choice in medical care systems and financing, voluntary insurance, facilitated or encouraged by fiscal arrangement, has grown apace, not least in Australia. Where there are gaps, the state can close many of them by providing purchasing power. And private insurance is most securely based to resist direct government control.

In the UK voluntary purchase of medical care (and welfare services in general—education, housing, pensions and so on) would certainly have developed if the state had not extended its welfare services from the low-income categories to universal provision for all categories (who qualified by age, location, etc.) independent of income. The eight provident health insurance associations would by now have increased to perhaps 30 or 40, covered far more than 2 million people, and perhaps drawn more than an average of £12 to £16 from each of 800,000 subscribers. And the hospital contribution associations would have helped to equip, extend or build hospitals with more than the £1 to £2 15s a year they draw on average from 4 million contributors covering 15 million people. Insurance for private medical care has grown steadily from the 50,000 subscribers of the three largest associations (BUPA, PPP, and WPA) in 1948 towards perhaps one million by 1969, covering perhaps 2.5 million people. With more graphic advertising, more extensive marketing, income-tax rebates, direct "subsidies" and vouchers, and not least, more competition and more competitors, the number insured

23. The criticism of doctors for restrictive attitudes and practices is particularly severe in the USA, not least from economists generally favourable to private initiative and independence from government regulation, e.g. Professor Reuben Kessel, "Price Discrimination in Medicine," *Journal of Law and Economics*, October 1958; Professor Milton Friedman, *Capitalism and Freedom*, University of Chicago Press, 1962.

might grow to 10 or 12 million in 5 years. Even that advance would still leave a large gap to fill. The formidable distance to be covered has led a former Minister of Health, Mr. Enoch Powell, to suggest that reform of the NHS in the direction of wider choice of medical care financed by private insurance would be practicable only if there were:

> a widespread conviction, based on the concrete evidence of experience, of the superiority of an alternative.[24]

The emphasis on demonstration and experience in practice is well-founded. But the extent to which the population has been able to sample alternatives has itself been largely determined by politically created public policy. More favourable—or, more correctly, less unfavourable—legal, institutional and fiscal conditions could have been accompanied by faster expansion in private medical care and financing. Not least, if taxation had been lower, voluntary purchase of welfare—stimulated by example and exertion—would have created much larger private sectors in education, medical care, housing and pensions.

Nevertheless, the doubt must remain whether in a country with compulsory tax-financing of a state health service for 20 years, everyone who can pay for private insurance, or who can be enabled to pay, will insure even if taxation is reduced correspondingly, or cash grants are distributed to maintain the redistributive effects of the fiscal system. Hence the ground for considering two alternative situations.

The first is compulsory insurance. This solution would be regarded with reluctance, if not repugnance, by many who have helped to develop voluntary insurance. Its unattractiveness could be ameliorated by three conditions: first, there would be competition between private insurers; second, there could be competition between private insurers and a state insurance organisation (or regional public insurers); third, the compulsory condition could be temporary, for say, five or seven years, until the habit of shopping for health insurance had been formed.

But the instinctive reaction against compulsory insurance may be well-founded. In reply to the first proposition critics would point to "a captive market" which might encourage complacency, acquiescence in high medical bills, building excessively cautious reserves. Second, state agencies suffer from the occupational temptation to dip into the taxpayers' pocket to disguise deficits or subsidise themselves to evade competition they cannot

24. *Medicine and Politics,* Pitman Medical Publishing Co., 1966.

otherwise meet. Third, "temporary" state conditions tend to become permanent.

Not least, compulsory insurance, even competitive and temporary, invites government control.

8. Cash or Vouchers?

If compulsory insurance is rejected in Britain, a second alternative to voluntary insurance is return or redistribution of tax revenue in the form of tied or earmarked purchasing power. By definition, income tax rebates would not suffice, since most wage-earners pay all or most of their taxes indirectly on their purchases; and cash refunds would not suffice since the assumption is that many would not insure, not that they are financially unable to insure.

The method of health vouchers has, to my knowledge, no precedent anywhere in the world, although the principle of earmarked purchasing power is familiar in Britain in luncheon vouchers, book tokens, and other forms. The health voucher could be distributed to everyone to purchase a choice between insuring with the state for the NHS or, possibly with an additional sum paid out of pocket or private insurance, with a private insurer. (It might also be used to insure with the state for private medical care or with a private insurer for the NHS.)

The proposal has been discussed in the political parties as one of several methods of stimulating private insurance. It may be of interest to record that a field survey in April, 1967, among a quota sample of men and women aged 16 to 65 replied as shown in Table III to the question:

> Some people have said that rather than give free or part-free benefits, it would be better to give people cash or a voucher for use to buy the services they prefer. Which would you think best?
>
> Free or partly free services
> Cash to buy services they prefer
> Voucher to buy services they prefer.

The case for the voucher in the UK is threefold. First, the advantage in terms of the present discussion is that it would be a more certain method than tax rebates or cash refunds of ensuring that recipients would use it to insure for medical care.

Second, a more particular advantage of the voucher in the context of domestic discussion in the UK on "social divisiveness" is that it would confer equality of status as a consumer or purchaser of medical insurance, although

Table III. Preferences in Social Benefits: Services, Cash, Vouchers

		Age				Socio-Occupational Group			
	Total	16–24	25–34	35–44	45–64	Semi-Skilled & Unskilled	Skilled	Lower Middle	Upper Middle & Middle
Sample	2,022	414	396	426	786	253	385	823	561
	%	%	%	%	%	%	%	%	%
Free or partly free services	49	54	51	47	46	57	51	48	44
Cash	12	18	13	10	10	7	10	12	16
Vouchers	37	27	35	42	42	34	37	39	38
Purchasing power (general and specific)	49	45	48	52	52	41	47	51	54
Don't know, etc.	2	1	1	2	2	3	2	1	2

(There was little difference in preferences between men and women.)

Source: Seldon, *Welfare and Taxation, Research Monograph* 14, IEA, 1967.

quantity of medical care would vary with income and with its distribution (within each income group) between expenditure on medical care and other consumption and investment.

Third, in a country in which a state service and the taxation required to pay for it are deeply entrenched, it may require more than tax refunds or cash grants to create new habits and to direct expenditure into new channels. After 20 years the roots of the NHS may now be so deep that they require an instrument as pointed and penetrating as the voucher to dig them up and re-plant them.

9. Using the Market

The evaluation of a comprehensive structure of health insurance in the UK, and perhaps in other countries, confronts the criticism that it is incapable of covering the unusual risks. To a degree the state must act as a long-stop for the exceptionally chronic, the exceptionally costly, and the exceptionally poor. But not all psychiatric sickness is long-term; not all chronic treatment remains beyond the reach of insurance; not all the poor are incapable of learning, with financial aid and independent advice, how to insure.

If the state provides purchasing power, many people, risks and treatments might be brought within the ambit of private insurance that are now treated in state-provided, "tax-financed," "free" institutions. The exceptional people, risks and techniques may require exceptional premium loadings. If the state supplies the finance with which to pay loadings, private insurers could, in many cases, provide the insurance.

Insurers would then need to make more use of the market, by applying experience rating, to cover categories formerly provided for by the state or excluded by private insurers because of physical characteristics or medical history. The rules excluding or restricting subscribers beyond a stated age or with a pre-existing condition could be replaced by premium loadings so that subscribers could decide for themselves whether the additional premiums were worth paying for the peace of mind they could buy. And the state could finance the loadings for people whose means were too low to bear them.

V. Supply and Demand: A Synthesis

The economist is taught that production normally takes place in anticipation of demand. It is the pressure of demand that creates the conditions in which it is profitable (in either a commercial or a non-commercial sense) to create the supply.

But in the UK the extension of facilities for medical insurance may have both to anticipate and to precede the supply of medical facilities. There are risks in over-expanding insurance before the manpower and facilities for private services are available to supply them. The growth of private insurance since 1948 largely reflects increasing dissatisfaction with a state service that is praiseworthy in emergency but that otherwise suffers intensifying congestion. Negative reasons for expansion in private insurance and medical care could be supplemented by positive reasons. Expansion would be accelerated if more of the population had personal (or even second-hand) experience of the higher standards that could be provided by increased funds and resources channelled into medical care through private insurance. One of the most effective methods of publicising and persuading people to buy a hitherto unknown service is to give samples or demonstrations. That method is hardly practicable for medical care. But the local availability of private facilities and their increasing use by the public is itself a precondition for more rapid expansion in private insurance.

In the UK, BUPA is "integrating backwards" by establishing Nuffield Trust nursing homes for its subscribers (and subscribers to other provident associations as well as members of the public who pay fees). It may also assist the expansion of private accommodation elsewhere, especially if the number of beds available to paying patients in state hospitals is further reduced. State hospitals contain some 450,000 beds, private hospitals and nursing homes 10,000, Nuffield homes 450. The Minister recently announced a reduction of 1,000 in the 5,600 private beds in state hospitals. Consultants differ on the extent of the demand for private beds in state hospitals, and insurance officials on the rate of increase in the demand for beds in the private sector. But if two-thirds of the British population have never heard of private health insurance, an even larger proportion of younger people aged under 20 have no knowledge of doctors or hospitals outside the NHS, and middle-aged and older people remember "private" doctors and voluntary hospitals as they were before the war. Experience of doctors who can give more than five minutes to initial consultations, or of a choice of surgeon, or of timing non-urgent treatment, or of hospitals where the patient is treated as a customer rather than a "beneficiary" is rare. That is the case for demonstration and publicity of responsive medical care as an inducement to insure and for pushing ahead with insurance as a stimulus to the supply of tailored medical services.

If the demand for private treatment continues to grow, charitable funds for hospital building may increasingly have to be supplemented by commercial funds raised on the capital market.

VI. The Outlook

The future for private health insurance and medical care in the UK (and elsewhere) will be shaped by arbitrary, unforseeable, even capricious political influences that make assessment for the future hazardous.

Yet three developments seem tolerably clear: first, incomes will continue to rise (at 4 per cent a year they would double by 1984); and expectations of higher standards, improved quality and personal services will continue to grow. Second, the contrast between privately-financed, market-provided abundance in every-day consumption and publicly-financed, state-provided stringency in welfare services will intensify. Third, countries outside the UK, in Europe, North America and Australia, whatever their imperfections, difficulties, and excesses, will provide living demonstrations of the advantages of personal choice, competition, and freedom from direct, detailed governmental control.

On these grounds it is not fanciful to foresee a growing place for private insurance and medical care in the UK. Efficient, responsive, ample, health services will entail rôles to be played by governmental and independent individuals and agencies. The rôles assigned to them, and the relationships between them, reflect principles that go to the roots of free society. In countries where choice in organising and financing independent medical care is common, its shortcomings are properly discussed, often perhaps indulgently. We in Britain should heed warnings as well as learn lessons from other countries. But we must now also reconsider whether it was wise to make government almost the sole provider. Government creates the legal and institutional framework on property, contract and exchange within which private individuals and organisations are free to arrange voluntary, spontaneous relationships as buyers and sellers of medical care; it provides services that individuals cannot arrange otherwise; it could redistribute purchasing power, so that, with few exceptions, all can pay with consumer authority; it lays down requirements and standards. Whether the relationship between government and private organisation is described as co-operation or partnership is less important than that, except in wartime or other emergency, government shall facilitate rather than frustrate personal sensitivity in sickness as in health.

February 1968

EPILOGUE

An International Impression

Five weeks' study in other countries of alternative approaches to medical care has dramatised the contrast with the deficiencies in the British system. The NHS is failing because the ideals set for it by economists and politicians who should have known better—not least that of providing "the best possible" medical care for everyone—cannot be achieved under any system, state or private, centralised or decentralised, priced or free; because it destroyed instead of improved the price mechanism that is indispensable to record preferences and allocate scarce resources in response to them; because it replaced the weaknesses of pre-1948 medical services with different but more stubborn defects; not least because it substituted for inadequacy of *individual* purchasing power which denied medical care to a gradually diminishing *minority* of families a more persistent inadequacy of *collective* purchasing power which denies improving medical care to the large *majority* of families who could pay for it directly but who are not prepared to pay for it through taxation.

The NHS is wrongly blamed for faults that lie ingrained in human nature, although it gave new or enlarged scope for political favouritism, capricious advantage and jobbery. And it is wrongly praised for technical advances that might have been even more impressive if the buyer were not a government department. Its central tragedy is that it did not have to intensify political influence or monopolise organisation or centralise initiative in order to channel more material and human resources into medical care and lessen the inequalities in its distribution between individuals, families, age groups and areas. And our tragedy as its intended beneficiaries is that we shall never know what benefits we might have enjoyed in its absence. What we do know is that for the common man in the street it has continued the subjection of the consumer to the producer, from which he could have expected emancipation by rising income, and instead consolidated it by embedding medical care in political regulation at worst or political paternalism at best. No matter how high his income rises the man in the doctor's surgery or hospital bed will find difficulty in asserting his sovereignty as a consumer so long as he remains in the NHS, for which he will have paid indirectly, because he will confront a seller's market in which the doctor will exert his technical authority and in which the politician has ultimate veto.

Escape from dominance by the politically-financed supplier will be possible only in private medicine competitively financed by insurance. And rising incomes will intensify the urge and the capacity to escape. That is the impression confirmed and strengthened by talks, sometimes intensive and compressed, sometimes expansive and leisurely, with people in Israel and Hong Kong (and a fleeting visit to India), in Australia, and in New Zealand and the USA. Scrutiny of documents brought away from these meetings, collected from conference delegates in Sydney, or received from authors dealing with other countries, has reinforced this impression. All the countries I visited or discussed, though they differed in social structure, religion, size and distribution of income, degree of industrialisation and economic organisation, were yielding their populations rising incomes, though at varying rates of acceleration. From the capitalist-bolstered socialist siege economy of Israel, through bicycle-powered Delhi and archetypal free-market Hong Kong to loin-girding Australia, mixed-economy New Zealand to increasingly obstructed but unstoppable private enterprise in America, there was little sign that doctors or patients were looking to the NHS as a model to adopt or adapt in their countries. British experience was being watched, sadly but almost with relief, as a warning of what to avoid.

There were critics of domestic medical care in plenty. Some Israeli doctors wanted fees for units of service instead of salary (even a senior medical civil servant, who rather liked capitation, also wanted reimbursement of patient-paid fees as in Sweden). In Hong Kong doctors, and an influential legislator, complained that the people had plenty of money for clothes and cars but had been spoiled by politicians to expect medical care for nothing, and a courageous civil servant was arguing in public for an increase in medical charges. Australian economists criticised their voluntary insurance system for lack of competition (where they were right, although competition is inhibited by the law) and for failure to cover the low earners and high risks (where it is wrong to expect the *suppliers* of medical insurance to compensate for deficiencies in *demand* that are the province of government). A New Zealand medical elder statesman blamed doctors for resisting government reorganisation of health services, though he was disenchanted with the results of abolishing charges (for hospitalisation) in retrospect. And my former family doctor, whom I had travelled 12,000 miles to see, showed me his surgery, with only three waiting chairs but ample equipment, his fees book, which recorded higher charges for home visits than for surgery visits and for barristers than for pensioners, and not least the more relaxed family life and the more satisfying professional life he leads than he did under the NHS. He explained that he could afford to install equipment with which to diagnose and treat: he was now practising medicine instead of sorting symptoms. He is a man of acute Christian conscientiousness who had ended many days in England exhausted at 9 o'clock; his wife's anxiety for his health had induced him to decide to abandon either England or medicine. He migrated in 1966. In New Zealand he missed his family, his cultural pursuits and his country. He was resolved to return to England for a visit, but not to the NHS. I do not know how far his experience is common.

Finally in California, Chicago, Washington and New York there were critics of American doctors, hospitals and insurance organisations (non-profit-making as well as commercial) among economists, civil servants, and journalists with philosophic sympathies Left, Right and Centre. Rising medical costs were worrying everyone. A senior public official criticised the American Medical Association for opposing payment by salary, but scoffed at the NHS for levying no payment at all. And the absurdity of universal state welfare was dramatised by the spectacle of the affluent retired business executive who changed TV channels and opened his garage doors by expensive remote control and enjoyed the benefits of Medicaire at the expense of the young, the poor and the sick.

But none of the defects or abuses I heard of independent medical services and financing were irremediable. Some, indeed, were the results of government policy in acts of omission—notably the failure to maintain competitive conditions—as well as in acts of commission—not least the grant of monopoly power. And nowhere, except among doctrinaire collectivists or among casual visitors to England who were grateful for free medical care, was there a disposition to look to the NHS as a model to copy, not even among the Australian economists who had developed the most refined critique of voluntary private health insurance. On the contrary, the NHS and its failures had in several countries become a bogey that was thought to inhibit any reform of private medicine—even in the direction of removing its obstacles—for fear that government might enlarge its interference and influence in medicine.

Four impressions crystallised as I journeyed on. One was that the criticisms of other health systems arose from human weakness, political failure or natural scarcity of resources rather than from decentralisation in initiative, independence in organisation, or the use of market pricing; indeed, decentralised initiative was producing exhilarating experimentation difficult to conceive expeditiously in the NHS. Second, every other system had imperfections, but they were imperfections assessed in terms of an ideal system. Third, few critics of private medicine thought of patients as consumers with a say in the services they paid for. Fourth, where efforts were made to compare medical systems abroad with those in other countries, including Britain, they were based on *quantitative* measures, usually in national or regional averages, that throw little light on comparative *quality* of medical care. Numbers of doctors per thousand of the population, or of patients per doctor, for example, may mean little without detailed knowledge of the time a general practitioner commonly gives a patient (often 5 minutes under the NHS, more generally 15 minutes elsewhere), the equipment at his command, and his capacity to follow the patient to and through hospital treatment. Statistical comparisons are tenuous and precarious in the extreme: they are the beginning, not the end, of scientific enquiry and inference. I shall not forget the outraged disappointment of the senior medical official in Asia who responded as best he could to a recent imaginative questionnaire from Britain, confessing he had to "pluck some of the answers out of the air," but who nevertheless began to read the resulting book avidly in the hope that it would enable him to compare his experience with that of other countries and who finally abandoned it barely half-way through because he judged the comparisons worthless.

Nothing I heard or have read in the wide range of criticisms of private medicine and insurance seems as fundamental as the defects of the NHS. And I now wonder whether we are likely to find any that are. There may be. But I doubt it. What seems clear is the failure of the NHS to reach finances that are accessible to private insurance, voluntary as in the USA, Australia and other countries, or compulsory as in some countries in Europe. Whether Professor J. M. Buchanan and economists who think like him,[1] or Mr. Houghton and other Labour politicians who have reached much the same view, are right or not, it may be argued that taxpayers can be persuaded to pay more in tax for state medical services. But again I doubt it, because they must share the NHS with other taxpayers who may waste and abuse it. The behaviour of people in other countries suggests they will not. They

1. In the *Inconsistencies of the NHS* Professor Buchanan argued that individuals as taxpayers are not prepared to provide in "free" health services as much as they demand as consumers.

may, of course, be forced by compulsory saving or taxation: Czechoslovakia has a high ratio of doctors to patients and other Communist countries have fine modern hospitals; but their methods hardly commend themselves to Britain.

It was depressing on return to find "the high priests of universalism," Professors R. M. Titmuss,[2] B. Abel-Smith,[3] and P. Townsend[4] stubbornly continuing their intellectual rearguard action in defence of an outworn, inhumane, profligate principle (though heartening to see the Fabian Society at least allow a penetrating thinker like Professor Mark Blaug to refute them). It would seem that fewer listen to them. They have little to offer supposed beneficiaries of state welfare but stringency, injustice, and chains. They obstinately refuse to see that the more poverty they uncover the more irrelevant universalism becomes. They have no escape from their dilemma.

The advocates of universal "free" services may continue their wishful thinking that the common people will willingly pay in taxation for state medicine that, paradoxically, denies them the freedom of choice that could accompany rising incomes. But the expectation is, indeed, the very opposite. People in countries with widely differing but rising incomes seem to want more *individuality* in medical care (and in other welfare services) to go with their expanding choices in ordinary everyday or household consumption. Aneurin Bevan saw the truth clearly when he told the Labour Party conference in 1945:

> If we were rich enough we would not want to have free medical services: we could pay the doctors.

Most British people are now "rich enough"; more are becoming "rich enough"; and people with low incomes could, perhaps by a reverse income tax, be made "rich enough." It is the politicians who are holding them back. But they will not be denied for ever. That, in a word, is why I think the days of a "free," tax-financed NHS are numbered.

6 June, 1968

2. *Commitment to Welfare,* Allen and Unwin, 1968.
3. *The Listener,* 30 May, 1968.
4. *Social Services for All?* Fabian Tract 382, Fabian Society, June 1968.

THE GREAT PENSIONS "SWINDLE"

THE GREAT PENSIONS "SWINDLE"

Is "Swindle" a fair title?

Mr. John Boyd-Carpenter, for the Conservatives, replying to Mr. Richard Crossman, Secretary of State for Social Services, in a House of Commons debate on Pensions: "He will recall that Mr. Stanley Orme . . . mentioned today that in his degenerate days he [Mr. Crossman] referred to that method of financing as a swindle. . . . if those who were responsible for that scheme were responsible for a swindle it was a very small peccadillo compared with the scale of swindling operations for which Mr. Crossman is responsible. The operations of Savundra or Whittaker White appear as that of mere amateurs compared with Mr. Crossman if there ever were any validity in the charge which, with remarkable frequency, he used to make in those days."

(*Hansard,* Cols. 742–3, March 6, 1969)

To the working classes
among whom I was born
in the faith that capitalism
will save them from paternalism

ACKNOWLEDGEMENTS

I owe my interest in pensions to the late Philip Fothergill who in 1947 asked me to steer a committee of three (with Lord Amulree and Barbara Shenfield) on the economic and social problems of the aged for the Liberal Party.

I have to thank Richard Sleight for informed advice and corrections on technical matters, Barbara Marlow for resourcefully assembling the statistics for some of the charts, Kenneth Smith for almost instant discovery of references and sources, and Janet Henderson for rapidly producing with Scottish imperturbability a coherent text out of increasingly illegible longhand and uncomplainingly retyping it after revision.

My wife, as always, listened readily to repeated rehearsing of phraseology and suggested *les mots justes.*

I am indebted to the Classical Economists and to the present-day economists who have inherited the classical tradition—its insight into human nature, its common sense and its understanding of the conditions of liberty—for inspiration.

Errors will remain despite willing assistance and conscientious checking. For the imperfections I am solely responsible.

24 December, 1969. *A.S.*

Above this race of men stands an immense and tutelary power . . . absolute, minute, provident, and mild. It would be like the authority of a parent, if . . . its object was to prepare men for manhood; but it seeks . . . to keep them in perpetual childhood . . .
. . . such a government . . . provides for their security, foresees and supplies their necessities, facilitates their pleasures, manages their principal concerns, directs their industry, regulates the descent of property, and subdivides their inheritances—what remains, but to spare them all the care of thinking and all the trouble of living?

Alexis de Tocqueville, 1841

. . . the mode in which the government can most surely demonstrate the sincerity by which it intends the greatest good of its subjects is by doing the things which are made incumbent upon it by the helplessness of the public, in such a manner as shall tend not to increase and perpetuate but to correct that helplessness . . .
. . . government aid . . . should be so given as to be as far as possible a course of education for the people in the art of accomplishing great objects by individual energy and voluntary cooperation.

John Stuart Mill, 1848

. . . universal pensions . . . do not contain . . . the seeds of their own disappearance. I am afraid that, if started, they would tend to become perpetual.

I regard poverty as a passing evil in the progress of man; and I should not like any institution started which did not contain in itself the causes which would make it shrivel up as the causes of poverty shrivelled up.

Alfred Marshall, 1893

An Open Letter to Mr. Richard Crossman
Minister for Social Services

Dear Mr. Crossman,

In the Explanatory Memorandum on your National Superannuation and Social Insurance Bill[1] you say, in a passage which reads more like your drafting than a civil servant's:

(i) "Public discussion . . . has produced suggestions that social security should develop along quite different lines . . . "
(ii) "but there has been little criticism of any major feature of the scheme . . . "
(iii) "given that the general approach [of your scheme] is right, as the Government believe it is . . . "

It is not true that your scheme has escaped (or withstood) criticism. And this short book crystallises criticism of its "major features" that you cannot rebut and emphasises others you have avoided. But even if the scheme were unassailable in feature and detail, it is defective in its *rationale.*

Throughout its history in this and other Western countries, with the main exception of Australia, "social insurance," as you call it, has been used to raise government revenue for purposes that have had little to do with insurance—*or poverty.* It may have begun as a humanitarian device to alleviate poverty but it has been made a political instrument to establish, by degrees, an increasingly egalitarian, centralised society. In the process public attention has often been shifted from "general approaches" to "major features," from ultimate objectives to technical *minutiae.* You have, perhaps unwittingly, also distracted attention away from its main, but most objectionable, feature—compulsory contributions and benefits related to earnings—by secondary proposals, such as attendance allowances for the disabled, that are indeed overdue but that have nothing to do with it and could have been introduced separately.

It may suit you now to brush aside examination of your "general ap-

1. Cmnd. 4222, December, 1969.

proach" or of "the quite different lines" that some believe preferable, and to fasten attention on your "major features." But your scheme would be a fundamental reconstruction of social policy with far-reaching economic and political effects that could last 50 years. You must not be allowed to put the cart before the horse. You cannot expect the country to discuss your scheme before you have satisfied it that your general approach is "right." Its "rightness" is *not* "given." You may think it is right. The public has not yet said what it thinks—because 999 out of 1,000 do not understand what you are up to. The handful of technical specialists you have consulted in the life assurance companies, the pension funds, the Confederation of British Industry or the Trades Union Congress do not know what the pensioner of the future thinks, because they have not asked him. Have you? Have you asked the individual pensioner of the future how *he* would like to save for retirement? Have you told *him* how your scheme would work? That it is *not* insurance? That what his employer and the State pay in will eventually come largely out of *his* pocket as a consumer and a taxpayer? That the higher paid in the scheme, including wage-earners and moderate salary-earners, will be paying for the lower paid because it is too late for you to suppress occupational schemes in which the highest paid are saving for retirement? That the National Superannuation Fund would *not* have a fund of contributions invested for his retirement? That it is no more than a tank topped up with his contributions that will be paid out as fast as he pays them in?

Not least, have you explained that your scheme, which you have urged because some people have no occupational pension, might make it certain that they never will have one and that they will therefore be wholly dependent on the State for their income in retirement? How do you propose to explain this governmental blessing for the "social divisiveness" against which you and your advisers have long inveighed?

The "expert" and the "spokesman" (often combined) are becoming more the tyrants and autocrats of our society than the advisers and servants. And particularly in "social insurance" they develop organisational attachments and ideological commitments that generate disdain for the common man's inability to understand their arcane expertise and create resistance to his urge to understand where he is being led. Politicians have used and capitalised on the experts to serve their short-term purposes instead of disciplining and defying them to serve the people.

So first things first. Ends before means. Tell the people where you are going; then, *if they agree*, discuss the ways of getting there. Before you entangle Parliament in details for the next few months, the onus is on you to persuade the country that your general approach is not merely "right," whatever that means, but the *best possible* for the years ahead and the advancing social and economic conditions they will bring.

I don't think you can do that. British social history, logical reasoning and common sense, the reality of political institutions, human nature and overseas experience are against you. You speak as though all were now over save the details. You can use your parliamentary majority, now four years old, to force one more distended inflation of "social insurance" into law. But you may win a Pyrrhic victory because you will not have persuaded the people. In my judgement they would not want your scheme if you tried.

You may say the people do not understand, even cannot understand and should leave such complicated matters to you, the civil servants and the actuaries. Then you should say so. And take the consequences at the General Election.

The people are concerned not only with the financial and technical detail of creating pensions in retirement, but also with the ethical, moral, economic and political implications of your scheme for the province and power of government in a democracy, and with personal liberty.

The last is not the least. Not long ago a former Minister of Pensions asked: "Why do you care so much about personal choice?" She may not know, or recall, John Stuart Mill; but you will remember *On Liberty.* This passage may help to remind all of us what the argument on pensions (and every government policy) is all about.

> The human faculties of perception, judgement, discriminating feeling, mental activity and moral preference, are exercised only in making a choice . . .
>
> . . . he who lets the world, or his own portion of it, choose his plan of life for him has no need of any other faculty than the ape-like one of imitation. He who chooses his plan for himself employs all his faculties . . .
>
> It really is of importance, not only what men do, but also what manner of men they are that do it. Among the works of man which human life is rightly employed in perfecting and beautifying, the first in importance surely is man himself.

That, to repeat, is what it is all about. In enlarging national insurance you would be reshaping the social, economic, political and moral framework of society. You would not merely be showing whether or not you are better than the insurance companies, or investment experts, or private enterprise generally at organising pensions. You would be helping to make Britain a more centralised, a less spontaneous society, in which man would have less and less power to learn by experience how to perfect himself. And that would be a heavy price to pay even if government were cleverer at pensions.

In the House of Commons on 4 December, 1969, a Labour backbencher said you "could reasonably hope to be regarded as the Beveridge or the Bismarck" of your time.[2] Beveridge cared about human security but also about freedom, individuality, independence. Bismarck cared more about power. The Prussian/German genesis of social insurance is hardly a happy augury for British democrats, conservative, liberal or socialist. If your Bill passes into law, you may be remembered in history less as a Beveridge than as a Bismarck. You would not be the first politician who, with the intention or pretext of alleviating human want, enacted human repression.

Yours sincerely,
Arthur Seldon

Godden Green, Kent
24–25 December, 1969

2. Mr. A. Palmer, *Hansard,* Col. 1780.

CHAPTER I

Why This Book?

This short book was drafted in early December and revised by early January. If I had had more time I should have dealt more fully with the arguments shrewdly marshalled and deployed by Mr. Richard Crossman, with academic acumen but with variations according to his audiences during 1969, for the massive inflation of state pensions he proposes in the National Superannuation and Social Insurance Bill, 1969. If the die is not yet cast, if there is still time to reflect, a short reminder in non-technical language to people in Parliament and at home that the world in which we live makes inflated, compulsory and universal state pensions unnecessary and undesirable might do more good than a longer book that came later or too late.

This Bill embodies the thinking of a small number of people—mostly sociologists[1] and politicians—speaking for themselves, not even for the Labour Party, possibly not for the Government, and certainly not reflecting the aspirations of the rising wage-earner.[2] Their intentions may vary from the praiseworthy but fallacious—the desire to avoid "two nations" in old age and the fall in living standards in passing from earnings to state pension on retirement; through the expedient but question-begging—the raising of revenue for the badly-battered National Insurance Fund and for current retirement pensioners; to the calculating but problematic—the desire for political popularity and re-election in 1970–71. But they stare blindly at the growing dichotomy between the increasingly satisfied demands of the emerging wage-earner as a consumer of commercial goods and his frustration as a "beneficiary" of state welfare. When confronted with chronic deficiency in state pensions, education, medical care, they mindlessly mouth "More money! higher taxes!" and, on a lower moral plane, "but let's call it social insurance."

1. Also known as "social administrators." Note on Sour/Sentimental Sociology, page 221, Appendix B.

2. A Note on Rising Social Expectations, page 119.

But the sponsors of the Bill do not really care what the mass of the people want. If they did, they could hardly doubt that the growing but unsatisfied demand for higher standards, better quality and personal service in welfare will in time provoke unease, resentment, rejection and explosion. The men and women who find comfort, attentiveness and choice in the shop, the hairdresser's salon, the airport terminal—where the worker's pound is as good as any man's—will not for ever tolerate the rationing, queuing and discomfort, the officious condescension and patronising arrogance in the state school, the National Health Service hospital, the Council Housing Manager's office, or the local branch of Mr. Crossman's Department of Social Services. The days of this twilight world of "double standards" are numbered.

But they can be prolonged. This is what the National Superannuation and Social Insurance Bill, 1969 would do. Emancipation by rising incomes, choice of service and competition between suppliers has been familiar in everyday consumption and has been spreading to saving for retirement. Mr. Crossman, therefore, is anxious to see his Bill become law, not merely for what may seem a patently electoral reason but for the more profound socio-economic one that if the deed is not done soon it may be too late in another five years.[3] Most salaried men are accumulating occupational pensions and wage-earners, though lagging behind, would have been covered in the near future; the introduction of inflated state pensions that would retard occupational schemes would therefore be an act of discrimination against the working people Mr. Crossman claims to champion. Having caught them in the state cage, or prevented them from escaping, he would use *them,* rather than the contracted-out salaried man he cannot catch or the taxpayer at large, to keep the lowest paid.

If the scheme could be made voluntary, or could be wound up after a short trial, it would not be objectionable in principle, even though still damaging. But politicians all over the world are better at expanding national insurance than at adapting it to meet social and economic change. That is perhaps the most telling lesson from almost every country in which it has been tried[4] (an honourable recent exception is New Zealand which scrapped its social security tax in 1968). If the National Superannuation and Social Insurance Bill 1969 becomes an Act, and the scheme is begun in 1972, the tan-

3. The *New Statesman* is engagingly disarming, "the private sector has grown so large that we have to live with it. . . . The Swedish solution [chapter XIII] is not now available." Editorial, 24 January, 1969.

4. Chapter XIII.

gled skein would not easily be unravelled, or the legislation repealed and reversed. The more Western countries have resorted to national insurance the more it becomes a mindless monster and the less a sensitive, humane and refined instrument of social policy for succouring people in trouble. It has become a one-way ticket on a non-stop passage, a balloon that can only be inflated—or pricked. Even though incomes will go on rising in the 1970s and 1980s, and more people will be able, and eager, to save for retirement in ways they prefer, reasons would be found—political impracticability, administrative complexity, constitutional convenience, financial continuity, or perhaps a group of fishermen in the Outer Hebrides not covered by a pension scheme—for preserving it long after the circumstances that gave it plausibility were lost to memory. Mr. Crossman triumphantly points to other countries as precedents. Their lessons are precisely the opposite. They are warnings, not exemplars.

It is essentially because the Crossman compulsory earnings-related scheme flouts common (though not always articulate) aspirations that it should be rejected. It looks like bringing out the best and the worst in the political parties. Conservatives may rightly oppose it because it endangers independent institutions, but shrink from condemning it on principle because it can be represented as an enlargement of their 1961 graduated scheme. Liberals rightly oppose it because it invades private saving, but propose an earmarked tax to finance the "flat-rate" pension. Labour members of Parliament will want to support a government measure, but they must also have disconcerting mental reservations. Let me reinforce them. I put it to Douglas Houghton, Brian Walden, Raymond Fletcher—to Messrs. Gunter, Marsh, Taverne, even Roy Jenkins—and other Labour Members that the wage-earner has not asked for the scheme; that if you asked him he would not want it; that it would do more damage to him (by keeping him tied to the State) than to the salary-earner and profit-receiver, who will continue to build up occupational pensions despite discouragement, and save for retirement in other ways; and that providing for married women and widows, or helping them to provide for themselves, need not be part of a new scheme embracing everyone else. The Labour Party is bringing in a measure that is not for the working man. Desmond Donnelly has left the Party because its conception of the welfare state would tether the wage-earner to government benevolence for all time. This is not what the English social democrats intended.

The Crossman scheme would not prevent "the two nations" in old age (once the *raison d'être* for "national superannuation" where the better-off have occupational pensions, and the workers have not) but consolidate and crystallise them. Unless the Government proposes to prevent or inhibit other forms of saving, the middle- and higher-income earners with over £2,000 a year will continue to differentiate themselves by private savings from the under £2,000 a year with state graduated pensions. The Crossman scheme must fail in this—a main—purpose of creating one nation in old age because occupational pensions have by now spread too far and because they are not the only way to save for retirement.

(How far the abolition of "the two nations" is still a main purpose has been made obscure by Mr. Crossman's recent Fabian Tract in which he propounds the intriguing notion—which I call the Theory of Social Damage—that it is proper for pensions to vary with earnings but not medical care or education.)[5]

Social and economic advance makes a vast expansion from flat-rate to earnings-related state pensions outdated. If the Bill is rushed into law by July, 1970, historians of the twentieth century will marvel that it took so long for its politicians to allow for the replacement of widespread poverty in 1900 by widespread opulence in 1970. From the perspective of history they will wonder that the 1960s, while preoccupied with the immediate but dwindling problem of poverty, were oblivious to the opportunities for winding up obsolete forms of government welfare and turning to new ones.

The Bill will slow down the clock of social advance. But its frustration of underlying aspirations will sooner or later be met by increasing evasion. Rising incomes will multiply forms of saving for retirement. In time, perhaps in 20 or 30 years, the scheme might be rejected.[6] In the meantime let it at least be made known to future generations that it was a political artifact based on sociological jaundice and historical myopia, not the will of the people of 1970.

For there is something radically wrong with a political system which can put into law a universally compulsory method of saving for retirement which few except several score actuaries, civil servants and politicians understand, which would be rejected on principle by the mass of the citizenry, and which is unsuited to the social order for which it is framed.

5. *Paying for the Social Services,* Fabian Tract 399, Fabian Society, December, 1969.

6. Mr. Rudolf Klein, a perceptive journalist whose sympathies do not rule his head, suggests the rejection may come earlier. In a preview of the 1970s he says: "The difficulty of maintaining the standard of living of old people persuaded the 1978 Labour Government to scrap Mr. Crossman's pension scheme . . ." *The Observer,* 28 December, 1969.

A Note on Rising Social Expectations

The aspirations of the rising wage-earner are central to the argument of this book. There is visible evidence of it in everyday experience, and the sociologists research into it earnestly. To judge from the final chapters in their two reports, a group of sociologists from the Universities of Cambridge, Essex, Edinburgh and Sussex conclude from a study of well-paid wage-earners in three large Luton firms that, although affluence has not produced "middle-class" political allegiances, their "central life interests are to be found in the cultivation and enjoyment of their private domestic lives";[7] they "define their work as a means of gaining resources for the pursuit of . . . largely familial ends." This is hardly a surprising finding. What is significant is that the process is still in its infancy.

Affluence is still young, even in Luton. The opportunities for realising their expectations are restricted by removing a third of incomes in taxes and providing "free" state education and medical care and subsidised housing and pensions in return. This development is not yet applauded as reflecting the natural desire of parents to endow and enrich the family but rather scorned as social climbing or condemned as queue-jumping. But the increasing emphasis on family life is largely confirmed by Mr. Raymond Fletcher's view, based on his constituency, Ilkeston in Derbyshire, that "aspirations that once had to be expressed in social terms (the organised demand for more schools, more welfare . . .) are now personal or family ambitions. . . . The Welfare State no longer generates enthusiasm among the workers. . . ."[8] Further evidence is provided by the annual Family Expenditure surveys of the Ministry of Employment and Productivity, by the findings of field surveys that indicate a desire for choice in welfare as well as in consumption, and by common observation of the curtains, cookers and cars of the working people of England, the accents at airport terminals and European beaches, and the clothes worn by the younger generation of office and factory boys and girls who are centuries ahead of their grandparents. Their aspirations and horizons are not now fixed for all time.

7. *The Affluent Worker,* Vols. 1 and 2, Cambridge University Press, 1969.

8. *Encounter,* November, 1969.

CHAPTER II

What Is at Stake

On 17 December, 1969, a Bill was published that may become an Act by July, 1970, unless it is purged or withdrawn on its course through Parliament in the next four months. Yet although it would affect everyone in the British Isles, few understand it, or sufficiently so to know how it will influence their lives.

It is being heralded as a great advance in British social policy. I believe it would be a tragic error. But since January, 1969, when a White Paper[1] indicated its contents, its main consequences have been obscured by a smoke-screen of statistics, secondary (not unimportant but still unrelated) appendages and forbidding detail.

The Act would require almost all employees (about nine out of ten) to pay weekly sums, varying with individual earnings, for a state pension varying with average national earnings. The payments would begin in 1972. The pension would begin in 1973, but on a very small scale, and increase for 20 years until it reached its full amount in 1992. (The size of pensions is shown on p. 152–53.)

The main object appears admirable, reasonable and long overdue. A state pension for the whole community of more or less half of average earnings over the working life seems modest compared with the pension of two-thirds of near-final earnings that more and more salaried people in the civil service, the nationalised industries, local government and private industry can hope to accumulate. Moreover, the state pension, unlike many private occupational pensions (in "public" as well as private employment), would be made safe by being preserved or transferred if the employee changed jobs; and it would keep pace with rising prices after as well as before retirement. Or, at least, so Mr. Crossman says. There would be several additional attractions; not least, two-yearly reviews of pensions being paid, better pensions

1. *National Superannuation and Social Insurance,* Cmnd. 3883.

for widows and divorcees, married women and children. But it is mainly as a civilised advance on the Beveridge scheme of uniform ("flat-rate") contributions and pensions, which had to be raised every few years to keep pace with inflation, that the scheme is being urged by the Government and sold by the Minister of Social Services.

"Sold" may sound more cynical than "urged." But it is more accurate. And it reveals a truth that "urged" conceals. The new scheme is not merely being "urged" by political leaders in a democratic society as a good idea, an improvement on the existing system, and one that should be adopted by the people after reasoned consideration, discussion and debate. It is being "sold" in three senses. First, in the *commercial* sense that the State pension would not be a gift from government but a purchase to be paid for by contributions. There is nothing necessarily wrong with that: if government made more of their activities commercial they would waste less of our money—and would lessen their activities. But, second, this scheme is being "sold" in the *economic* sense that the Government is competing with all the other ways in which we can spend or save our money. It is hoping we will accept the scheme graciously, not grudgingly, because we think it better than other methods of accumulating a pension—or saving for retirement in other ways. And third, the Government is "selling" the scheme in the *political* sense that it hopes to win popularity by it—more popularity than it would by asking for public money for any other social benefit, and more than the other political parties would win by any better scheme for accumulating income in retirement.

Such political "salesmanship" is also not necessarily objectionable, though it is often made so in practice by exaggeration, suppression and irresponsible promise. It is unavoidable in a parliamentary democracy in which political parties compete for electoral favour and power. But it is a truth too often overlooked that politicians, no less than the businessman whose activities and methods they often condemn, are competing. The businessman makes a profit by selling goods that find favour in the market place; the politician acquires power by selling policies that find favour in the polling booth.[2] And in both cases any other alternative would be worse. If businessmen did not compete, the alternative is monopoly that might be difficult to control by legislation. If politicians did not compete, the alternative is a

2. Economists have studied the "entrepreneurial" behaviour of politicians in a new branch of economics. The development is traced by Professor T. W. Hutchison, *Markets and the Franchise,* Institute of Economic Affairs, 1966.

dictatorship that is usually impossible to discipline except by revolution. But the lesson remains: politicians may burn with a zeal to do good, but they cannot exercise it without power, and to acquire and keep power they must be political "salesmen." In the past year Mr. Crossman's gradually-aroused critics had admired his salesmanship even when they became increasingly doubtful about, and progressively dismayed by, his thinking.

But there is a wide gulf between the Government's objectives and the means Mr. Crossman proposes. Of course it is desirable to have pensions near half pay that are not lost on a change of jobs and that go on rising after retirement. That does not mean Mr. Crossman's proposals are the best way to arrange them. Indeed, the 13 years of argument on state pensions since 1957, when Mr. Crossman first announced his thinking on "national superannuation," have held back other and better ways, by creating uncertainty about what politicians would do, as distinct from what they said.

Beveridge can hardly be blamed for evolving a scheme that failed to anticipate inflation. The period he had in mind when he wrote his 1942 Report on social insurance was the 1920's and 1930's when the obstinate evil was deflation. Inflation was a post-war device applied as the lesser evil to ward off the worse evil of unemployment. It is difficult to maintain the value of money, and therefore stable prices, when the rest of the world is inflating, but since 1945 British politicians have not seized every opportunity for resisting inflation. Beveridge came to see the havoc that inflation had wrought with the pension he had devised to be based on real national insurance and built up gradually over 20 years. (Mr. Crossman's scheme promises the same 20 year "build-up," but post-war politicians ignored Beveridge's advice and paid the pension earlier; it is unlikely that Mr. Crossman's 20 years would ever see the light of day.)[3] Over dinner in the Reform Club, where Colin Clark, Ralph Harris, Graham Hutton and I had met to discuss a letter to the Editor of *The Times* in October, 1961,[4] he talked to us of inflation, politics and pensions. He has become known as the architect of post-war social security, but he saw it as subordinate to liberty—a juxtaposition that has not always been observed by politicians who have traded on his name or misapplied his teaching.

Pensions are not merely a matter of actuarial calculations (of insurance premiums), rates of interest (earned by insurance funds) and life tables (calculations of the expected duration of life and retirement). They invade the

3. Chapter VI.

4. The main paragraphs are reproduced on pages 124–25.

whole of individual and social life: the treatment we mete out to present-day pensioners who could not save during their working lives (which covered the slump years of the early 1930's); the freedom we enjoy in providing for retirement by personal or occupational pensions, life assurance, buying a house, investing in national savings, Building Societies, unit trusts, stocks and shares; the effects of occupational schemes on relations between employers and employees, on industrial costs and on the supply of savings for investment in industry; not least, the political consequences of the periodic enlargement of national insurance which is no longer insurance but taxation, and its effects on incentives to work and save, on the public finances of government, on the power of politicians to rule our lives.

These are the essential issues. Yet for month after month discussion has been fogged by figures of "contributions," "benefits," "opting out," "partial abatement," and other financial or technical detail. The Government has not emphasised the importance of these less obvious but more fundamental aspects. The pension specialists in the Life Offices Association, whose members largely insure the medium-sized and smaller pension schemes, in the National Association of Pension Funds, which mainly represents the larger funds run by the larger firms and by public authorities, and in the Confederation of British Industry, which represents employers, have, perhaps naturally, been pre-occupied with financial calculation and assessment. But when the National and Local Government Officers Association (NALGO) spoke out in August, 1969, the prospective pensioners acquired a direct and vocal spokesman.[5] The wider, less immediate but more far-reaching repercussions have generally come second to individual financial effects.

It is to emphasise these far-reaching repercussions for readers as savers, taxpayers, electors and citizens that this book has been written. It will not go over the detail of how much pension for how much contribution individuals can expect by what date, if partially contracted-out or wholly participating, if male or female, married or single. These figures have been discussed in numerous newspaper articles by informed writers, notably Dryden Gilling-Smith and Richard Sleight. But they depend on projections, estimates and guesses by civil servants and undertakings and promises by politicians who may be senile or dead by 1992. And the figures, which look reassuringly solid when they are printed, can be changed a year or two after 1972, or even before the scheme starts, as in 1961.

5. On 9 January, 1970, a NALGO conference narrowly rejected a motion on strike action urged by 50 branches unless the Bill were revised to protect members' occupational pensions.

It is possible to agree with Mr. Crossman that his scheme would comprise a fundamental reform in British social policy. He argues it is necessary, desirable and overdue. This book replies that it is unnecessary, undesirable and out-of-date. I suggest that the last third of the twentieth century requires not more national insurance but less, not obstacles to private saving for retirement but encouragement, not aggrandisement of the State by still more taxation revenue for political authority to spend but emancipation of the individual by widening choice in spending and saving.

This debate cuts across conventional party divisions. In 1961 the Conservatives introduced a graduated pension scheme; in 1966 they said they would repeal it. In 1957 no trade union voice was raised against national superannuation; in 1969 trade unionists spoke up. The CBI supports the principle of relating national insurance contributions and benefits to earnings. Labour MPs are finding that their traditional supporters are showing strange symptoms of acting and thinking like middle-class, bourgeois capitalists with a stake in property and an urge to acquire more, although only one MP has had the insight to express in graphic words[6] what social surveys have been finding for years:

> the workers . . . have little enthusiasm for the expansion of the social wage at the expense of their individual wage packets. . . . In the last two decades their collective aspirations have waned and their individual aspirations have waxed.

Mr. Crossman's pension scheme would further inflate the social wage.

From *The Times*, 20 October, 1961: A More Humane Society Apportioning State Benefits

To the Editor of the Times

Sir,—At the Conservative Conference, the Prime Minister said that the Government was considering how the social services could be remodelled "to ensure that public resources are concentrated on those to whom they do most good, and that the benefits are not wasted by being dispersed too widely."

May we suggest that the Government should be thinking along the following lines:

6. Mr. Raymond Fletcher, *The Times*, 9 July, 1968.

(1) There should be no further increases in general social benefits; any further increases should be confined to people in need.
(2) Existing benefits paid to people not in need, and who have not earned them by contributions, should be reviewed. By definition, this would not involve either hardship or injustice.
(3) Assistance rates to people in need should be raised.
(4) More vigorous steps, including the use of the broadcast services, should be taken to ensure that all who need assistance know how to get it.
(5) People with adequate means should be required to pay for social services now supplied free or below cost. This should apply not only to health services but also to education, school meals, housing, libraries, and others.
(6) The resultant saving in public expenditure should be used to increase national assistance, strengthen neglected services (such as mental and child care), and reduce taxation.
(7) Methods of contracting out of the social services should be devised for those who are able and wish to provide for themselves.
(8) Excusing the relevant social insurance contribution, returning the notional cost of the service not used, allowing the cost of private service against income tax, and other methods of encouraging self-provision should be examined.

18 October, 1961

Yours faithfully,
Colin Clark,
Ralph Harris,
Graham Hutton,
Arthur Seldon

CHAPTER III

"Swindle"?

Before we go into all this more deeply, why "swindle"?

This is not my word. It has been used in Parliament by the politicians about each other's pension schemes: the 1961 graduated scheme and the proposed 1972 earnings-related scheme. (There is no essential difference between "graduated" and "earnings-related." "Graduated" means related to earnings. "Graduated" was used to describe the 1961 scheme and "earnings-related" the 1972 scheme.)

The word appears to have been used not in the strict legal sense of cheat but in the financial sense of (not) value for money and in the moral sense of deception. On 27 January, 1959, when the House of Commons was discussing the general principles of the National Insurance Bill, Mr. Crossman said:

> When we were discussing the White Paper it was still possible to have doubts. I think those of us—certainly this applies to myself—who on first reading described the White Paper as a counterfeit or bogus imitation of the Labour Party's plan were under-estimating how bad it was. On reflection, we now realise that if we were to call this Bill a swindle we would not be exaggerating.
>
> (*Hansard*, Cols. 993–4)

And he explained:

> It is a deliberate attempt to persuade the people that some improvement in pensions is being carried out and that, for instance, wage related pensions are being introduced, when, as has been conclusively shown by my hon. Friends, the whole aim and object of the Bill is a fiscal arrangement to reduce the Exchequer liability and to redistribute the burden of pensions so that it falls predominantly on the middle range of wage earners.
>
> (*Hansard*, Col. 994)

Ten years later, on 6 March, 1969, the former Minister of Pensions of 1959, Mr. John Boyd-Carpenter, replied to Mr. Crossman, who had introduced the January White Paper on "earnings-related social security":

> . . . in the financing of the scheme the right hon. Gentleman has adopted, as he admitted, the practice from the 1961 Act of applying to the payment of current flat-rate benefits revenue raised by contributions to a wage-related scheme. He will recall that one of his hon. Friends, with singular lack of tact, mentioned today that in his degenerate days he referred to that method of financing as a swindle.
>
> . . . if those who were responsible for that scheme were responsible for a swindle it was a very small peccadillo[1] compared with the scale of swindling operations for which the right hon. Gentleman is responsible. The operations of Savundra or Whittaker White appear as that of mere amateurs compared with the right hon. Gentleman if there ever were any validity in the charge which, with remarkable frequency, he used to make in those days.

Mr. Boyd-Carpenter went on to explain his charge:

> There is . . . a dodge in this scheme . . . It is the redistribution element. . . . The 1961 Act was, of course, weighted in favour of the poorest. But that was done openly and fairly by the use of the Exchequer contribution. . . . Each brick, each unit, of contribution brought and bought the same benefit no matter what point in the scale of earnings it related to. It had that element of an insurance scheme. But that is not so with this scheme. [He went on to explain that the pension would not be proportional to contributions.] How can the right hon. Gentleman describe that as a pension contribution?
>
> (*Hansard,* Cols. 742–3)

In this parliamentary exchange "swindle" seems to have referred to the misleading use of the word "insurance" to obtain contributions by pretending that they would pay for a state pension "related" to them and therefore to the earnings of which they were a percentage. Mr. Boyd-Carpenter maintained that the pension was related to contributions in his scheme but not in Mr. Crossman's. Mr. Crossman counter-charged that the real aim of

1. Rendered by Soule's *Dictionary of English Synonyms* as: "Petty fault, slight offence, petty trespass, slight crime." 1961 Edition, p. 378.

Mr. Boyd-Carpenter's scheme was not to devise a new pension scheme but to raise government revenue.

Later he seems to have thought more kindly of it; on 25 November he told a meeting organised by a trade union: "Pay-as-you-go was one of the few good things the Tories did." But Mr. Crossman's change of mind does not make it right. "Pay-as-you-go" may have been unavoidable (and politically convenient) for *past* pensions; it is not unavoidable for *future* pensions and it is politically obnoxious.

"Graduated" and "earnings-related" can be used in two senses: "strictly proportional" and "varying generally." Mr. Boyd-Carpenter claimed that his pensions were graduated strictly according to the contributions. Mr. Crossman can claim that his pensions would be related to earnings, but this would be true only generally, not strictly. So far, the charge of "swindling" they levelled at each other seems to be a matter of degree.

But on both sides "national insurance" conceals the true purpose. Both have dressed up government fund-raising as "insurance." The fundamental question is: since contributions, like taxes, are compulsory, why do politicians mount the charade of acting like insurance salesmen rather than tax gatherers? Because it is politically easier to raise funds by promising pensions in return? Here Mr. Crossman has been more candid than Mr. Boyd-Carpenter in confessing the politician's difficulty of raising taxes by calling them taxes. The "dodge" is not simply that *part* of the contributions are transferred from some contributors to others (the "redistributive element") but that the *whole* of the contributions are taxes called by another name that politicians hope would smell more sweet. It is the very practice of presenting "national insurance" as insurance rather than as a form of taxation that is objectionable because it is deceitful. That is the source of the national insurance "swindle."

Lord Robbins once caused Harold Laski offence by writing (of communism): "Lillies that fester smell far worse than weeds."[2]

National insurance might have been a good way to pay for pensions, perhaps better than general taxation. But nowhere in the world does it work like insurance. Everywhere it is abused. It is time to accept that there is something in the political control of insurance that makes it go bad. It might have been a beautiful flower. But everywhere—in Europe, America, Britain—it is festering.

2. *Economic Planning and International Order,* Macmillan, 1937.

CHAPTER IV

The Strain on Political Institutions

What is at stake is more than the virtues or vice of Mr. Crossman's brand of "national insurance," and whether it is morally more objectionable or less objectionable than Mr. Boyd-Carpenter's. The exchange of verbal gunfire in the recurring Parliamentary/political battle conceals a deeper *malaise.* It is the very repute and dignity of the Parliamentary institutions within which the party system operates, and the respect in which they are held by the British electorate and the outside world, not least in the former Dominions and Colonies, that are damaged by increasing resort to manipulation of national insurance, the politicians' solace and opiate.

The damage to British political institutions is all the more severe from policies that subject the politicians to pressures that no fallible human can resist. Such a policy is the use of national insurance, at first from 1925 until 1948 in apparent good faith, but lately in barely more than name, to raise tax revenue in return for pensions to be paid for by people decades ahead who are not consulted and whose wishes cannot be foretold.

On paper the state could run an insurance system no less than private organisations, with some advantages and drawbacks, but with a fund of accumulating income and interest out of which to pay the pensions. This was the intention until as late as the Beveridge Report of 1942. But *in practice* the pensions promised outrun the contributions; pensioners increase in numbers; living standards rise; prices rise; the fund runs out; general tax revenue has to be mobilised; then, to avoid unpopularity or to win votes, the insurance system is itself prostituted by increasing current pensions and raising the revenue for them by enlarging the contributions beyond the sums required; finally, to placate *future* pensioners, contributions are varied with earnings in return for pensions in the future. Hence the birth of "graduated" (Conservative) or "earnings-related" (Labour) pensions. They are no more glorious, no more compassionate, no more imaginative than that. Their origin is prosaic, commonplace, perhaps mercenary, but nevertheless urgent and unavoidable: the Government's need for money—more money than it can raise by ordinary taxation. To make the promises persuasive, complex formulae tie the pensions to prices, earnings or both. And to demonstrate the solemnity of the undertaking, actuarial spells are intoned and Acts of Parliament gravely commit people yet unborn and governments yet unformed.

C'est magnifique; mais ce n'est pas l'assurance. A government may properly tax its working/earning citizens to provide for its old people; but it should do so without assurances of specific rewards, returns or benefits. There is an understanding, or an expectation, that the State will continue to defend its citizens from external enemy, internal civil commotion, catastrophic fire or flood, supply street lighting in the towns and cesspool drainage in the country. But no government can guarantee that its citizens will receive £24 11s 8d a week for a couple or £14 7s 10d for a bachelor, spinster, widow or widower if average lifetime earnings were £48 a week by 1992. The actuarial projections for the 1946 and 1961 schemes now make sad—or comic—reading.

Governments and politicians reduced to such devices cannot hope to command the respect of the populace that sees their pompous promises unceremoniously reviewed or revised or abandoned year by year. There is a telling parallel. Inflation of the currency remains controllable so long as it appears to be controlled and temporary. When it accelerates without end it becomes uncontrollable because it forfeits belief. When politicians make promises they do not keep, they may be forgiven for a time; when they make promises for others to keep, they are sooner or later distrusted and discredited. Each generation reviews afresh the obligations it inherits. It honours those it approves in the light of its circumstances, mores and aspirations. Tradition, caution, cultural inertia may continue outward forms and peripheral practices. They will not ensure the satisfaction of costly financial undertakings made 20, 30, 40 or more years previously to ease the passing embarrassment of politicians who shirked unpalatable decisions for fear of losing power.

This is what is now threatened. The real reason for full, "earnings-related" pensions in 1992 is to raise money in 1972 for a diminishing minority of poor pensioners born in 1907, 1897 and 1887. It is *not*, as Mr. Crossman claims, primarily to prevent a fall in the living standards of people retiring after 1972 who, although earning enough to maintain their standard in retirement, would fail to provide for it unless ordered to "contribute" to the State's "national superannuation." It is *not* to ensure that pensions rise with living standards before and prices after retirement. It is *not* to ensure that pensions are preserved on a change of job. It is *not* to provide more generously for people who retire before 1972, or for widows, or married women at work. *None* of these requires compulsory, universal, earnings-related "national superannuation" benefits. Nor do they require earnings-related contributions.

The main objective—more generous pensions for retired people in need—requires more taxation, a rechannelling of current expenditure to people in need, less government expenditure, or all three. These solutions government has shirked. Instead it is tempted to raise revenue by calling additional forced levies "national superannuation contributions" and committing their successors to repay them in pensions. This practice would not be new in 1972. Nor was it new in 1961. It has been going on since 1946, when the Government ignored Beveridge's advice on building up pensions gradually out of contributions. For 20 years or more British politicians have promised larger pensions than contributions could support. The temptation to raise taxation without tears has been too strong. Even men of high principle have succumbed. But a dodge it remains. It is in this sense a pretence, a deception, a fiction, a "swindle."

It is no defence to point to other countries that practice similar deception. In almost every country where national insurance was begun, ostensibly to ensure income in retirement, it has degenerated into a political device for very different purposes: to save them from financial embarrassment or further the ideology of politicians temporarily in power.

All who care for political democracy—not least British Parliamentarians of all parties—must be alarmed by the damage to British political institutions and the integrity of British political life wrought by the intensifying resort to "national insurance" as a substitute for taxation. It must transcend the financial conundrum of finding money for existing pensions.

There is some evidence of the unease. In the House of Commons on 4 December, 1969, Mr. Douglas Houghton, Chairman of the Parliamentary Labour Party and Minister for the Coordination of Social Services from October, 1964, to early 1967, rebuked both Front Benches, as a Conservative speaker later described it:

> For the sake of the prestige of, and confidence in national insurance I hope that we will stop talking about "the Tory swindle." It is not good for national insurance and does not happen to be true . . . the truth is that the 1959 scheme [begun in 1961] was redistributive, but the Tories of the day dared not say so. They pretended that the graduated contributions were value for money when they were not. But the scheme as a whole was value for money. I am always surprised that the Tories let that label stick.
>
> (*Hansard*, 4 December, Cols. 1804–5)

He explained his exoneration as follows:

> The scheme as a whole is value for money today. There is no deferred annuity of the level of the national insurance pension which can be bought in the market for the price paid by the insured person in the scheme. That will be true of the future as well.
>
> (*Hansard,* Col. 1805)

This exculpation of Mr. Boyd-Carpenter makes a further distinction between the poor financial return on the graduated contribution, which repeats Mr. Crossman's criticisms, and the good financial return on national insurance contributions as a whole. Mr. Houghton did not say why he thought the national insurance pension was good value for the contribution and, he implied, far better than could be obtained in any occupational pension scheme. This may be true for older men nearing retirement; and on paper the state could give very good pensions. But in practice there is a fundamental difference between state pensions and private ones bought in the open market. On a long view it would be surprising if, in a working life of 40 to 45 years, annuities deferred to retirement could not be better at recent high rates of interest. (Of course, if a man moved between several jobs, he would benefit only if he carried his accumulated pension wherever he moved.) It is the interest earned on invested pension funds that enables occupational schemes to give very high pensions. The power of interest to make savings grow can be illustrated most simply by example: £100 earning 7% a year will double in 10 years, earning 10% in 7 years. Occupational funds have been gradually raising their earnings for 15 years or more. It is true some have been slow because they were uncompetitive or over-cautious, but they have gradually followed the more enterprising. The pension fund run by one large British firm[1] has earned around 10% a year for some years from investment in industry, and its pensioners have benefited accordingly—much more than a government can be conceived to pay out of what are normal contributions and taxation. This is perhaps the most prolific, profitable and prosperous pension fund known in Britain. But it shows that very profitable investment at very high yields is possible. State pensions are not closely comparable with occupational pensions because each has ancillary features the other may lack: for example, state pensions are more easily transferable and have given widows' pensions more generally; occupational schemes commonly carry life assurance on death before retirement and often lump sums

1. Imperial Tobacco; the pension fund has been managed by George Ross Goobey.

on retirement. But I doubt whether the State could ever match the best of the occupational schemes.

Mr. Houghton's anxiety was echoed by a Conservative Front Bench spokesman, Mr. Paul Dean:

> I hope that we have for all time got rid of this dreary argument about the Tory swindle.
>
> (*Hansard*, 4 December, Col. 1825)

Mr. Dean, who normally speaks with informed good sense on medical care and pensions, seems to have missed Mr. Houghton's distinction which, right or wrong, repeated Mr. Crossman's condemnation of the 1961 graduated pension. But whatever the balance of argument on the financial aspects of the 1961 and the proposed 1972 schemes, even if Labour and Conservative spokesmen now agree on whether or not there was or is going to be a "swindle," the political repercussions remain, and cannot be suppressed, because they have become part of British history.

Beveridge was more aware of the dangers of "national insurance" than the politicians who first praised and then condemned him as outdated when they sensed that the disciplines of the "flat-rate" contribution and pension would cramp their efforts to attract electoral support by raising government funds faster than they could spend the revenue they levied by taxation. But the "contribution" principle was questioned when the Beveridge Report was barely translated into the legislation of 1946 and 1948 that created the post-war welfare state. In 1950 an American study pointed to the deceptive labelling of "national insurance" that, if perpetrated by private industry, would have brought down the moral condemnation of the mass of British *literati* and social observers. It said:

> adoption of the term "insurance" by the proponents of social security was a stroke of promotional genius. Thus social security has capitalized on the goodwill of private insurance and, through the establishment of a reserve fund, has clothed itself with an aura of financial soundness.[2]

In the proposed 1972 scheme, although a surplus of contributions over outgoings is envisaged in the early years, it is not considered an essential element of the scheme, which is designed to pay out substantially all the income it receives in each year. And this procedure is rationalised by supporters of

2. L. Meriam and K. Schlotterbeck, *The Cost and Financing of Social Security*, Brookings Institution (Washington), 1950.

"pay-as-you-go" who applaud the absence of a fund and of the financial restraints on political control.

In 1952 Professor Alan T. Peacock concluded from a study:

> it is difficult to regard British national insurance as genuine "insurance" in any strict sense of the word . . . as it is compulsory and there is no adjustment of premium to risk.[3]

He emphasised "the misleading analogy between private and national insurance." This analogy is again exploited in the current debate on the Crossman 1972 pension scheme.

In 1953 Dr. Colin Clark, until recently of Oxford University, wrote:

> governments, both Labour and Conservative, have been promising old age and widowhood pensions of a value far beyond actuarial contributions . . . no government . . . put even inadequate contributions into a proper reserve fund, as any prudent administrator of an insurance scheme would do, but spent the money as fast as it came in . . . political parties . . . have been guilty of promising pensions which they knew could not possibly be paid out of the contributions received.[4]

Dr. Clark has left England for Australia after years of fertile and fearless teaching and writing that brought him no recognition or honours. But he has done Britain more good than if he had compromised with what politicians thought "politically possible."

Other Western countries have introduced, developed and inflated national insurance, with results that can be seen in Germany, Sweden and elsewhere in Europe. Some people in the USA would follow the same course and take—or welcome—the same risks of uncontrollable political power, unnecessary taxation, the inhibition of independent insurance, private saving, and capital for industry, and the standardisation of social life.[5] In Australia, which continues to resist national insurance, and New Zealand, which has recognised the impracticability of segregating social security from general tax revenue, voices urge the same errors that have been made "in socially more advanced countries." Mr. Crossman quotes earnings-related national insurance in other countries as examples for Britain to follow. They are lessons on what to avoid.

3. *The Economics of National Insurance,* Hodge, 1952.
4. *Welfare and Taxation,* Catholic Social Guild, 1954.
5. Chapter XIII.

CHAPTER V

How It All Began

Little sense will be made of the debate on pensions in the coming months if we cannot see the ultimate objective of it all. There is little point in examining proposals, plans, statistics and projections if we do not know where we want to go, or whether they will lead us there. We must refuse to be confused, bemused or diverted by detail. We must insist on knowing where the politicians are leading us.

The hard-headed, practical, common-sense, "pragmatic" man is inclined to dismiss objectives with the obvious truth: "we must start from here." That is only a beginning. It is more important to know: *Where do we go from here?* Movement "from here" has no virtue in itself. If it is to be better than staying put, it must shift us nearer where we wish to go.

The tragedy of much British social policy, not merely for the quarter of a century since Beveridge and 1948 but for a whole century since the Forster Elementary Education Act of 1870 which introduced the State directly into the *provision* (in contrast to the *financing*) of schools, is that it has started "from here" *but has largely led away from where we want to go.* It has tackled immediate social abuses or shortcomings in an apparently humane, workmanlike, practical manner, but left a legacy of undesirable effects that have not merely plagued succeeding policy-makers, but, more important, frustrated the children, grandchildren and great-grandchildren of the very people it was designed to help. It has comprised a series of first-aid treatments that have inexorably debilitated, inhibited and disabled the patient. Now, after 100 years of increasing state education we are told that parents are incapable of choosing schools; after 55 years of rent restriction and increasing council house building they are unpractised in selecting a home; after 35 years of national insurance pensions millions have no personal or occupational pension; after 22 years of the National Health Service they must not be allowed to pay for medical care more than they can be made to pay in taxation. Earnest, well-intentioned, troubled, burdened, but also vote-conscious, short-sighted and sometimes misinformed politicians have tackled urgent "problems" and devised solutions to satisfy their consciences, their parties and public opinion. But it is their occupational hazard that they cannot look very far ahead. In doing what good can emerge from the maelstrom of principle, expediency and opportunism that is the stuff of party politics, they have often done harm to people, society, the economy and political institutions in the years that followed. Economists have lately studied, and become alarmed at, the "social" (as distinct from the "private") consequences of industry in congestion, pollution and noise. The social consequences of politics last for decades. In *Julius Caesar,* the supreme analyst of human nature makes Mark Antony say:

> The evil that men do lives after them,
> The good is oft interred with their bones . . .

We like to remember the best in our politicians, but the worst is often not known until long after they have passed on. Any good they do in their lifetimes is usually apparent; the evil they do is not known for long years and is often buried in undocumented human experience.

We must "start from here," but we must know where we are going. If we cannot agree where we want to go, at least those who do not want to go where governments want to lead us, and who think the people would not want to go there if they knew, can in a democracy say so, and hope to persuade them to change direction. And governments will have to listen.

This conflict between good intentions and the harmful consequences arising from the anxiety to do something about pressing problems is vividly exhibited in the history of British pension policy. Before it is examined more closely let us note the main objectives of pension policy in a civilised, liberal, democratic and increasingly wealthy community.

First, above all it would desire to ensure as high a standard of living as possible to those of its old people who could not in their working lives save sufficient for their retirement.

Second, it would allow and encourage people to save for retirement as much as and how they wished, provided they did not frustrate the desire of others to do so.

Third, it may require them to save at least enough to avoid dependence on more thoughtful people who have saved more. Since earnings normally vary widely, and the amount of saving people think desirable varies with their judgement on how far they wish to enjoy their earnings while young or middle-aged and how far they wish to ensure comfort, security and tranquillity in their later years, they may save very different amounts. The community would not set a ceiling on how much they saved, whether, say, half, two-thirds, as much as, or more than, they earned in their last few years of work. A person may "need" less after retiring, but he has leisure to spend more to do all the things he could not do while he worked. At 65 a man can expect to live for 14 years to nearly 80; a woman of 60 can expect to live 19 years to about the same age. For perhaps at least the first 5 or 10 years they can lead a more varied and interesting life than before. Retirement is retirement from work, not from life.

British politicians have had to accept these inalienable rights and irrepressible differences in human nature: although many of them still urge equality in education and medical care there is no pretence that everyone should retire on the same pension and Mr. Crossman has evolved a new theory to rationalise this inconvenient obstruction. Indeed Mr. Crossman's scheme would *force* most of them to save *different* amounts through the State, thus perpetuating "social divisiveness" in retirement.

How far have these objectives of a civilised, democratic and increasingly wealthy society guided British pension policy?

A century ago people in Britain did not accumulate pensions. Some were rich enough to dispense with them. But most had no retirement. They worked until they died, some in their forties. If they lived longer but could not work they were supported by their families, by Friendly Societies through which they had saved small sums, by charity, or by the local authorities; these gave them cash, food and clothing, and shelter in a "workhouse" or care in a hospital infirmary.

Since the 1850s economic advance, social improvement and medical science have lengthened the expectation of life at birth from 30 or 35 to around 70 (a little less for men, a little more for women). In 1840 there were 800,000 people over 65 in Britain out of 18½ million, or only 4½ per cent. By 1900 there were 2¼ million out of 37 million, or 6 per cent. Now there are over 7 million out of 54 million, or 14 per cent. A century ago many people died before they could retire; now most live on well after retirement. In 1850 or 1870 there was almost no problem of income in retirement; now retirement is a 15-year- or 20-year-long phase of life to which many people look forward with pleasure and anticipation (see figure preceding Table A, p. 138).

Most of this improvement has taken place since 1900. The expectation of life (at birth) was then still only 45 to 50. But more people were surviving into their 60's and 70's. The problem was that many had little or no certain income from private sources.

In the 1890s social reformers increasingly thought that the State would have to step in. And it did. A Royal Commission in 1905 recommended state

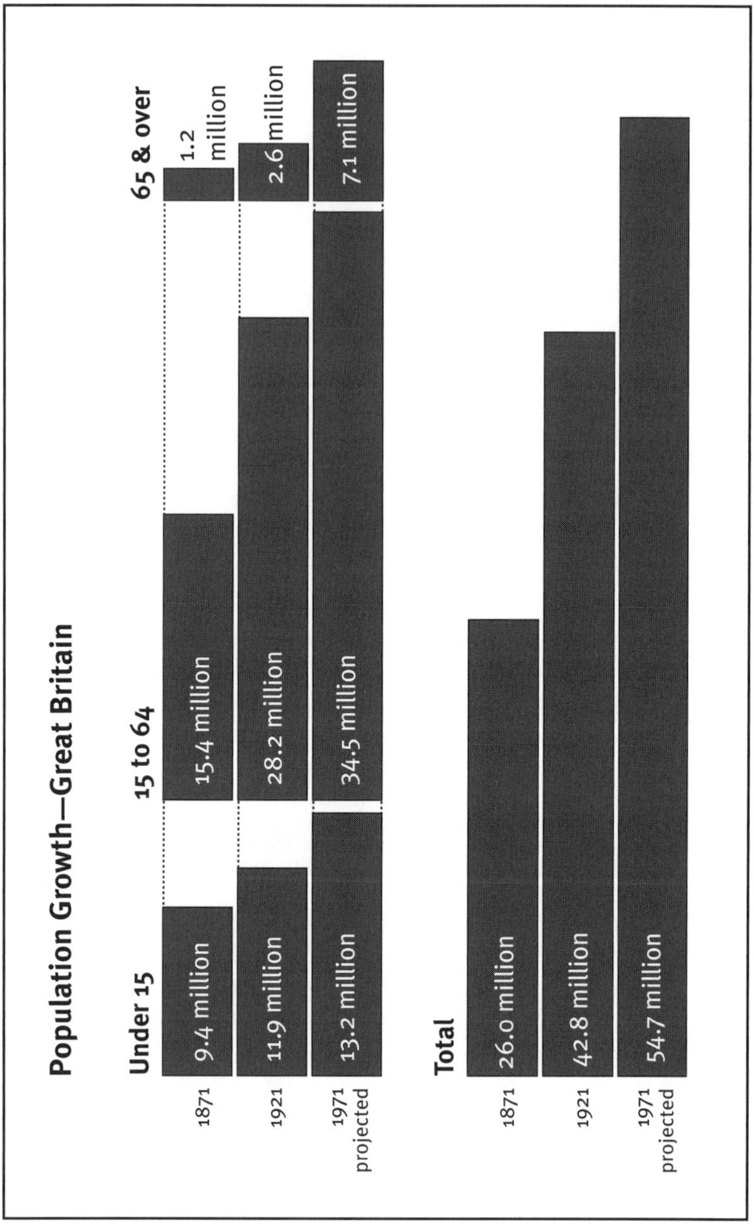
Population Growth—Great Britain
Under 15
15 to 64
65 & over
1871
9.4 million
15.4 million
1.2 million
1921
11.9 million
28.2 million
2.6 million
1971 projected
13.2 million
34.5 million
7.1 million
Total
1871
26.0 million
1921
42.8 million
1971 projected
54.7 million

Table A. Population—Great Britain (millions)

Year	Under 15	15–64	65 and over	Total
Censuses				
1861	8.3	13.8	1.1	23.1
1871	9.4	15.4	1.2	26.0
1881	10.8	17.5	1.4	29.7
1891	11.6	19.8	1.6	33.0
1901	12.0	23.2	1.7	37.0
1911	12.6	26.1	2.1	40.8
1921	11.9	28.2	2.6	42.8
1931	10.8	30.7	3.3	44.9
1941 (war: no census)				
1951	10.9	32.6	5.3	48.9
1961	11.9	33.3	6.0	51.3
Projections				
1971	13.2	34.5	7.1	54.7
1981	14.1	35.9	7.9	57.9
1991	15.4	38.2	8.1	61.8

The figures are rounded to the nearest decimal, so that the total may differ slightly from the sum of the items in each year.

aid and Lloyd George introduced the Old Age Pension of 5s a week for a man or woman of 70 with inadequate other income. In 1909 580,000 old people drew £7.5 million. In 1920 the pension was raised to 10s where it remained until 1946.

Thus far the State paid the pension on a means test and out of taxes, and the method made good sense. Everyone contributed to its cost roughly according to their capacity to pay, and the pensions went to people in most need. There was argument about the size of the pension and the age at which it should be paid, but the principles governing who should pay and who should receive were clear and civilised. There was debate also about the distribution of taxes (indirect taxes on purchases weigh more heavily on people with lower incomes).[1] But the Old Age Pension, paid by people who could pay and received by people who should receive, was like Portia's gentle rain

1. Dr. E. G. West argues in *Education and the State* that if working men had paid lower taxes they would have been able to pay for at least part of the "free" education (and other social services) the state created for people who could not pay; that is, the state was taxing people to provide services for people who in large part could not pay *because* it taxed them!

from Heaven in *The Merchant of Venice:* it "blesseth him that gives and him that takes."

In 1925 there came a big change. The 1908 Old Age Pensions were to continue to be paid out of taxation, but there would be new Old Age Pensions based on national insurance. The 1908 pension required no "contributions" from the pensioners. The 1925 pension would be paid to men and women at 65 who earned them by their contributions from wages and from their employers. There would also be some help from "the Exchequer" (that is, the taxpayer), but only in the early years. The Government Actuary calculated that if the contributions were raised three times every ten years and invested they would generate enough capital and interest in 30 years to pay for the 1925 pension (and for the 1908 non-contributory pension) by 1956. But the essence of insurance—that the fund is built up before the pension is paid—was thrown overboard. The pension was paid before enough had been accumulated and the deficit was to be covered by an Exchequer grant (£4 million for ten years).

In 1946 when the pension was raised from 10s a week to 26s on Beveridge's 1942 recommendation, much the same happened. Again, the contributions required for the pension were calculated actuarially. This time the Exchequer Supplement was fixed at one-sixth of the contributions. Again the insurance contribution principle was ignored, despite Beveridge's advice that the pension be built up over 20 years (a period that recurs in the Crossman Scheme).

Why 20 years? The main reason is that that is how an insurance system is run. The contributions mount up into a fund which is invested and used, with the interest it earns, to pay the pensions as they fall due. And for the particular reason that after the war there were bound to be large demands on government revenue for at least a few years and it was desirable to keep down the cost of pensions. If the contributory pensions had been paid at once they would have gone to *all* pensioners—then about 5 million, whatever their age and whether they could be regarded as in need or not. To limit the cost therefore meant confining an increase in pensions to people in need, and financing it for general taxation.

Beveridge made these two reasons clear later.[2] The acceptability of his Report turned on the financial cost of his proposals, especially for pensions for people in or nearing retirement. The Beveridge Committee started work in July 1941. By the summer of 1942 it was seen to be envisaging a financial re-

2. *Power and Influence,* Hodder and Stoughton, 1953.

construction of social security rather than an administrative in-filling. In July the Treasury became interested, and

> There followed a series of discussions and interchange of notes, between Keynes,[3] Robbins,[4] Epps[5] and myself, with the finance of the scheme coming ever more clearly to depend on what we did about pensions for those already at or near the pensionable age.

This problem of paying current pensions is the bug-bear of pension policy reform. No politician has yet found the solution except by promising pensions for *other* people. It is the problem from which he runs away, as Mr. Crossman is now doing.

On 12 August Beveridge made what he called a "deal" with Keynes:

> The gist of the deal was that Keynes promised to support my Report if I would keep the additional burden on the Treasury down to £100,000,000 a year for the first five years; after that, he said, the Treasury should have no difficulty in meeting rising charges. I found myself able to satisfy Keynes's condition for support, provided that I spread the introduction of adequate contributory pensions over a substantial period of transition. I wanted to do this *in any case*... (my italics)

Why "in any case"?

> It seemed to me right to make pensions as of right... genuinely contributory; for pensions there must be a substantial period of contribution.

The "substantial period" he recommended in the Report was 20 years. This advice was ignored, how far for political, administrative, "stigma" or other reasons we shall never know. But what about current pensioners?

> Those who were already nearing the pensionable age would have to be covered, and could rightly be covered, by assistance pensions subject to a means test.

But the 20-year contribution period was not honoured.

> The deal depended on a long transition period for pensions as of right. That has not been applied in practice. Our deal went west.

3. John Maynard Keynes, 1883–1946, the leading economist of the period, then an adviser at the Treasury.

4. Now Lord Robbins.

5. Sir George Epps, the then Government Actuary.

And he concluded sadly:

> When the Report had been made it passed . . . into the hand of men exercising or seeking political power. This proved . . . a less pleasing world.

The result of ignoring this advice? Failing to build up pensions slowly and in the meantime paying pensions only to existing pensioners in need meant a rapid accumulation of insurance deficits. Instead of enough money to pay all pensions in 1956, or about £15,000 million, there was only £1,500 million, or a tenth, in the National Insurance Fund. By 1970 the deficit must be over £30,000 million, or about as much as the whole of the National Debt. Again one can imagine the outcry that would have been created by the *literati,* spiritual leaders and social workers if such a blunder had been made by insurance companies. They would have condemned "the commercial capitalists" as irresponsible, callous and defaulting enemies of old people in particular and society in general.

But who now blames "the men of 1946" for irresponsible, callous default? At least the insurance offices have no power to force people to insure with them. The men of 1946 had power to force everyone to insure with them. Of course, luck was against them. The slump of the 1930s had reduced the contributions; the war of 1939 to 1945 and post-war inflation and rising living standards among the working population made it necessary—and politically attractive—to raise the pensions.

But was there no bad management? Was the National Insurance Fund invested wisely? It was not. It was used as an instrument of government financial management to buy gilt-edged securities. And by governments of both parties. This is a telling example of the irresistible pressures on them to take a short-run view and deal with an immediate problem, like Charles Dickens' Mr. Micawber, in the hope that sooner or later something would turn up to save the day—or at least the government's face. Pensions are the graveyard of the politician's reputation. Even the great Winston Churchill offered widows' pensions in 1926 far in excess of the value of the contributions and despite warnings from the Government Actuary. Even the high-principled Hugh Gaitskell tried to explain away the 1946 failure by arguing that 20 years was a long time to wait and that the general public would not have approved an increase in other national insurance benefits without a parallel one in pensions. Now Mr. Crossman is proposing a new kind of pension with a 20-year build-up and is trying to persuade us that the promises he makes in 1972 will be kept by politicians and taxpayers in 1992.

Well, anything is *possible.* Gaitskell's explanation, or excuse, must be examined closely. If trouble is built up for future politicians, taxpayers, social insurance contributors and pensioners, can a politician be forgiven for short-sighted policies by passing the buck to public opinion? If it was right to pay the higher insurance pension immediately, was it not the politician's duty to explain to the general public that the only way to do so was to levy higher taxation, politically unpopular though this may have been? If higher pensions are desirable for old people in need, is it essential to give it to everyone, politically popular though the course may (or may not) be? Was the purpose in 1946 to protect old people from seeking the then National Assistance and its supposed Poor Law stigma? Was the purpose to further the political doctrine of equal state pensions no matter what differences there were in needs, means or other individual circumstances? Or was it, simply, understandably, but cynically, vote-catching?

Historians will debate the motives that determined the decisions of 1946. They may never distinguish the real reasons from the excuses. But public opinion must now weigh up a similar battery of motives, promises and probabilities that underlie the Crossman pension proposals of 1970. What is clear so far is that history is not on his side.

Moreover, there is a large difference. At least until 1946 there was the intention to base the pension on a fund of national insurance contributions with some assistance from "the Exchequer," the contributors being able to say that they had paid for the pension in much the same way as the owner of a private insurance policy who accumulates a pension or buys an annuity. The pensioner is then dependent on a fund of accumulated premiums (or contributions), topped up by interest and perhaps an increase in capital values resulting from careful, clever investment. He may suffer from bad luck or bad management, but he is not dependent on politicians or taxpayers 20, 30 or 40 years in the future.

Since about 1957 this pretence has been abandoned. Mr. Crossman had the clarity of insight, the academic urge and the *Realpolitik* to see that what his political mentor and coadjutor, Aneurin Bevan, had described as a myth and "bunkum" could no longer be described as a reality. The National Insurance Fund, which by 1957 had about a tenth of the capital sum "projected" in 1925, could never be reconstructed sufficiently to pay the state pensions. The future accumulated state pensions could never be "replaced"; they would have to be based on annual assessments: each year the cost of pensions would be assessed and the contributions calculated accordingly. The actuaries call this system "assessmentism": public relations men and politicians have tried the seductive but deceptive "pay as you go." I think the prospective pensioner must call it "pray as you pay": for his contributions do not go into a fund, but, like the proverbial Epsom Salts, straight through the system and out. There is no systematic fund, no profitable investment, no interest and no capital growth. There is Mr. Crossman's (and his colleagues') assurances and undertakings, that politicians and taxpayers unknown will pay the pension in 1972, 1982, 1992, 2002, 2012 . . .

There can be two opinions about whether "pray as you pay" is more or less secure than funding. But there can be no doubt that it is very different. The difference can be minimised or exaggerated. The funded pension may be said to rest on a financial fund of invested contributions; and the "pray as you pay" pension on a political fund of goodwill from the younger and middle-aged of, say, the 1990s to the older people of that decade. But Mr. Crossman is not sure about it himself. He has had to abandon the insurance principle but wants to go on calling it insurance. Indeed, he says he wants to re-create the insurance system by replacing taxes with social insurance contributions which create a real claim to a pension. Sometimes it is called "the contract of the generations," "a contract no Chancellor can ignore"; sometimes a "semi-contract."

Is this a loss of faith in the political "social contract" in which taxes paid into a common pool during the working life pay for pensions drawn from the common pool in retirement? Is it a return to the notion that the right to the pension is not secure unless it is based on a *financial* contract in which identifiable and recorded contributions pay for identifiable and recorded pensions? If so, are "contributions" paid out almost at once any different from taxes? Do the contributors see them differently? Have the contributors been told, honestly, frankly and sincerely, in the Prime Minister's phrase, that this sort of "national insurance" is very different from the insurance they know? Do they understand the difference between the funded pension based on a *financial* fund of investments and the "pray as you pay" pension based on a *political* fund of promises, undertakings, assurances, understandings?

CHAPTER VI

Crossman's National Superannuation

Politicians who condemn economic activity outside the State—private enterprise, "capitalism"—covet and capitalise on its institutions, practices, even language. "Insurance," "contract," "fund," and "saving," which have well-known meanings in private industry, have been used to advocate *national* insurance and national "superannuation." Why? Because they are trusted by the people. The advocates of state control have tried to cash in on them.

Consider each of the three words in the grandly-named National Superannuation Fund in the 1969 Bill. Even the use of the word "national" is misleading. It is meant to convey an impression of wisely-inspired, public-spirited, "official" good intention to take care of people in old age. It recurs in "in the national interest." In practice, it means *state* insurance and superannuation or *government* insurance and superannuation run by politicians, civil servants and public officials. Their intentions are usually, or sometimes, good; their performance is not necessarily good and is often bad. And it is by their performance that we must judge them.

Then, "superannuation." Another splendid word much used by governments that *sounds* much more impressive than "pension," which private schemes are usually content with. But it is not as good a word; it is more grandiose and pompous but it has much less reputable connotations. A "pension" is an allowance or annuity, that is, a form of income. To be "superannuated" can mean to be on the retired list but also

> decrepit, anile, aged, imbecile, doting, antiquated, effete, rusty, time-worn, disqualified, unfit for service, *passé*.[1]

Not least, "fund." There's a comforting word, rather like nest-egg, reserve, savings, property, a word designed to convey reassurance, peace of mind, a sense of security. "Fund" normally means a stock of money or assets care-

1. Soule's *Dictionary of English Synonyms.*

fully accumulated, set aside and ready for specific purposes or perhaps to meet emergencies. But the National Superannuation Fund is not a fund in this sense. It is a tank, filled by contributions by one pipe and emptied almost at once by pensions out of another pipe. It is not even a reliable tank, with a more or less constant level of water. It goes up some years, down other years, almost dry in some periods, almost overflowing in others. The contents may be taken out for purposes that have little to do with pensions. And it would be at the mercy of politicians often at their wits' end to find money for quite different purposes. What sort of "Fund" is that?

"National superannuation" was invented in 1957 by Mr. Crossman with the assistance of academics described as "social administrators," a species of sociologist.[2] Sociology covers a wide range of studies, from rigorously scientific at one extreme to extremely sentimental at the other. Mr. Crossman's academics have deployed sentimentality that often seems to dominate the science. Sociologists of this kind "care" about the "under-privileged" (a nonsense word if you examine it closely: if privilege is bad, people who have less than others should not be helped to have more—except on the equally nonsensical supposition that anything is good if it is owned equally). In this branch of sociology "compassion" infuses thinking to the point at which almost anything is justified by good intentions—inadequate statistics, faulty reasoning, unstated assumptions, selective evidence. This is almost as objectionable as the Marxist notion that the ends justify the means. Certainly this kind of sociologist, of whom there are many in British (and overseas) universities (whose former students sometimes bemuse social policy overseas), misjudges human nature, does not understand the working of economic systems, and is out of sympathy with the aspirations of the rising working man (and woman) to the point of contempt.

These faults show in the development of "national superannuation" from a conference resolution in 1955 to the White Papers and the National Superannuation and Social Insurance Bill of 1969.

The 1955 resolution led to the 1957 report *National Superannuation,* described as Labour's Policy for Security in Old Age. It argued that there were two nations in old age; those with an occupational pension in addition to the state pension and those without. So it proposed that everyone should be required to save through the state for a pension related to his earnings. People with a good occupational scheme might be allowed to contract out, although on terms that were ominously vague and that could not be so favourable that the state scheme would be endangered. (Is it not remarkable

2. A Note on Sour/Sentimental Sociology, page 221, Appendix B.

that politicians, who are servants of the people even when they lead them, think of themselves as "allowing" people to have liberties? No true servant of the people would make that mistake. But the habit of thinking of the people as subject rather than sovereign has grown for so long that the mistake is made by politicians of all parties.)

The document also revealed the strange ambivalence in Mr. Crossman: clear thinking and academic candour disfigured by dogmatism that brushes aside unwelcome argument and evidence, and an undemocratic disposition to dismiss the aspirations of the people for whom he "cares." Hence the sometimes engaging and sometimes disagreeable gallimaufry of almost embarrassing frankness and stubborn obscurantism. "Pension rights must not become . . . subject to the whims of politicians," said *National Superannuation*. But the new graduated pension was not designed to have a financial fund, as those on which occupational schemes are based. Then what was to be the pensioner's guarantee? ". . . confidence can be placed in the survival in perpetuity of a government in Britain." From a political scientist of Mr. Crossman's stature, this is a claim that not everyone will accept without a lot of convincing argument and evidence. If government is a continuing entity it is also supreme; if it can keep its word, it can also break it. "The State," said Aneurin Bevan in 1954, "is a sovereign body and can alter the terms of the contract when it wishes without asking anybody. It did it in 1931, and it has done it over and over again." British politicians have hardly always honoured their promises.

Observers must speculate about the motives of politicians. They are not demi-gods, but fallible beings who must be continually put in their place. Mostly they are a mixture of good, bad and middling, a *pot-pourri* of altruistic idealism and selfish lust for power; men no better when out of office than the rest of us. No doubt the wish to see the poorer with higher pensions was one aim of *National Superannuation*. But other consequences would follow. One was that a lot of money would be collected in graduated contributions from the higher-paid that would be more difficult to raise in taxation: so electoral unpopularity would be avoided. Second, the National Insurance Fund would be kept going with some semblance of the insurance principle, although Aneurin Bevan had clearly stated the truth in 1954:[3]

> There is no such animal as "the Fund." It does not exist. It is a pure myth. . . . Let us get behind these figures to the economics of the situation; . . . let us get rid of this bunkum about insurance.

3. 9 December, 1954. *Hansard*, Col. 1152.

Third, the contributions would yield so much more than required for pensions that the surplus would for a time form a National Pension Fund to be invested in industry. With what purpose? To increase production so that the pensions could be paid without depressing the standard of living of future generations, said Mr. Crossman and the sociologists. On paper, impossible to deny. But in practice a distinguished Labour banker, the late Lord Piercy, showed that in several countries the funds were often used to support government borrowing, and the interests of the "national insurance" policyholders took second place. (Another sidelight on the astigmatism of politicians: when private firms borrow their pension funds they are denounced with fine moral fervour. Sauce for the state goose is poison for the private gander.)

Whatever its trimmings, National Superannuation, vintage 1957, was not so much national insurance as redistributive taxation. This was its Achilles Heel, as it is the Achilles Heel of National Superannuation, vintage 1970.

But as Mr. Crossman did not acquire political power until 1964, nothing came of National Superannuation 1957. Instead 1961 brought a modified version in Mr. Boyd-Carpenter's scheme of graduated state pensions. The National Insurance Fund was running relentlessly into the red and money had to be found somewhere or other. The main purpose was to find more money for existing pensions, so the scheme was decked out with implausible excuses of which the most uproarious was that it was intended to encourage the development of occupational schemes. The main principles were much the same as in National Superannuation, except that there was a bad official under-estimate of the number of employees who would be contracted out: instead of 2¼ million, over twice as much, or about 5¾ million. In all, this scheme will comprise no more than a short, inglorious page in British social history. The Conservative Party said in 1966 that it would be abolished; the Labour Party proposes to scrap "graduation" to make way for bigger, and hopefully better "earnings-relation."

The episode provokes a fundamental reflection: what if the Conservatives in the years from 1951 to 1964 had concentrated on providing generous state pensions for people in most need and helping occupational or other private pensions to expand, so that by now almost everyone who wanted a private pension was covered? Would the Labour Party be able to argue for national superannuation? If they did, would they be heard? (A Conservative Act of 1956 provided some encouragement for annuities for people who are self-employed—shopkeepers, builders, window-cleaners, accountants, barristers, writers, etc.—or employed by firms with no pension schemes. But the tax concessions have not been sufficient to attract, in 14 years, more than 250,000 out of several million who could be covered by such annuities.)

Still more fundamental: the remaining pockets of absolute poverty must be removed if society is not to be regulated increasingly by successive rounds of centralised control on the ground that, since *some* people are poor, or ill, or ill-housed, or ill-educated, we must *all* be provided with money, or medical care, or housing, or education by the State. Since *relative* poverty will always be with us as long as incomes differ, it must be prevented from being used as the pretext for progressive government interference in our social and economic life.

And so to 1969. It has taken Mr. Crossman from 1964 to reach the seat of office from which he could launch his brainchild of 1955. In January a White Paper announced the broad outlines. Apart from the apparent abandonment of a National Pension Fund for investment in industry, they were substantially as foreshadowed in 1957. But there was a fundamental omission: the terms for contracting out by firms that had better schemes. Mr. Crossman invited the pensions industry to consultations—the Life Offices Association (LOA), the National Association of Pension Funds and the Society of Pension Consultants of the Corporation of Insurance Brokers. The CBI and the TUC were also consulted as representatives of the employers and employees.

The nature of these consultations was obscure. Initially they seemed to be talks between equals, an impression created and reinforced by the use of the term "partnership" by both sides to describe the relationship between state and occupational pensions. Even in the early days it must have been clear that the hopes of many insurance officials that they were embarked on a purely technical, actuarial exercise, were unfounded. The Director of Public Relations of the Life Offices Association wrote a newspaper article on the White Paper in words that were gushing and naïve or deceptively tongue-in-cheek:

> It is vital to take a long cool look at it, and not to down it impulsively for particular shortcomings.
>
> The life offices have described it as "realistic in principle." It certainly has one outstanding merit. It does make an honest effort to see people as human beings—individuals with widely varying tastes and needs.
>
> . . . it sets out to create a pension system which will keep all retired people out of real poverty and still give them a chance as individuals to enjoy retirement at the kind of living standard they have been accustomed to while working.

What better commendation than that? Not a word so far about the financial purpose—to find money for *existing* pensioners. But more in the same vein of bonhomie:

> For largely administrative reasons, no State scheme can treat everyone as a special case. . . . This is something that "occupational" schemes can do.
>
> [They] cannot however by any means do the job for everyone: they are not by a long chalk within everybody's reach.[4]

This formula not only surrendered the position, but also surrendered it unnecessarily, because occupational schemes are still spreading and would do so further if unimpeded: and, more important still, they are *not* the only way to provide private pensions. But this, in brief, was the superficial thinking on which the short-lived honeymoon between the life offices and Mr. Crossman was based. For much more than this was at stake: a political principle, the Government's standing with its supporters, its hopes of appearing to improve on Beveridge, and perhaps the reputation of an able Minister who had invested 15 years in an idea. I voiced these doubts on 6 March in a debate, organised by the Chartered Insurance Institute of London, with a member of the LOA's committee negotiating with the Ministry.[5] Later in March Sir Paul Chambers, a former head of the Inland Revenue, was also critical of the Crossman scheme.[6]

The "discussions" continued into the spring and summer. The "interests" were consulted separately, and they were not encouraged to exchange notes. But it may have been Mr. Crossman's innate academic approach that caused him, in April and May, to blurt out hints on how his mind was working on the terms for contracting out. The insurance experts' comments became perceptively sharper and a shade less politely formal. The most colourful description of the hinted terms, by an austere actuary with fighting spirit who led the LOA, Gordon Bayley, was "peanuts." Not a day too soon the LOA said contracting out was not "a concession" but the essence of "partnership" between state and occupational pensions. Other pension people also became alarmed and restive, but they were silenced by membership of one or other of the organisations being consulted. At last Mr. Crossman was being seen as a consummate tactician in psychological warfare as well as a politician with a care for the "under-privileged."

4. "Your Pension and You . . . ," *Evening Standard,* 19 February, 1969.
5. Report in *The Policy Holder,* 4 April, 1969. Reproduced in Appendix A, pp. 217–20.
6. *Forward from Beveridge,* later published by the Institute of Statisticians.

In May Mr. Crossman announced that to pay for the higher pension and other benefits promised for the autumn, and to avoid increasing deficits in the National Insurance Fund, £430 million a year would have to be found from higher contributions, and they would be graduated with earnings in the 1961 scheme. In a speech on 25 November he explained that to pay for the increased pensions he had increased the employee's contribution by 1s a week and put the rest on the graduated pension instead of increasing the employee's and employer's contributions by 3s 6d a week each. This arrangement he described as: "wangling the Boyd-Carpenter scheme . . . stretching it to the limit. . . ."

It may have been this interlude which aroused further disquiet about what might be in store in 1972. In June a highly respected elder statesman of the pensions world, T. A. E. Layborn, spoke out in a sharply-worded address to a meeting of business executives. In August the National and Local Government Officers (NALGO) published a statement indicating widespread alarm among its 400,000 members employed by local authorities. Other unions—the Transport & Salaried Staffs Association, the National Union of Journalists and the Association of Post Office Executives—joined its criticisms at the Trade Union Congress in September and the Labour Party Conference in October.[7] In September the Pension Consultants declared against the principle of graduated pensions. In November criticism spread to the CBI when the contracting out terms were announced in a further White Paper (Cmnd 4195). Finally, the Bill and accompanying White Paper (Cmnd 4222) were published on 17 December, 1969.

The details have by now been amply publicised and discussed in the newspapers and on the broadcasting channels. They will not be repeated here because we are concerned with what they *imply* rather than what they *say* (in any event, they will almost certainly be changed before the scheme is due to

7. By January 1970 not many other unions, with members likely to be affected no less than NALGO's, had voiced doubts or unease, at least in public. Among the main ones are the Association of Scientific, Technical and Managerial Staffs (Secretary, Mr. Clive Jenkins), 75,000 of whose 115,000 members are in occupational schemes, the Clerical and Administrative Workers Union, and the Union of Shop, Distributive and Allied Workers (Mr. A. W. Allen). The National Union of General and Municipal Workers (Lord Cooper) has 250,000 members in occupational schemes. The Draughtsmen and Allied Technicians Association (Mr. George Doughty) has 80,000 in occupational schemes. The Society of Graphical and Allied Trades has 230,000 members, most in occupational schemes. The Amalgamated Union of Building Trade Workers has 23,000 in steel industry and local government schemes and some in building industry schemes.

start). But for convenience the main figures as they were in December 1969 can be summarised and the question asked "but who pays?"

(a) *Contributions* (for employees not contracted out):
  (i) employees (men and women) would pay 4.75% of earnings[8] for the "national superannuation pension," 1.7% for unemployment, sickness and other "social insurance" benefits, and 0.3% to the National Health Service, making a total of 6.75%;
  (ii) employers would pay 4.5% of *total* earnings, 1.7% and 0.6%, plus 0.2% for redundancy payments, total 7%;
  (iii) taxpayers would add 18% of employees' and employers' contributions.

(b) *Pensions*
  (i) single persons:
    60% of average working-life earnings up to half of national average earnings;
    25% of average working life earnings from half to 1½ times national average earnings.

These figures mean that, roughly, the few people earning up to half of the national average in 1992 will have a pension of 60% of their average life earnings, people with or near the national average about 40%, and people with 1½ times the average about 35%. (There would thus clearly be a good deal of switching about of money in this scheme: whatever it is, it is not a straight pension scheme. There is a good argument for saying that people with less than average earnings should get a higher percentage of them in pension than people with higher earnings. But that is not the point. The question is; *is this the best way?*)

  (ii) married women—a choice of:
    (*a*) as for a single person;
    (*b*) a reduced pension based on husband's life average earnings plus 25% of her life average earnings.

(c) *Partial contracting-out*
  (i) Pension "abatement" (gobbledygook jargon for "*reduction*"). Men 1% of earnings up to 1½ times national average. Women 0.55% of earnings up to 1½ times national average.

8. Up to 1½ times national average earnings (now about £1,900, but probably rising to over £2,000 in two years).

(ii) Contribution abatement:
Employer 1.3% of earnings up to 1½ times national average.
Employee 1.3% of earnings up to 1½ times national average.

The figures seem disarmingly simple. What lies behind them? The employee/employer/government contribution arrangement seems cosy. It is used, with variations, wherever governments raise money by "national insurance." But it is one more of the fictions on which the system is built.

Employees, employers and "the Government" may pay these sums in the first place, but that does not mean that they suffer all the cost. Economists speak of "impact" and "incidence" to differentiate between the initial and the ultimate effect. The two are different because the contributions can be shifted to other people. As indicators of who "pays" in the last resort, these figures mean very little.

(i) The employee's contributions, which would be a proportional tax on earnings, would not necessarily be paid by having them deducted from wages or salary. If a union is strongly organised, or an individual worker is in high demand, or a firm is stuck with capital equipment it cannot leave idle, or makes a perishable product so that it cannot stand industrial friction or stoppages, the contribution could be passed back to the employer, who may bear part of them out of profits as a smaller loss than would result from interruptions to production.

(ii) If the employer sells a product in strong demand, or the general economic situation is inflationary, there are several ways he could pass on both the employees' and his own contributions (another tax on earnings); by resisting higher costs or raising prices; alternatively he may lower quality, or produce a narrower range of sizes, shapes, models, colours, etc., etc. Although the employee does not receive it, the employer's contribution is part of salary or wages; it is paid *for* the employee; if it was not paid, salary or wages would tend to be higher.[9]

(iii) The government's contribution does not come from gold mines underneath Downing Street or Whitehall. It comes from the pockets of taxpayers. Taxes on income or wealth are progressive; they are borne more than proportionately by the better off. Taxes on purchases—beer, tobacco, petrol,

9. "I wish the Minister of State [Mr. David Ennals] would give up talking about those in occupational schemes as 'privileged'. . . . They have had to pay for their pensions and they go on paying for them from the start to the finish of their careers." Mr. A. Palmer, (Labour), *Hansard*, 4 December, 1969, Col. 1781.

clothes, household goods—are regressive; they are borne more than proportionately by wage-earners. Apart from a probably small part that may come out of profits, *all* the contributions come ultimately from the pockets of the employee either as a customer or taxpayer—or his wife in her shopping. But no one knows how much out of which pockets. The contributions would be switched and shifted about from some groups of employees to employers, from them to other employers and employees; from some industries and regions to others, and so on. No *individual* can know how much he would be paying. The neat array of figures is a gigantic concoction of monumental make-believe. Certainly most individuals who think they could be getting a good bargain should think twice. The only thing that is clear is that most people would be paying, as taxpayers and consumers, more than they think they would as employees. Young people especially will be paying in contributions for 30 or 40 years that could have brought them really high pensions if invested at high yields of interest. Mr. Crossman has not found the secret of King Midas.

CHAPTER VII

Eight Principles—Eight Fallacies

Apart from Mr. Crossman's persuasive salesmanship at innumerable conferences, meetings, dinners and confrontations during 1969, the new scheme has been launched by a series of White Papers, press conferences and booklets. Explanation, information, education and propaganda have been mixed in judicious proportions. The facile distinction between information (good) and persuasion (bad) applied to commercial advertising would have been no easier to apply to this flow of governmental advertising which showed often masterly deployment of information and argument.

In January, 1969, Mr. Crossman published a booklet, "Pensions—The Way Forward," a summary of the White Paper, and in November revised and republished it as "The New Pensions Scheme: Latest Facts and Figures with Examples," price 1s. (Why not free? Is not the shilling a socially divisive, regressive charge that bears more harshly on the poor man than on the rich?—Was it intended as a deterrent to frivolous, wasteful demand? Which commercial insurance company would expect its customers to pay for a brochure explaining a pensions scheme? Of course it could not make them pay, or join, as a state monopoly can.) The booklet provided more than facts, figures and examples; it laid forth objectives, principles and proposals. But even while the scheme was being discussed the figures had changed: the January edition was based on average national earnings in April, 1968, of just over £22 per week; the November edition used the April, 1969, figures of £24 (a rise of nearly 8%). The scheme becomes more out-of-date for more people each year as incomes rise and they can save without being told how, or how much, by the State.

As the "basic objectives" the booklet proclaimed "Eight important principles for the pensions of the future."

"1. Rights to benefit must be earned by contributions."

The argument: pensions financed wholly by taxation would be too low because "people are prepared to pay more in a contribution for their own personal or family security than they would ever be willing to pay in taxes."

The reply: an important truth, but only if applied to contributions to *private* insurance. This is an effort by government to cash in on the trust in private insurance. The distinction is obfuscated by clever academic talk about "pay as you go," creating a new kind of insurance; but what matters is the attitude of the contributor. There lies the difference. The contributor to a private pension regards the premium as a payment out of income. The contributor to a state pension regards the contribution as a deduction from income. Mr. Crossman's sociologists cannot see a difference between the two. The individual who joins a firm is normally expected to join its pension scheme after a period (and he is usually pleased to do so when aged 30 or 35); if he were not, Mr. Crossman would complain he was one of the "underprivileged." But the scheme is run by the firm where he works and he is closer to it than to a state scheme. He feels he has more of a say in it through spokesmen (or directly) than in the "national superannuation" scheme on which he is never able to express an opinion except at infrequent General Elections when it is one of 68 or 127 other policies. A man who sees his premium to an occupational scheme rise can feel he is saving more for the future. And if he does not like it—or anything else about the firm—he can move to another. He may not always take his accumulated pension rights, but in full employment he can usually change to a new job. A man who sees his "national superannuation deduction" has risen regards it not as a payment for something he will receive but as a loss of earnings. If he does not like it there is nothing he can do. (Of course, he can protest, organise, demonstrate, but unless he can get many hundreds of thousands or millions to think as he does he has to lump it because there is nothing he *himself* can do.) Small wonder then that he sees little if any difference between his national insurance and his PAYE tax deduction: both are monies taken by the State for services or benefits he cannot identify. He cannot see which part of his income tax or his beer tax or petrol tax pays for his local school, or hospital or refuse collection. "National insurance" may originally have had the noble intention of making more efficient and more comprehensive the private insurance that grew up for over a century in friendly societies, mutual societies and insurance companies; *but in making insurance national it transformed it into taxation.* Many people of integrity, like Mr. Douglas Houghton,[1] regret the dilution of social insurance by taxation because it seems to establish a claim to benefits that can be regarded as "earned." But in no country in the world, including the ones Mr. Crossman refers to as examples to commend his scheme, is national insurance self-contained. Everywhere it is not merely dependent on general taxation (private insurance is also often aided by concessions); its central weakness is that the constant struggle to keep its funds separate usually ends in failure. And everywhere politicians sooner or later succumb to the temptation to use it to raise revenue, not least by graduating "contributions." The significant difference is between payments to *the State* and payments to *private* organisations: because payments to the State are unitary, compulsory and cannot be identified with the services which they buy, but payments to private organisations are various, voluntary and can be identified. There is one state scheme; even if there were only two private schemes there would be a choice. In practice there are hundreds, with thousands of variations.

Here again the politician is out of touch. However much he may wish he could make national insurance different from taxation and like private insurance, the man who pays senses it *is* like taxation. A letter from a steelworker to the Editor of the *Observer* on 7 December, 1969, is more indicative of his attitude than is the wishful thinking of politicians.

> To the Editor of the *Observer*
>
> Sir,—I have a pain in my neck from shaking my head at Mr. Crossman's Fabian Tract, reported by Nora Beloff in your last issue, including his solemn intoning of "reducing or postponing the spending power of those at work" as a necessary evil.
>
> Where he gets the belief that those at work accept paying higher social security contributions with less hostility than higher taxes, I do not know.
>
> I work in steel and know more about industry and workers than Mr. Crossman and the Fabian Society put together and multiplied by 107. And although I know nowt of office workers, I can tell you that if Mr. Crossman expects any man to accept with anything less than naked rage the reducing or postponing of his spending power after a hard week shotblasting, turning, milling, grinding, or operating a windy hammer or whatever, then Mr. Crossman is going to get the usual surprise of those

1. *Paying for the Social Services,* Institute of Economic Affairs, 1967, Second Edition, 1968.

who try to replace incentive with an ideal that never has worked to anyone's satisfaction and never will.

As one old foundry hand put it when the contribution did its great leap forward recently: "Aye, one day we'll go to the pay office an' get some tickets fer us dinner, some tickets fer the housekeepin', some tickets fer fags an' nowt else."

That seems an exaggeration now, but it's the logical end of letting kind but impractical dreamers like Mr. Crossman loose on the social services.

Leicester. *J. Macdonald.*

Some Labour MP's are beginning to reflect similar views. Mr. John Forrester, Stoke-on-Trent, North, said in the debate on the November White Paper:[2]

> My experience has been that anything taken out of the wage packet at source of the average working man or woman is regarded as income tax . . . If these contributions are to be deducted in the same way as PAYE, the general population will look upon them as just another piece of taxation.

And these deductions have become so large that they cannot pass unnoticed. Perhaps in the 1920s when they were a few pennies a week, or in the 1930s when they were a few shillings, they might have been ignored or forgotten. But now that they are one or two pounds a week, politicians can hardly hope that they can be tucked out of sight and out of mind (Table B). And when it is clearly explained to the employee that, in all, including the contribution the employer pays for him, the new scheme would forcibly relieve him of nearly a tenth of his pay for "National Superannuation" and a seventh including "social insurance," and that these proportions would rise down the years, and possibly approach those in Germany and Sweden, the welcome for Mr. Crossman's Bill may be less than enthusiastic.

Earnings-related national superannuation contributions are a tax on earnings, or, in more familiar language, an income tax. In shifting the financing of British state pensions from a standard rate of contribution to an earnings-related contribution, Mr. Crossman has evolved a new form of income tax. It is true that it could be represented as an extension of Mr. Boyd-Carpenter's 1961 scheme, but that was based on Mr. Crossman's of 1957. It is also true that the idea is not indigenous but copied from other countries. But if the Bill is described as heralding a great advance in British social policy it

2. *Hansard,* 4 December, 1969, Col. 1770.

Table B. Employees' Contributions

National Insurance Pension, 1948–69 (not contracted out)

		Men		Women	
		s	d	s	d
Year	1948	4	7	3	7
	1951	4	9	3	9
	1952	5	5	4	3
	1955	6	4	5	3
	1957	5	7½	4	8½
	1958	7	4½	6	2½
	1961 (graduated scheme)	7	3½	6	3½
	1963	8	3½	7	2½
	1965	10	2½	8	10½
	1967	12	1½	10	6½
	1968	12	8	11	0
	1969	13	7	11	10

National Superannuation (Pension) and Social Insurance, 1972 (not contracted out)

		Proposed		Present	
		s	d	s	d
Earnings per annum	£1,000	26	0	27	2
	£1,250	32	5	30	5
	£1,500	39	0	33	0
	£1,900 and over	49	5	34	0

should also be recognised as introducing a new form of tax on earnings. At a time when direct taxation on income is regarded as economically harmful and is increasingly resented by wage- as well as salary-earners, earnings-related national superannuation may earn fewer bouquets for the benefits it promises than brickbats for the tax it exacts. If it were calculated as an electoral asset, which some of Mr. Crossman's supporters have hoped it might be, it may after all prove an electoral albatross.

That national insurance is different from taxation is, on paper, a plausible hope; but in practice it is a pretence that is not maintained even by officialdom. National insurance contributions are usually lumped together with general tax revenue in official statistics. No doubt good men will go on hoping that there is, or could be, a difference. But the truth is stated in one of the last pronouncements of another failure of recent government, the Department of Economic Affairs. In its "Progress [*sic*] Report," No. 55, dated August 1969, it said:

> Social security contributions are included [among taxes] because they are compulsorily levied by governments, and public social security schemes must be regarded as an instrument of public policy rather than as a trading activity comparable with private insurance schemes.

Some politicians value the national insurance principle as an idea they wish would work in practice to make state pensions safe from politics. Mr. Crossman told the NALGO conference that taxation would put the pension "at the mercy of the Chancellor," but the scheme would create "a contract that no Chancellor can ignore." Other politicians value it as a financial expedient in producing money they cannot raise by taxation and in giving them more power to run the economy. There are politicians of both kinds in Britain, and some with mixed motives. Other countries struggle to make national insurance work, but their politicians cannot easily lose face by confessing failure. Some in the USA and elsewhere claim its difficulties would become manageable if only it covered still more benefits and people. New Zealand has abandoned its 30-year effort to run a social security tax related to earnings. Australia has never used national insurance at all.

"2. Benefits and contributions must be related to the contributor's earnings."

The argument: the more a man (or woman) earns, the more should be saved for retirement.

The reply: this is the paternalist autocrat at his worst. The mischief was started by the Conservatives in 1961 and my criticism of it is reproduced in Appendix C. Government may require a man (or woman) to save at least enough to avoid having to depend on more far-seeing people in retirement. But beyond that the State has no business at all. How much more people want to save is their business. Many or most may want to save enough to continue their living standard after retirement, which means an income of not far short of their earnings in, say, the last five years before retirement. But man is mortal. If he dies before retiring, his self-denial in all his working life has been in vain. To tell a man he *must* save (beyond the minimum) is an invasion of a basic human right to live life as he pleases. Politicians of this sort should be put in their place. So, ideally, should firms that make membership of a pension scheme (beyond a minimum) compulsory, though the latter is less objectionable since men can change firms: the State is inescapable. Every man should be able to contract out of saving more than a minimum in specific pension rights, and to tell him he must save more than this minimum *through the State* is to aggravate the impertinence. Even if there were a case for compulsory saving above the minimum, he should at least be allowed to save how he pleases.

The notion that pensions must be earnings-related is a transparent pretext dragged in to make graduated national pensions sound humane. It should be seen for what it is: a shallow rationalisation.

"3. Benefits must normally be sufficient to live on without other means."

The reply: Yes—if this means a minimum income in retirement. But it is the same for everyone. It does not require a compulsory *earnings*-related pensions scheme. The community is hardly obliged to keep a retired skilled worker in a larger car than a semi-skilled man, or a retired office manager in smoked salmon because he was accustomed to it.

The doctrine of maintenance of living standards in retirement is one of the most meretricious propositions that has emerged in recent years. What it does to the notion of the "socially divisive," which compulsory earnings-related pensions would perpetuate into retirement, must be left to the consciences of the confused sociologists who have inveighed against it for so long.

Here Mr. Crossman has resourcefully come to their rescue: he has enunciated a new theory of "social damage."[3] People should not be able to pay for better education or medical care, for that would do "social damage." But

> We think it doesn't do social damage in pensions or housing for people to be allowed to do this . . .
>
> . . . as Socialists we say that people should be able to buy themselves something better.

This *sounds* like a remarkable development in political thinking. Is it a profound proposition worthy of an academic's tome rather than a politician's sentence in a party lecture? What are its origins? What is its *rationale?* What

3. Fabian Tract 399, p. 20.

is its intellectual and philosophic lineage? What would be its implications for other government policy? Is it a great new truth shared by Mr. Crossman's colleagues in the Cabinet? the Government? the Parliamentary Labour Party? the Coventry East Labour Party? For, observe, Mr. Crossman says "*as Socialists,* we say. . . ." But what say the ghosts of Karl Marx, Lenin, Harold Laski, Aneurin Bevan, John Strachey and Kingsley Martin?

This is not as lofty a proposition as it sounds. It seems suspiciously like a piece of resourceful improvisation devised to make sense of the widening gulf the Government has to face in social policy. In pensions 12½ million people—half the labour force and two-thirds of the men[4]—are accumulating occupational pensions, and many more are saving in all sorts of other ways for retirement. It is too late to force them all into a single pension mould on the ground that, although differential earnings may be a regrettable necessity for incentives, differential pensions would be repugnant as an unnecessary source of social divisiveness in retirement. And 9 million people own their homes—half of the total. Some live better than others, as do some tenants than others. Here again it would be far-fetched to suppose that all householders could be squeezed into a common, standardised "accommodation unit." Hence the convenient theory that differential housing and differential pensions do no "social damage."

But only 5% are privately insured for "something better" than the National Health Service (not that everyone has exactly the same treatment: advantage can be bought by power and influence as well as by fees). And only about 8% of children are at private schools to get "something better" than state education (not that they always do; and nor do all children get the same at state schools).

Now that is politically a very sizeable difference: 50% in "better" housing and pensions; only 5–10% or so in "better" medical care and education. It is therefore not politically feasible to prevent "earnings-related" housing and pensions. But it is politically feasible to prevent "earnings-related" education and medical care. Or at least it may be politically profitable to appear to show concern about their "social damage" as a result of queue-jumping and other disagreeable practices.

Now suppose that half the people had "earnings-related" education and medical care as well as housing and pensions. This is what would have happened if it had not been prevented (and *everyone* would have had better medical care and education: Mr. Crossman is not arguing that earnings-

4. These are the proportions reluctantly conceded by Mr. Crossman. But they are much larger if younger men under 25 or 30, who should not necessarily be forced to save for retirement, though they may want life assurance if married, are omitted.

relation will *reduce* the lowest pensions). Should we then be hearing about a Theory of Social Damage? Since we may have more private "better" medical care and education by 1992, as well as more extensive "earnings-related" (private) housing and pensions, how does Mr. Crossman propose to prevent "social damage"?

Moreover, while it is too late to suppress "earnings-related" housing and pensions as dangerous competitors to state-approved and state-provided housing and pensions, even small competitors from private education and private medical care are "disturbing elements" in the attempts to organise centralised state education and a National Health Service.

The Theory of Social Damage could be demolished by a first-year undergraduate of economics or political science, although a student of sociology might have more difficulty. Perhaps it should not be taken seriously but dismissed as an aberration or political trimming.

"4. Benefits must take into account changes in price levels and in general living standards."

The argument: the risk that money will change in value must be pooled, and pensions should share in rising living standards.

The reply: as a general objective this is unexceptionable. It may require help for people with low earnings and a requirement to save for people disinclined to save. But for the rest it should be attained in the ways people prefer: it does not require compulsory *state* saving for *everyone.*

The statement presumes that money will continue to fall in value year by year and prices continue to rise. That is a political risk, arising from the inability of politicians to maintain the value of money. But if prices continue to rise, so do the yields of investments, and, although some were slow and unenterprising, pension funds have increasingly been invested in the most profitable enterprises, some of which have much more than kept pace. Mr. Crossman offers the taxpayer of the 1980's and 1990's a guarantee of future pension values. (Nothing is more likely than that such a guarantee, if it were believed, would weaken resistances to inflation.) I prefer the investment manager of 1970, because there is a choice of managers and investments and the failures can be changed.

Further, a given rise in pensions can be arranged beforehand by paying a larger premium to cover an assumed rate of growth in living standards. Oddly, the Inland Revenue limits approved schemes to 2½% a year.

But—who is to say that benefits "must" take into account rising prices and living standards? That is for the individual to decide for himself. To repeat: he has only one life; no-one is better equipped to decide how to apportion his earnings between the 40 to 50 years of work and the 15 to 20 years of retirement—if he survives.

"5. Women will contribute on the same basis for men and earn similar benefits."

The argument: married women now may choose whether or not to pay the flat-rate national insurance contribution. But many considering part-time work would doubt whether it was worth working at all if they had to pay it. Under the new scheme women who earn little would pay little. They would no longer have to choose between a flat-rate contribution that takes a large proportion of their earnings and not insuring at all.

The reply: here again, there is a curious use of words. If it is desirable to give married women with low earnings from part-time work the opportunity to insure at a lower level, *those who wish* can be given it without bringing in *every* married woman (about 2¾ million) and forcing her to insure whether she wishes or not. Again the exceptional few are used as the pretext for extending the State system to all.

If the low-earning married woman is to have a benefit larger than earned by her subnormal contribution, it should be found from general taxation. Again the scheme is self-condemning as an abuse of insurance to disguise taxation.

Women's circumstances may differ—their range of dependants is usually smaller—yet they will be compelled to insure as though their circumstances were the same, and whether they wish or not. It is arguable that they should be able to insure against the risk of widowhood and not depend on their husbands. But this scheme would leave them no choice. There is a difference between being able to insure and having to insure. The suspicion is that Mr. Crossman is more interested in extracting their contributions than in providing them with pensions.

This arrangement is described as "The new deal for women." It is "new"; but "new deal" normally means "better." What sort of philosophy is it that regards compulsion as better than choice? or compulsion for all justified by the exceptional requirements of the few?

"6. The scheme will be run on the 'pay-as-you-go' principle."

The argument: the contributions are fixed to meet the expected cost of pensions in each period: since they vary with earnings they will produce more income as earnings rise so that pensions can be raised with prices and incomes and therefore without an "excessive" burden on future contributors.

The reply: This proposition naïvely, or subtly, begs the whole question underlying the task of accumulating retirement income in an increasingly opulent society. The seven million pensioners of 1970, with the two million or so in need of higher pensions among them, will have passed on by 1990 or 1995. People reaching 65 in 1980 and beyond will mostly have lived through times of full employment and high pay out of which they could save for retirement. Many have done so; most could do so. To give higher pensions to the relatively few who did not or could not save does not require everyone to be enrolled in a new, larger, growing scheme in which they will accumulate state pensions for themselves.

Since earnings, as Mr. Crossman's booklet says, will be rising, people will be able to save for retirement in the various ways they themselves prefer. The sane thing to do in a civilised society is to let them, or encourage them. And that would free government for the jobs that only government can do, but which it now neglects because its characteristic defect is that it is reluctant to relinquish the power it exercises in mothering people who want to grow up.

That is the essence of the matter. The practical problem that should engage the thoughts of statesmen in a liberal society is that of changing from compulsory state pensions, which may be appropriate when most incomes are low and people will not or cannot save, to a more flexible system in which people could save how they wished—and how much they chose (beyond a minimum). The task of statesmanship in a free society is to decide at which age people shall be weaned from the State system and be freed to accumulate retirement income by pensions, endowment assurance, house purchase and investments of various kinds.

Why have politicians—in Britain and other countries—thought of extending only national insurance even though social and economic advance have made it out-of-date? That is the question that has hardly been asked, still less answered, by the advocates—or the critics—of bigger and better national insurance. Yet it is the question that the British people must ask. Is it because the administrative problem of change is complex? Or because national insurance can be used to distribute governmental favours? Or because it is a convenient method of raising revenue without the unpopularity of asking for higher taxes? Or because it expands the power of politicians by enlarging the domain of government?

However well-intentioned the proposed expansion in state pensions can be made to appear, these are questions that should not be left unanswered in the next few months. But they will not be answered unless they are asked, insistently and repeatedly. The detail of who pays how much for what seems immediate and urgent; but much more is at stake than who gains a few shillings at whose expense: a 1970 version of Lloyd George's ninepence for fourpence. This argument is an effort to escape from the dilemma of "pay-as-you-go": that it builds up nothing—except easy promises for someone else to keep. But there is no escape. Aneurin Bevan saw the truth: in the House of Commons on 9 December, 1954, he said:[5]

> The universality of social security in Great Britain completely destroys its insurance character. The only way one can save for the ageing population is by investment.

The vain effort to escape derives from the failure to see that there are two classes of pensioners: the present and the future, and their pensions require *different* methods of financing. As long as they are not separated, growing financial confusion will follow.

"7. The State scheme will work in partnership with employers' pension schemes."

The argument: the "important part" that employers' schemes have to play in partnership with the State scheme is recognised in the arrangements for partial contracting out. The new State scheme "is designed to assist the long-term development of employers' schemes," but they will have to undertake "some re-adjustment."

The reply: the relationship between State and occupational pensions is fundamentally competitive, not complementary. If there is "partnership" it is between a senior partner who makes the rules and a junior partner who observes them. If the junior partner grew too big for his boots he would be disciplined by a change in the rules. It may suit the senior partner to allow his junior partner a little rope, but the junior partner would soon be reminded that he survived on sufferance.

The occupational schemes, whose managers initially thought they could outwit the Minister in the partnership game, would soon see how much rope they would be allowed if they contracted out (*partially*) on a scale larger than suited the finances of the state scheme. If they did, the income of the state scheme would sag, and either the national pension contributions would

5. *Hansard*, Col. 1156.

have to be raised sooner than the Minister has been saying; or more money would have to be found from taxation (which it is the central purpose of the scheme to avoid); or the promised pensions would have to be postponed. What more natural than for the Minister, Mr. Crossman or a successor, to show that all these disagreeable consequences could be avoided by a single device: by making partial contracting out even more partial by altering the terms so that it became too difficult and costly to satisfy them? The "partnership" game is replaced by the power game.

If the Government now recognises that occupational schemes have "an important part to play," it is a reluctant acknowledgement of a development it had not foreseen and does not welcome. They are an unwelcome intruder, not a long-hoped-for guest. They provide a large amount of private saving which helps to fend off inflation and equip industry with risk capital. Although other forms of saving might develop in time, the demise or drying up of occupational pension saving would make the Government's financial management of the economy more difficult and higher taxation necessary to mop up the purchasing power it distributed for consumption through "pay-as-you-go" pensions.

Whatever these refinements of monetary and budgetary policy, the Government, despite Mr. Crossman's Theory of Social Damage and the exoneration of differential pensions, would want fewer occupational schemes, fewer employees covered by them, less money going into them, and fewer employees looking to private industry for their income in retirement rather than more. The claim, therefore, that the new State scheme is "*designed*" to assist the expansion of occupational schemes can hardly be taken seriously.

The philosophic predilections of the parties to the pensions debate cannot be brushed aside. The controversy is not merely technical, or financial, or economic. If Mr. Crossman thinks occupational schemes are now "important" it is not because he values them as a method of accumulating retirement income. Twelve years ago he thought they were dying out and the prospect did not depress him, although they were "important" then. If he could choose now, he would like them to have died out because he prefers State to private pensions. Although he now thinks that paying for better pensions would not do "social damage," he would not facilitate their starting if they did not exist, nor help them if they waned. He may have indicated his underlying feeling in a revealing phrase at the NALGO meeting, where he spoke of "a mushrooming of occupational pensions" since 1957. It is unwanted vegetation that "mushrooms."

Mr. Crossman's talk about "partnership" between State and occupational pensions is political salesmanship. The relationship is not a partnership but an uneasy equilibrium in which the political influence confronts and frustrates the economic tendency: the political power is poised in reserve to maintain and expand state pensions whatever difficulties they confront from rising incomes and the consequent urge to independence from state tutelage. Such a confrontation cannot be resolved in favour of independent choice if the State is run by people who believe that the State and not private individuals, or commercial insurance organisation, or industrial employers should provide pensions.

"8. People changing their employment will be legally entitled to have their pension rights from their employer's scheme preserved."

The argument: there are no universal or comprehensive arrangements for "safeguarding" pension rights in an occupational scheme on a change of job. The Government intend to require all employers' schemes to preserve pension rights for employees who so wish. Other employees will continue to be able to withdraw their contributions.

The reply: strictly this is another part of remuneration that is agreed between employer and employee (or employers' association and trade union); both sides know the terms of the contract and can avoid them if they are unacceptable.

On general economic grounds there is a strong case for preserving or transferring pension rights in order to encourage mobility of labour. Employees should be able to choose between taking accumulated pension rights or their contributions (and their employer's) in cash. But the Government's proposal, to allow withdrawals of contributions, conflicts with its criticisms of employers who fail to preserve pension rights. Withdrawal of contributions is being confused with accumulation of savings. The Government, says Mr. Crossman's booklet, "sees considerable merit in leaving an individual free to decide whether or not to withdraw his contributions." Its commitment to freedom in that respect conflicts oddly with its neglect of freedom in others. If individuals should be allowed to withdraw their contributions *they should be free to do so from the State scheme if they can use them to better effect elsewhere.* In principle withdrawal from State, as well as private, schemes should be permitted provided the contributions are used to accumulate savings in some other form which the employee prefers.

The Government is itself an employer. Civil servants normally take their pension rights if they move to other public (or sometimes quasi-public) employment. But not if they move to private employment before the age of 50, when mobility is most likely and beneficial. In this respect the Government has itself been more at fault than private employers who preserve or transfer pension rights after a minimum period *wherever their employees move.* Mr. Crossman's booklet was silent on this shabby treatment of civil servants but the criticism has struck home. The Bill (Clause 109) requires pension rights to be preserved for employees aged 30 who have been in an occupational scheme in industry. It excludes civil servants, members of the armed forces and "analogous employments," but the Explanatory Memorandum says it intends to preserve pension rights for them from the beginning of their employment. Why not put this promise into the Bill? Is this one more government "undertaking"? How often have civil servants been disappointed?

These are the "eight important principles." More could be said against all of them. Even where they make sense as *objectives* they do not make a case for the *policy* of a compulsory state pension scheme that draws in almost everyone (about nine-tenths of those earning up to 50% over the national average), men and women, however much they wish to save, and whether they wish to save through the State or not.

CHAPTER VIII

Humanity for the Aged

I suggested above that the primary object of government pension policy should be to ensure the most generous possible assistance to old people who cannot help themselves. The Crossman scheme would "revise" the existing basic State pension every other year to take account of rising prices, and leave it to the discretion of future governments to adjust for rising incomes. This proposal falls short of what is humanely desirable and financially possible in Britain.

The pension for a man and wife has risen from £2 2s in 1948 to £8 2s in November, 1969. Yet notions of what is desirable for a couple, as reflected in Supplementary Benefits for people in need, have risen with rising prices and general living standards, so that two million out of the seven million pensioners have their pensions supplemented. Pensioners receive sums varying from a few shillings up to £12 10s a week in Supplementary Benefit. It would cost £220 millions to raise the basic pension to the point where Supplementary Benefit can be dispensed with. Even if this additional money could easily be found from National Insurance contributions or taxation, much or most of it would go to the remaining five million pensioners not drawing Supplementary Benefits. Some of them should be given more, but many of them are comparatively well-off. Even though they pay tax on the pension (as earned income), if they numbered, say, three million they would receive in all additional hundreds of millions of unnecessary aid that could help pensioners in more need and reduce taxation.

If the relatively affluent pensioners were few in number, it might make sense to distribute the pension universally to every retired person at 65 (or 60 for women) and retrieve some of it from the affluent pensioners by taxation. But their proportion may be around half of the seven million, and it will grow in the next 10 and 20 years as people now earning accumulate income in retirement from occupational pensions, other forms of saving, and perhaps part-time work. The tax "claw-back," on which the Government preens itself in family allowances as though it were discovered in 1968, will then be seen, *first*, as increasingly requiring unnecessarily high taxation, *second*, as administratively wasteful in the to-ing and fro-ing of a money shuttlecock from the pensioner-taxpayer to the Government and back again, and, not least, *third*, as inhumane since it would be distributing too much money to people with enough and too little to people with too little.

How does Mr. Crossman reconcile this patent inhumanity with the compassion he professes for the poor and "the disadvantaged"?[1] (a fatuous term). The answer is that he is caught in the dilemma of conflicting objectives: compassion for the poor and passion for equality. As an egalitarian who believes that conditions or systems are acceptable only if they are shared equally, he cannot foreswear the universal, equal pension as a right. He rationalises this attitude by claiming that any further effort to relate State assistance to individual circumstances in means and needs would be as reprehensible, obnoxious and unacceptable as a means test.

There are so many flaws in this attitude that they must be stated briefly. First, the reasoning reveals a confusion about the meaning of words. Equal pensions to people with unequal needs and means is not equality of treatment of human beings in any intelligible sense. *Equal* pensions to people in *unequal* circumstances give *unequal* help. Second, is it compassionate to acquiesce in the notion that people carry a social stigma if they accept means-tested pensions *even when their needs are larger?* Third, do pensioners themselves prefer equality of status to more generous assistance? Mr. Crossman and the Government do not know, because they have not asked the pensioners. And when they are asked they do not give the answer Mr. Crossman supposes. Let the Government use the Social Survey to find the truth. Fourth, the State pension is not like an occupational pension, an income bought by "contributions." Most of it comes from the taxpayer: for new pensioners 80% or more. Only the rest can be described as a "right" earned by the pensioner's (and his employers') national insurance contributions. But that is no reason why the community of taxpayers should not give the pension with good grace, or why the pensioner should not receive it without loss of dignity or pride. Let the Government ask the people and base its policy on public opinion, not on superficial surmises.

The one condition for this relationship based on mutual respect is that the pensioner shall be in need despite honourable effort to make himself independent. No one objects to helping a man who cannot help himself.

1. *Paying for the Social Services*, Fabian Tract 399.

The relationship is soured only when the pensioner is not in need and could avoid dependence, as millions of pensioners are and can today. Provided help is accepted in good faith there need be no resentment in the giver or indignity in the receiver. Neither need the assistance be grudging or sparse. A prosperous community such as Britain could afford to give generously to old people who had no chance to save enough for retirement or whose living standards would otherwise be noticeably lower than that of the rest of the community. This is broadly the position in Australia, where there is no "national insurance" at all but where the whole of the pension is provided out of current taxation. It disregards other substantial resources of income and property and the pensioners harbour no sense of stigma.[2] The notion that national insurance replaces stigma by dignity is another myth fostered by politicians.

Mr. Crossman's proposal to revalue the pension every other year misses the target. However much the pension kept pace with prices (or living standards), some individual pensioners would continue to receive too little and many too much. And it is with individual pensioners—people with unique needs and means—that we should be concerned, not with abstract averages or notions of general equality that tolerate inhumanity to some and largesse to many more.

The Government, under the influence of Mr. Crossman and his sociologists, has had to recognise the callous neglect of individuals that is unavoidable in its doctrinal enthusiasm for universal, equal social benefits. But its traumatic incapacity to tear itself away from the 1930s and the household means tests makes it cling to the notion that although perhaps benefits should not be universal they should at least be based on "categories," "classes" or "groups" of people in recognisable special need—the old, the long-term sick, the disabled, heads of large families—and not on individual cases.[3] This shift from universality of social benefits to variation by "category" shows some progress from the rigid attitudes of four or five years ago when Labour listened to its academics, indulged its doctrines, and was not confronted by awkward evidence in making policy. But it is not good enough. There is again a ritual obeisance to words. "Categories," "classes," "groups" do not have needs or feelings. Pensions and other benefits are designed to help *individual* people; and not all people in a "category" are alike. A disabled or sick or old person is helped not because he is disabled, sick or

2. Chapter XIII.
3. *Labour's Social Strategy,* a discussion paper published by the Labour Party, August, 1969.

old but because his disability, sickness or age prevents him from earning enough for independence. That is the stubborn truth that confronts the universalists; they have had to abandon universality but still hope to save its principle (and their faces) by the compromise of "category." They should not be allowed to escape the logic of their dilemma: they must choose between compassion for people and their illogical passion for equality.

The Government's notion of helping "categories," "classes" or "groups" is thus a half-way house from political rigidity to compassionate humanity. But it is a half-way house in which people are still semi-sacrificed to obdurate dogma. To help *individuals,* social benefits must be adjusted to *individual* circumstances. Politicians who would continue to use the repugnance of "means test" as a political instrument are insensible ideologists out of touch with the people. If there is objection to being singled out for variable assistance, the solution of humane politicians would be to devise an anonymous indicator of deficiency, not to erect a 40-year-old fear of the 1930s as a barricade against social reform in the 1970s.

CHAPTER IX

Pensions in Industry

In 1957 *National Superannuation* argued that most people not then covered by occupational pensions in small firms, or apt to change jobs, or in seasonal trades, etc. would never be covered. Hence, first, the politician had to step in and, second, force them to accumulate pensions *through the State,* i.e. through national insurance suitably calibrated to switch income from the higher to the lower incomes.

It must have been advised badly. The sociologists may know something of poverty but little of industry. With a characteristic admixture of candour and ingenuousness Mr. Crossman has now to confess that:

> we had hopes that our great new scheme, though it would allow good [another question-begging word] private schemes to contract out, would be able to look forward to a dwindling amount of private insurance and be able to take over most of this field of activity.[1]

It is difficult to make sense of this expectation (except on the ground that industry would dry up its pension schemes for fear of Mr. Crossman's intentions). Sober examination of the labour market, in which pensions are the main ingredient of remuneration apart from salary or wage, and of the reasons for the expansion in the number and coverage of pension schemes since the late 1920s, could not possibly have led to such a conclusion. Here again the reason for the error was that Mr. Crossman's advice was sociological, spiced with wishful thinking, rather than economic. In the event, as he concedes sadly but resignedly,

> the situation had been transformed . . . in the decade before we took office and started work on national superannuation.[2]

Even then he underestimates and understates the transformation.

1. Fabian Tract 399.
2. Ibid.

From 1957 until the end of 1967 the number of employees covered by occupational schemes had risen from 8 million to nearly $12\frac{1}{4}$ million.[3] *National Superannuation* 1957 said that occupational schemes were designed mainly for salaried employees and that there was not much chance for wage-earners in many industries. By the end of 1967 $5\frac{1}{4}$ million out of $8\frac{3}{4}$ million wage-earners working for employers (private and public) with pension schemes had been covered. Table C shows the coverage of salaried and wage-paid employees, male and female, in private and public employment. Mr. Crossman's expectation or judgement or hope of 1957 was plainly very far out.

The coverage is by now certainly larger, probably over $12\frac{1}{2}$ million. And it would have been larger still were it not for the continuing uncertainty caused by the incessant political talk of ever-larger earnings-related pensions, especially since 1964. Moreover, these figures (and the Government Actuary's figures) understate the coverage because they show *all* employees of firms with schemes. But if men aged under 25 or 30 are excluded (in all 3.1 and 1.4 million respectively, or 21% and 9.7% of the total male labour force), on the ground that retirement saving need not start so young, the coverage is appreciably larger.

What had gone wrong? A glance at the USA, where pensions have for years been an ingredient of collective bargaining, might have suggested that it was reckless or hare-brained to envisage "a dwindling" in occupational pensions. It is true there have recently been thinkers in the USA, similar to Mr. Crossman, who would expand Federal pensions to the point at which they constricted further expansion in occupational pensions.[4] But it would take a strong force to dislodge them from the American labour market. And, if they had not been inhibited in Britain, they would have spread much further, not least because of their very flexibility.[5]

Then, again, although the expansion of British occupational pensions has been substantially aided by the tax concessions on employers' contributions, it was too late to remove occupational pensions from the British labour market even in 1957. A hostile government could reduce the tax concessions, and ominous allusions have been made "at a top level review at the Treasury"[6] to

3. Government Actuary, *Third Survey Occupational Pension Schemes,* HMSO, 1968.

4. The Chief Actuary in the US Department of Health, Education and Welfare has recently described them. See chapter XIII.

5. M. Pilch and V. Wood indicate the possible variations in occupational schemes in a study of 620 staff pension schemes to which wage-earners' schemes tend to approximate: *Company Pension Policies,* British Institute of Management, July, 1969.

6. *The Times,* 3 December, 1969.

Table C. Coverage of Occupational Pension Schemes—31 December, 1967

		Number employed by employers with pension schemes (million)		
Category of earnings	*Sex*	Private	Public	Sum
Salaried	Men	4.4	1.7	6.1
	Women	2.0	1.3	3.3
Wagepaid	Men	6.2	2.5	8.7
	Women	3.2	0.8	4.0
Total		15.8	6.3	22.1

Source: Occupational Pension Schemes, Third Survey, Government Actuary, HMSO 1968. The percentages rounded to the nearest 5.

"major tax anomalies" that would result if tax concessions were continued on occupational pensions contributions after 1972 but not on national superannuation contributions. This hardly reflects the spirit of "partnership" between state and occupational pensions that has been Mr. Crossman's theme and refrain since the White Paper of January, 1969. But it could be an early intimation of the pressure the Government could apply to the occupational schemes, if the new State scheme ran short of contributions by an inconveniently large adoption of (partial) contracting out.

The truth is that politicians, sociologists, actuaries and other pension specialists have not clearly understood the role of pensions in the market for labour, or the mechanism by which they are financed. Pensions cannot be divorced from pay and other non-cash or deferred forms of employee remuneration. If one element is disturbed the others will change to restore the total remuneration or, as economists call them, the "net advantages" of alternative employments. If occupational pensions were forced into the State "insurance" scheme, other forms of employee remuneration would be developed to take their place. If employers and employees were compelled to shift their contributions to state pensions they would not passively sit by and leave everything else unchanged. Mr. Crossman has seen that the sizeable contributions employers in Sweden (and Germany and other countries)[7] have to make have been shifted forward to the consumer in higher prices and

7. Chapter XIII.

Table C (continued)

Number covered by pension schemes (million)			*Proportion (%) covered*		
Private	Public	Sum	Private	Public	Sum
3.2	1.5	4.7	75	90	75
0.8	0.9	1.7	40	70	50
3.6	1.6	5.2	60	65	60
0.5	0.1	0.6	15	15	15
8.1	4.1	12.2	50	65	55

have thus raised the "cost of living." He does not seem to see that this would also be done by employees whose contributions have been inflated, although he sees that British trade unions would not desist from large wage claims on the ground that their members were provided with large pensions by employers' contributions.[8] The difference is not that Swedish trade unions are more public-spirited but that the British labour market enables trade unions to ask for higher wages in the knowledge that employers will be even more tempted to buy "industrial peace" if they can pass higher wages on to the consumer as higher prices. In that event trade unions could also pass on their members' higher national insurance contributions.

In spite of his past errors, some of which he now sees and engagingly concedes, Mr. Crossman insists that

> However much occupational pensions are encouraged there will always be about one worker in four who is not covered by them.[9]

It is not clear what he means by "encouraged." The removal of obstacles could itself accelerate expansion—not least the jungle of rules governing the procedure for approval of pensions schemes. The Inland Revenue enforces these rules as though its primary task was to avoid tax avoidance; I suggested in 1960[10] that it should shed this function to a different office whose task would be to expedite pension schemes. There are many other obstacles to the development of occupational schemes, some of apparently secondary detail

8. Fabian Tract 399.
9. Ibid.
10. *Pensions for Prosperity*, Institute of Economic Affairs.

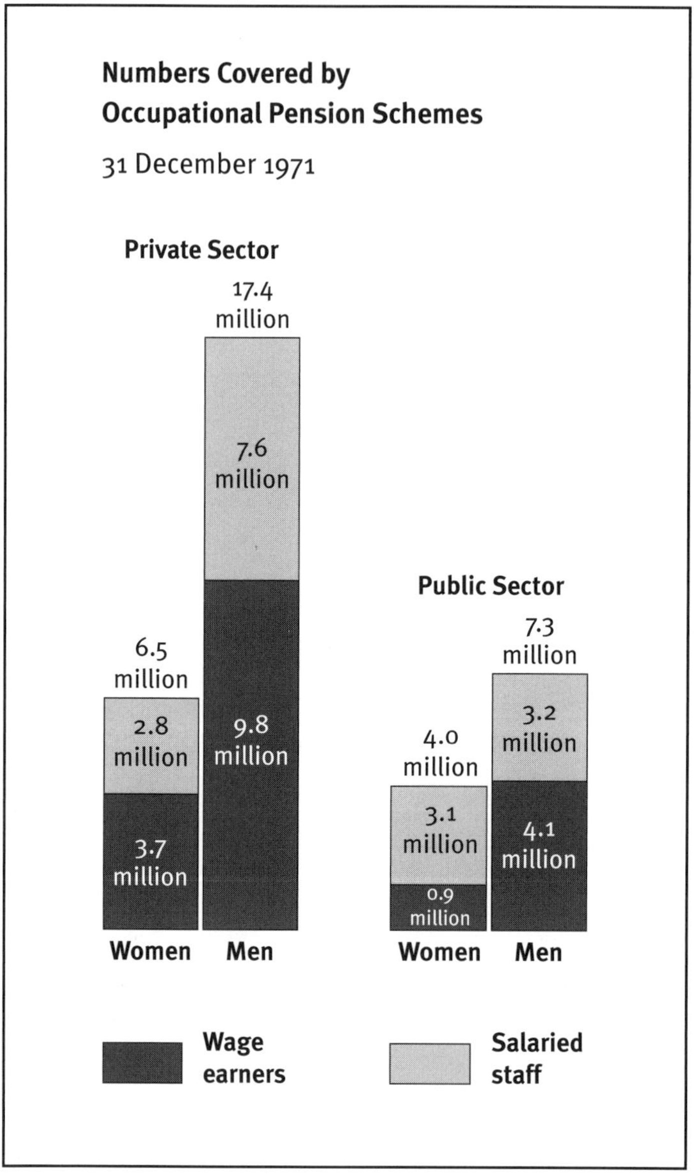
Numbers Covered by
Occupational Pension Schemes
31 December 1971
Private Sector
17.4 million
7.6 million
9.8 million
6.5 million
2.8 million
3.7 million
Women
Men
Public Sector
7.3 million
3.2 million
4.1 million
4.0 million
3.1 million
0.9 million
Women
Men
Wage earners
Salaried staff

but together comprising a formidable brake on occupational pensions. Then there is the special problem of small firms, often with seasonal labour, as in building, or intermittent labour, as in trawling, for which the solution would be federal schemes of various kinds.[11] Pensions could be based on *type of employment* rather than on single *employers* to facilitate preservation or transfer of pension rights on a change of job. Not least, there is no necessary reason why the pension should be based on occupation at all: it could be arranged by each employee in a manner to suit himself. This is indeed done, mainly by higher-paid employees, and it could in time spread to others. But it would be stifled by further expansion of graduated state pensions.

If the obstacles were removed, occupational pensions could in time cover all British employees who wanted them; the remainder would receive higher pay out of which to buy individual pensions. This would be the inevitable outcome in a competitive labour market, in which no employer can attract and keep employees unless he gives total remuneration that, in one form or another, is as good as that offered by competing employers. And this is especially true in full employment. There will always be declining firms, employees who like frequent changes, workers whose abilities do not command as much remuneration as the "norm," small firms with seasonal trade or intermittent work. Whether the workers in them number one in four, one in five, or one in six, it is hardly a good enough reason for disturbing the natural evolution of forms of payment that suit the other employers and employees. The intelligent solution, if no other voluntary method is evolved, is a residual State scheme for the unusual, uncommon or abnormal employee. A state scheme for everybody and anybody in order to make sure of covering the exceptional can hardly commend itself to a democratic and flexible society. But the notion that the old, sick, under-privileged or disadvantaged tail must wag the otherwise healthy and wealthy dog lies at the root of the argument for egalitarian centralisation in social, economic and political life.

11. "The Case for Federal Pensions," *Daily Telegraph,* 28 June, 1966.

CHAPTER X

Saving for Democracy

In arguing that the occupational pension schemes should be allowed favourable terms for contracting out, the insurance companies and the pension funds have pointed to the large amount of new saving they have generated—over £800 million a year, or two-fifths of all private saving in 1967. Government spokesmen have seemed to agree that occupational schemes are important for this reason and that the contracting-out terms are designed to enable them to continue. The new emphasis on private savings is considered by occupational pension spokesmen to indicate a substantial change in attitude by Mr. Crossman and his advisers, and to represent a victory, or at least a decisive advance.

There is nothing sacred about 1967. It happens to be the last year for which the Government Actuary reviewed the development of the occupational pensions. Government spokesmen have too often argued from a "still" rather than a moving picture, which may have suited their case but conveyed a misleading impression. The occupational schemes have loomed larger in the national economy than speeches inside and outside Parliament have indicated.

In 1963, the year of the previous Government Actuary Survey, the figure was much smaller, only £560 million. At this rate of expansion, it would have been getting on for £950 million in 1969 and exceeding £1,000 million in 1971. Table D shows the income and outgo of the schemes in 1963 and 1967 and the "projection" to 1971. If any readers are members of occupational schemes they may note with satisfaction—and, if not, with envy—that

(a) employers contribute about three times as much as employees
(b) the total contributions added about a third of each year's new contributions in interest—£480 million in 1967, up from £325 million in 1963
(c) the interest earned in each of the two years was itself almost enough to pay the pensions—up from £365 to £570 million,

Growth in Occupational Pensions — in £ million

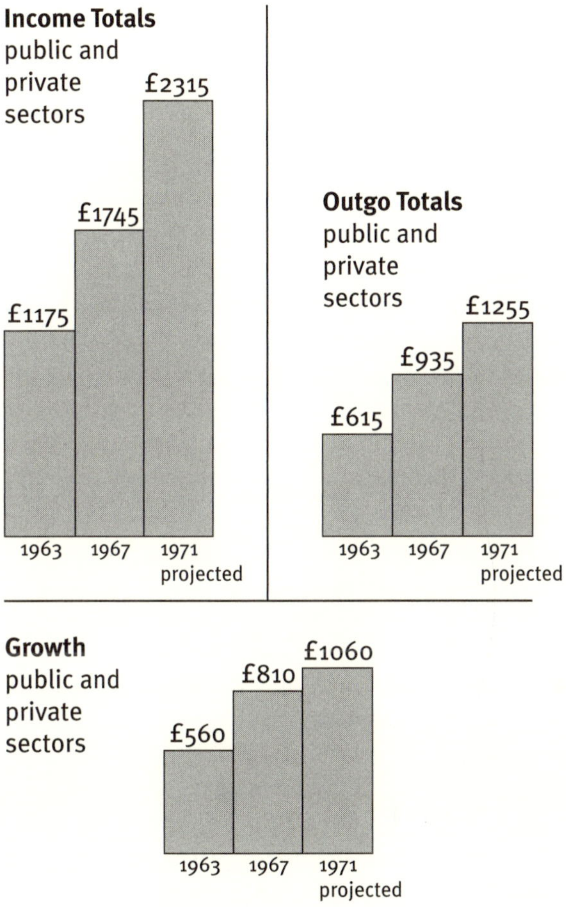

although there have also been other benefits and administrative costs

(d) the pensions in the private sector doubled in the four years, 1963 to 1967; in the public sector they rose by a third: private sector pensions are more recent (mostly from the 1930s) than public sector pensions (many began in the nineteenth century)

Table D shows what the income and outgo *would* be in 1971 if they went on rising as they did between 1963 and 1967. (In practice some of the items would rise faster, others more slowly.) Total contributions would rise to £1,680 million, interest to £635 million, total outgo (pensions, etc.) to £1,255 million, leaving a net increase in the fund, that is, a net increase in private savings, of £1,060 million.

"*Would* be." But they will be less in 1971 if Mr. Crossman's Bill is passed and the new scheme is introduced. Some occupational schemes will slow down, and some will shut down. There have been plenty of "assurances" about the safety of *past* benefits in national and local government (which are meaningless—unless the Government were contemplating confiscation) but no "assurances" about *future* benefits, which will probably be less than they otherwise would have been. Here again we are in a world of projections based on working assumptions which, if they are wrong, as they often are, will make the figures different, perhaps very different, from those expected. In 1961 the Government Actuary estimated that 2¼ million employees would be contracted out of the graduated scheme: in the event the number was over twice as much—more than five million. In 1969 it was estimated that 10,000 out of 65,000 occupational schemes may be closed down. They will probably be the smaller ones, so the loss of new savings will be proportionately less. But small schemes have often grown larger. And schemes that keep going would be changed so that the flow of new saving will fall away.

The Government concedes that the rate of *increase* in occupational pension saving would slow down, at least in the early years, given the amount of contracting out likely on the terms it has announced. The economics of saving are not as simple as the pension or the Government spokesmen have seemed to suppose. There can be differences of opinion about the effect of contracting out on private occupational pension saving. It has been argued that, initially, and probably in the long run, more contracting out would either raise the amount of saving[1] or reduce it.[2] And it is also possible to argue

1. D. Lomax, "Pensions: The major economic issues," *The Times*, 17 November, 1969.
2. T. Atkinson, "Pensions: The savings issues," *The Times*, 4 December, 1969.

Table D. Growth in Occupational Pensions 1963, 1967, 1971 (£m.)

	1963			1967			Projection 1971		
	Private	Public	Total	Private	Public	Total	Private	Public	Total
Income									
Contributions									
employees	120	110	230	190	155	345	260	200	460
employers	335	285	620	525	395	920	715	505	1,220
Total:	455	395	850	715	550	1,265	975	705	1,680
Interest earned	240	85	325	365	115	480	490	145	635
Total:	695	480	1,175	1,080	665	1,745	1,465	850	2,315
Outgo									
Pensions	125	240	365	250	320	570	375	400	775
Other benefits	140	110	250	210	155	365	280	200	480
Total:	265	350	615	460	475	935	655	600	1,255
Growth in invested funds	430	130	560	620	190	810	810	250	1,060

Sources: 1963 and 1967: Government Actuary's Surveys.
1971: projection at rate of expansion 1963 to 1967.

that a fall in the rate of saving through occupational schemes would not necessarily reduce *total* saving. The Government, by accumulating a surplus in the national insurance fund, or more generally through the budget (by raising taxation or borrowing more than it spends), would or could compensate, or more than compensate, for the loss. Professor E. Victor Morgan of the University of Manchester and Professor Jack Wiseman of the University of York,[3] for example, have argued that an increase in occupational schemes with funds (civil service pensions have no funds: they are paid out of taxes) would probably increase total saving, but that an extended state scheme that was only partially funded (and partially paid out of current contributions and/or taxes) might also possibly increase total saving.

Not surprisingly the Government has fastened on the *total* saving question. Mr. Peter Shore, the Minister without Portfolio and Deputy leader of the House of Commons, who replied to a debate in the House of Commons on 4 December, 1969, in the absence of Mr. Crossman through illness, claimed that total saving would not decline in the early years because much more money would come in contributions than would go out in pensions, and that the excess would be available for investment.

The total of saving is significant because it affects the total demand for goods and services, the general level of output and government budgetary policy. If savings fall away, consumption is likely to rise; and since Keynes the reflex reaction of government is to increase taxes in order to avoid inflation by keeping consumption down. At least this is the theory of some macro-economists,[4] who favour fiscal (tax) policy as the primary method of regulating the economy. (Whether it is a correct theory is another matter: for various reasons, not least that increased taxes can produce *more* consumption in the anxiety to avoid still higher taxes, the fiscal theory of economic management has been giving way to the monetary theory of economic management. This is led by Professor Milton Friedman of Chicago University and is gaining acceptance among British economists. It states that the economy is best regulated through the volume of money.)

But whether total saving is higher or not, what is also important—perhaps even decisive, since the argument on total saving is debatable—is *who owns the saving*—the people or the Government. A democracy requires gov-

3. Appendix to *The Future Relationship of State and Occupational Pensions*, National Association of Pension Funds, September, 1968.

4. Macro: total. Macro-economists think it important to study *total* output, *total* expenditure, *total* consumption, *total* saving, etc.

ernment to be disciplined by non-governmental sources of power and influence, which rest on ownership. If less saving is done by individuals and more by government, the State becomes more powerful and individuals less powerful. If corporate saving increasingly comes under government control, more money is put into—what? So-called gilt-edged stock to bolster government's weak credit status, with the interest of potential pensioners a poor second? Or into industry where it may earn more but get government entangled in business enterprise?

The savings argument has been discussed largely in its monetary/fiscal effect on the economy. Its structural effect on the centralisation and dispersal of power, which is essential for democracy, is more discernible and more fundamental. The earnings-related state pension scheme is probably vulnerable on the financial damage it would do the economy; it is unquestionably vulnerable on the political damage it would do to democracy in Britain.

CHAPTER XI

The Contract of the Generations

Since it became evident that, by bad luck and/or mismanagement, the effort to fund the State pension (and thus to create financial and legal rights to the pension) had to be abandoned, and the pretence that it was funded was recognised as Aneurin Bevan's "myth," the absence of funding has been transformed from a sad necessity into a lusty virtue. And it has been justified by two "explanations."

The first was that funding was not necessary for state pensions since the continuity of the State was a sufficient, if not better, guarantee of the pension: it could use its ultimate sanction as a revenue-collector and tax-gatherer. And unfunding was in some circumstances better than funding because the pension could be paid without waiting for the fund to be built up. This was the reasoning behind the 1957 National Superannuation proposals and the 1961 graduated scheme.

The second explanation has the more majestic title of "the contract of the generations." One generation pays national insurance contributions and taxes that go out in pensions to the previous generation, and it is in turn repaid by the contributions and taxes of the succeeding generation. Or, as the schoolboy was taught to add at the end of geometric proofs, *quod erat demonstrandum:* "which was to be proved."

These "explanations" do not so much elucidate as rationalise. There may be circumstances in which partial funding or even no funding is financially convenient, but to suppose that it is to be preferred to full funding is naïve. In almost every Western country where it has been tried, funding has broken down because it was *politically* difficult to maintain. If it were possible for the State to run an actuarially-based scheme in which a fund were built up to pay the pension, it would be a better guarantee for the pensioner than a state pension "guaranteed" by contributors and taxpayers unborn. It is because politicians everywhere have failed to run insurance as effectively as it is run by private organisations that they have resorted to "pay-as-you-go" and "the contract of the generations" as the best *they* could do, *not the best that could be done.*

Politicians are apt to resort to "assurances," "undertakings" and other expedients to disarm critics and avoid questions they cannot answer. They should have learned from history to display more humility. They can "bind" themselves, but that is hardly a guarantee since they may be out of office within a week; or they may "commit" the Government, although that is hardly more reassuring. But to pretend to commit politicians and governments that follow 10 or 20 years later is hardly to be taken seriously as a *guarantee.* The reason is not merely that politicians in difficulty proliferate "assurances" that can plausibly be ignored by the plea that circumstances they could not foresee had changed. Even more, the circumstances may indeed have changed, so that the "assurances" could not be honoured even if they had intended to do so.

It is presumptuous for a politician to suppose that personal "undertakings" are a substitute for power to enforce them. No doubt the word of a Minister of outstanding quality—a Pitt, a Gladstone or a Churchill—may outlive his term of office, or his life, for a time. But the history of every country is littered with "undertakings" that lived only so long as they were politically convenient. What is remarkable is that they should be accepted at their face value.

No one in Parliament who knows anything about the 25 years history of British state pensions really believes that the earnings-related pension would be built up in twentieths over 20 years from 1972 to 1992. To listen to Mr. Crossman explain the formula to an audience of journalists at a press conference—"in the first year the pension will comprise one-twentieth of the new and nineteen-twentieths of the old, in the second year two-twentieths of the new and eighteen-twentieths of the old, . . ."—is to imagine oneself at a congress of witch-doctors competing for the year's most potent placebo.

For how long will governments review the State pension every other year? The answer is as long as it suits them; or as long as they cannot politically do otherwise. The Bill contains 129 clauses, many with sub-clauses. How long will they remain the law if they survive unchanged into an Act? The only answer is: no one knows, not even Mr. Crossman. The substance of some were changed even in the short period since they were announced in the White Papers: employers, for example, are to pay 7% of their total payroll, not 6¾%, a "little" change that will add millions of pounds to their costs—or housewives' shopping bills. But the whole document is filled with a spurious flavour of certitude that would not survive a year if circumstances changed and made any part of it politically dispensable.

The Bill may be regarded at best as a bundle of good intentions and at worst as a bunch of promises that look inviting in an election year. The only guarantee that the pensions displayed would be paid is prospective pensioners' personal judgement about the conflicting interests in 1992 and beyond. Not least among them will be the sheer number and voting power of pensioners and the sheer number and voting power of people in work—complicated by the children at school and university who will also be costing the earners a lot of money.

As a rough guide to these numbers Table A (p. 139) shows age-groups under 15, 15 (16 from 1976) to 64 (60 for women), and 65 and over, and Table E the working population. The middle group is estimated to grow only from 25½ million in 1972 to 26⅓ million in 1981, an increase of 800,000 (the men from 16.6 to under 17 million, an increase of 350,000, the women from 9 to 9.4 million, an increase of about 450,000). The under 15's are estimated to grow from 13.2 to 15.4 million, or by 2.2 million, and the 65's and over from 7.1 to 8.1 million, or by 1 million. Who can say with certainty that the earners of 1992 will gladly support the pensioners of 1992 in the superior stations to which they deemed fit to vote themselves in the 1970 or 1971 General Election?

The rumblings of revolt have been heard in Belgium, Germany and the

Table E. The Working Population of Britain, 1939–81 (million)

	Men	Women	Total
1939[1]	14.6	5.1	19.7
1948[2]	15.7	7.1	22.8
1952	15.9	7.4	23.3
1956	16.2	7.9	24.1
1960	16.2	8.2	24.4
1964	16.5	8.7	25.2
1968	16.3	8.9	25.2
Projections			
1972	16.6	9.0	25.6
1976[3]	16.6	9.0	25.6
1981	17.0	9.4	26.4

[1] Men 14–64, women 14–59, excluding private domestic servants. [2] 15+. [3] 16+.

USA. It will no doubt grow in time, perhaps when and where "social security" takes 15% or more of their earnings from the young and middle-aged. Initially they may demand lower retirement ages at which to stop paying and start sharing in the largesse, or refuse (or avoid) higher contributions. In Britain the proportion would be 13¾% in 1972 but SET would raise it to over 20%. The breaking point is not postponable indefinitely. The resistance to periodic increases in "social insurance" contributions will begin all the sooner when the "contributors" realise they are paying not insurance contributions but an income tax.

The British standard of living in 1970 rests partly on the capital bequeathed by the Victorians and Edwardians. The Crossman scheme would divert Elizabethan saving away from the Charlesians. Gratitude may not be their strongest emotion.

There are other uncertainties. The 18-year-olds now have votes. Will they want more free university post-graduate training for well-paid jobs in preference to large pensions for people who have lived their lives? Who knows how much government will be required to spend on maintaining and improving "amenity" under the influence of persuasive writing, such as that of Dr. E. J. Mishan, which is gaining rapid ground? New medical discoveries will create insistent demands for government provision of equipment to save life, and drugs to stop or multiply it. The conquest of disease could accelerate the increases in the number of the retired. And suppose Britain joins the Common Market after all?—or Europe joins a North Atlantic Union? Whom is Mr. Crossman "binding" or "committing" then?

British politicians who inherit the incubus of being virtual defaulters on government borrowing (£100 invested in Dalton's "gilt-edged" Treasury stock in 1947 is now worth £32 at present day values and about £15 at 1947 values) must be strong men indeed to make promises based on the creditworthiness of governments. Social security promises have also been broken in Sweden, in the USA and elsewhere—all of course with convincing show of good reason.

Private schemes may also run into difficulties. But there is a significant difference. The choice in practice is between the political risk in a pension scheme with no reserve fund and diffused commercial risks in private schemes with reserve funds. Let the choice be explained in these terms. And let the people decide.

Not least, let it be clearly understood that "right" (to the pension) and "contract" are two more good words that have been made misnomers. A "right" to a pension that a man acquires by saving for it is unambiguous. The "right" a man has to an income when he can no longer work is of a different kind. The word has been re-defined to mean a moral right or claim on society. But transfers of income from one age-group, or class, or generation, to another represent decisions by one group, or class, or generation, to help another in need of help. No group, or class, or generation has a "right" in any absolute sense. It is the existence of need that creates a moral "right" to help in civilised, humane society. The well-fed man does not have the same "right" as the hungry man, the well-heeled pensioner as the shabby pensioner. People who accept from others what they cannot morally justify by need are taking not by "right," nor even by charitable grace, but by immoral acquisitiveness.

In civilised parlance "contract" means a voluntary agreement between two parties each of whom thinks it will gain. There is no such voluntary agreement between the generations on pensions. Indeed, there can hardly be one since future generations cannot be consulted; and if they could they would hardly agree since the terms are loaded against them. In the Crossman scheme each generation would have to pay a higher proportion of its pay to its pensioners than the preceding generation. In 1972 the cost for pensions alone would be not far short of 10% (employers' and employees' contributions) and it could rise to 12% by 1982 and 15% in 1992—figures approaching the bloated proportions in Germany. This is not a voluntary agreement, or a mutually advantageous bargain. It is an act of irresponsible abdication.

CHAPTER XII

National Insurance and the Civil Servants

Seeing "the Minister" flanked at press conferences during 1969 by six to ten senior civil servants, or accompanied by one or two at dinners, was dangerously conducive to the impression that "the civil service" was behind him, not only as technical advisers and executants but also in spirit. Such a deduction, although it may have been drawn unconsciously by some in the company, was, of course, wholly erroneous. They were there to help the Minister with information or to help answer questions, although he sometimes called on them to reply or comment. (How far this is a constitutional novelty I leave to others.) But they were not there as supporters of Mr. Crossman's "national superannuation."

Nevertheless, as they sat facing the audience, properly impassive (except in an unguarded moment when a smile or a frown might have indicated reservations), the observer could not help wondering what they thought of it all. On a far-reaching social reform that has evoked doubts among supporters as well as opponents, the able people who man the senior offices of the Departments of State must have private opinions. But they cannot express them in public, short of losing their jobs and sacrificing their careers—and losing their pensions if they resigned for private employment before the age of 50. (Two distinguished civil servants, Sir Leslie Rowan and Sir Henry Wilson Smith, resigned soon after 50 to enter industry.) Yet civil servants know better than most people what is being prepared. For everyone there comes a moment when their duty to their employers (and their careers) conflicts with their duty to their country (and their consciences). For men and women designated "public servants" whose work—in the words of Sir William Armstrong, head of the Home Civil Service—yields "the traditional satisfaction of service to the community," the conflict must be particularly acute.

Obvious difficulties would be created if a government had to work with senior civil servants out of sympathy with their policies or disquieted by their methods: and the 1964 and 1966 governments brought in academics and others, as temporary civil servants, for a specific measure or period although some did not stay long. If resignation is unnecessarily drastic, and transfer damaging, there may be a strong argument for allowing conscientious civil servants to make their doubts known in public (perhaps in hearings on legislation in process, as in the USA, or on more informal occasions) as well as in private memoranda to the Minister, so that Parliament, the press and the public have the opportunity to weigh them. There may be a thin dividing line between the furnishing of information, the provision of opinions and the statement of judgements by civil servants. The first is common, although information is less easily accessible to outsiders than to insiders in Britain. The second is not unusual. During the recent General Election in Australia, the Liberal/Country Party government may have been caused some embarrassment by the testimony to a Senate Committee of an official that the calculations used in proposals for compulsory health insurance, adopted and advocated by the Labour Opposition as a major election plank, were technically accurate. The third is rare, at least in Britain. In the USA there has recently been the remarkable example of a senior civil servant, the Chief Actuary, whose conscience has driven him to declare in public his doubts on social insurance developments.[1] His courage was the more remarkable because of criticism that he was at fault in so doing.

The traditional rigid view that the prestige of the British civil servant rests not only on his widely acknowledged integrity but also on absolute confidentiality, even about matters not risking national security, nevertheless appears to be thawing out. Civil servants were known to have had talks with Labour leaders in 1963 and 1964 near the end of the last Conservative Government, and similar consultations may now be taking place in reverse. So far from being condemned they have been approved on the ground of the desirability of continuity in the event of a change of government.

If resignation is too drastic, silence may be misleading or dangerous. A Minister may imply that his officials support him, but since the officials cannot speak the country cannot judge. On the crucial terms on which occupational schemes would be allowed to contract (*partially*) out of the earnings-related pension,[2] Government spokesmen have referred to the Government Actuary as though to an extra-governmental tribunal, and have left the im-

1. Chapter XIII.

2. The observer must record the remarkably dispassionate independence that has characterised the contributions to Commons debates of Mr. Douglas Houghton, the Chairman of the Parliamentary Labour Party (and Minister for the Co-ordination of the Social Services

pression that he would approve what the Minister was doing. In the 4 December debate, for example, Mr. David Ennals, the Secretary of State, said:

> . . . what should be a fair amount of contribution reduction to match up with the 1 per cent of pension abatement? This was obviously not a matter on which we, as laymen, could take a snap judgement. We therefore took the advice of the Government Actuary who, as an independent figure, reached his own conclusion. Sir Herbert Tetley's . . . conclusion was that a fair amount of contribution reduction would be 1.25 per cent [for the male employee and his employer separately]. This, he said, would be fair for the average scheme.
>
> We . . . decided to move beyond what the Actuary had thought was fair, and we moved to 1.3 per cent.

(At a press conference on the White Paper detailing the terms for (partial) contracting out, Cmnd. 4195, in November, 1969, Mr. Crossman also referred to the Government Actuary, sitting several places away on his right, as an independent expert.)

The Government Actuary had not said that the reduction in contribution should be 1.25%—which the Government then decided to better out of consideration for the occupational pensioners. Terms that were "fair" to the "average" (contracted out) scheme could massacre half (or more) of them—depending on where the arithmetic average came in the "array" of all the schemes. If only MPs of above-"average" intelligence were allowed to continue their membership of the Commons, half (or more) would lose their seats. If only Bills of "average" value to society were passed by Parliament, half (or more) could be scrapped. And the country might miss them less than it would half the occupational pension schemes.

The 1.25% was calculated by supposing that in the first years of the scheme newly-invested pension funds would yield 7½% a year in interest and the average yield on interest re-invested during the period until the employees retired was 5½%, that death rates would be common to all schemes, and that administrative expenses would amount to 7% of the contribution "abatement." Cmnd. 4195 said the Government did not challenge the Government

from October 1964 to February 1967). When on 4 December, Mr. Ennals, the Minister of State, said: "My right hon. Friend could, if he had wanted, have steamrollered our State scheme through . . . ," Mr. Houghton rebuked him: "My hon. Friend says that the Government could have steamrollered through a scheme without any contracting-out arrangements. Surely he knows that would have been politically impossible?" *Hansard,* Col. 1723.

Actuary's "advice" (the 1.25% "abatement") but questioned the assumptions, which it thought were "too tightly drawn" because the average scheme would have "no financial inducement . . . to contract out" and they would be "particularly unattractive to schemes with a membership older than average" (so that contributions were fewer and pensions larger than the "average").

However you read it, this comment on the Government Actuary's "advice" seems to suggest a difference of opinion, and implies a criticism. The difference is broadly measured by the decision of the Government that the "abatement" should be 1.3%. The implied criticism is that the Government Actuary's terms would have borne harshly on the "average" or slightly below-"average" scheme and that the Government had gone to 1.3% to help schemes with rather higher than average costs.

This show of generosity was gratuitous. Why 1.3%? If the Government was concerned about the occupational schemes, as it kept on repeating, why did it not go higher—to 1.4% or 1.5% (the figure suggested by the pension experts)? Because, if it had, more employees would have been contracted out and the contributions to the State scheme would have been less; the contributions from employees not contracted out would, therefore, have had to be raised earlier than the Government wished, and either the taxpayer's subsidy would have had to be higher than the 18%, or the Government would have had to reduce the pensions it had been promising. The whole edifice would have tottered and collapsed. On the other hand if too many occupational schemes closed down or dried up, private savings would slow down; the Government was then in two minds about whether it would regret the development or whether, as Mr. Peter Shore, another spokesman, said, the temporary surplus in the National Superannuation Fund would make up for it.[3]

In short, no issue of principle had been solved at all in all the palaver from January to November. The dilemma had not been removed because it was ineradicable. The notion of "partnership" was at last seen as the shallow charade it was: the contracting out terms would *have* to harm many occupational schemes or the Government scheme would not work. The relationship between the two was not cosily complementary but cruelly competitive. At last it became clear to all who before had been blind, or who did not wish to see, that money for state pensions must be taken from money for private pensions. The time for self-delusion had passed.

3. This reply misses one of the most important aspects of the argument discussed in Chapter XI.

But the Government cannot shuffle off blame to the Government Actuary. It was not his assumptions that were "too tightly drawn," but, as he politely put it, its terms of reference to him. In the first White Paper of January it said that the reduction in contributions to be paid for contracted-out employees should be linked to the reduction in pensions on the basis of *average* "commercial" cost. It is true that the three main elements in commercial cost are interest, death rates and expenses. But, with much respect for the able man who is the Government Actuary, these considerations are not merely "similar in many ways" to those used in assessing premiums for self-insured pension schemes. They are substantially the *same* considerations, but they have very different effects. A life assurance company which applies a common premium to be paid by all employees (and/or their employer) in a pension scheme is averaging the varying risks of the members depending on their ages, health, etc. If there are sizeable numbers, the risks cancel out for each insurance company running an insured scheme or each firm running a self-insured scheme, and employees who are older or less healthy than the average benefit at the expense of the younger and more healthy. This is a kind of rough, poetic justice, justified also by the administrative costs of otherwise calculating premiums separately for each employee. The internal subsidy is relatively small and acceptable because administrative costs per employee are lower in a group than for an individual (and the larger the group the lower the cost per employee).

But applying "averaging" to different *schemes* is very different from applying it to different *individuals* within each scheme. Applying an average premium to a scheme means that some members subsidise others. Applying a single contribution abatement to all schemes means that some will be able to carry on easily and others will not be able to carry on at all. It may be said: so much the better—they are not big and healthy. But pension schemes, like humans, are not static; they change over time. A small scheme today could thrive in three years.

The argument is not whether the Government Actuary's assumptions of 7½ (5½)% for investment yields, mortality rates, and 7% costs were too high or too low. *Any* such assumptions of *single* "average" figures applied to all pension schemes would make it impossible for some of them to continue. Rising from 1.25% to 1.3% may save some schemes but still kill off many and their unknown potential growth in the years to come. That is part of the price of national superannuation.

The Government has not shown magnanimity towards occupational pensions by allowing more generous contracting out terms than those calculated as "fair" (another question-begging word) by the Government Actuary. Its terms of reference were bound to produce "advice" that would enable them to kill off growing occupational pensions and private savings. If, as happened, the Actuary's "advice" was "too tightly drawn," Ministers could appear gracious and still repress the occupational pensions. If it had been more generously drawn they could have pleaded that employees not contracted out would suffer. National Superannuation enables Mr. Crossman to say: "Heads I win, tails you lose." The moral is that *national* superannuation is a strait-jacket that should not be forced on private schemes of varying sizes, and stages of development. It should be discarded as having no place in a variegated society.

CHAPTER XIII

Overseas Exemplars—or Warnings?

Mr. Crossman points to other countries that have earnings-related national insurance pension schemes to bolster his case for earnings-related pensions in Britain.

International comparisons are precarious because no two countries are alike. It is easy to find countries that have done what one considers desirable. For some years now the international "league tables" of tax burdens and social security expenditure have been exploited by everyone to "prove" everything. In some countries total taxation is heavier than in Britain (e.g. France and Germany, Sweden and Holland), in others lighter (e.g. the USA and Canada, Australia and Switzerland). Some countries spend more on state pensions than Britain, others less. So what? It does not follow that taxes in Britain should be lowered or raised, or social services enlarged or reduced. All that such cases show is that in *their* social and economic conditions such-and-such social services or methods of payment may be desirable and are apparently practicable. It does not follow that they would be practicable in Britain, nor that we should copy them. What matters more than a comparison with other countries is a comparison with Britain in recent times. Taxpayers in Britain will not willingly pay more taxes or social security contributions merely because the citizens of other countries do so. The case has to be demonstrated in terms of British conditions, attitudes and preferences. The question is: is government likely to spend £1 or £100 million additional taxes more wisely than the taxpayer?

The choice of countries as examples is also significant and not always convincing. The National Association of Pension Funds in a 1968 report[1] thought that a brief review of "developments in other countries of the Western world" was relevant; this was "of major interest because of Britain's application for membership of the Community"; and Sweden and the USA

1. *The Future Relationship of State and Occupational Pensions*, September, 1968.

were added "because of the important developments in their countries in recent years." It therefore briefly reviewed Belgium, France, Italy, the Netherlands, Sweden, the USA and West Germany.

If Britain joins the EEC it does not follow that she must adopt its pension systems, good, bad or indifferent. The EEC might with equal reason adopt ours, if it were better. Harmonisation has hardly begun, and if other countries act unwisely we are hardly wise to follow them. Germany's difficulties were mentioned in the NAPF report but not Sweden's. The USA account is now out-of-date. And there was no reference to New Zealand or Australia at all, two countries with which Britain might be thought to have more in common than with others in the NAPF list.

What has been happening in Germany, Sweden, the USA and Australia?

Germany (West)

Since 1957 Germany has in several respects been operating a pension scheme more similar than any other Western country's to that envisaged by Mr. Crossman. The pension is based on the employee's average life earnings and on the national average earnings; it is financed by earnings-related contributions by employee and employer and by the general taxpayer. Pre-1957 pensions are revised annually with the upward movement of wage-earnings generally.

The costs are higher than those contemplated for the Crossman scheme. In 1968 German employees paid 7% of their earnings and employers 7% of their total payroll; the Government provided about a quarter of the combined 14%. The corresponding UK figures in the first year would be 4¾% and 4½% making a combined contribution of 9¼%, plus nearly a fifth (18%) of the 9¼%, with increases after a few years.

What such a system can lead to is vividly shown by the German experience. The employee's contribution represents earnings postponed until retirement, although they may partly be passed on to consumers. The employers' contribution is probably passed on to consumers in large part. And the Government's contribution is provided by taxpayers, direct and indirect. The Federal Ministry of Labour has calculated that 60–80% of the Government's contribution is provided by the employee, that is the future pensioner. (This is rather like the position in Britain where most people in the middling ranges of income pay taxes within 10% or so of the value of their social benefits.)

Calculations by the Ministry of Labour and private insurance organisations suggest that from 1973 employees will be paying around 20% of earnings for pensions insurance. Dr. Wilhelm Claussen, State Secretary in the Federal Ministry for Labour from 1957 to 1965, estimates[2] that, in addition, sickness insurance takes 10%, unemployment insurance 1½%, direct taxes 10%, and indirect taxes a further 10%. Thus "social security" paid for by taxes of all sorts would take about half of employees' income. What would British workers think of following this example? Yet Germany is a country to which advocates of higher taxation and expanded social insurance in Britain point to show what is possible and desirable.

The system has worked reasonably effectively since 1957 because the high rate of growth in incomes has yielded contributions sufficient to pay pensions. But the pension system is becoming a bloated form of saving in which the politically-promised pensions of the future seem to be increasing faster than those of the present-day contributors. Dr. Claussen calculates that a young man who joined the German State scheme in 1968 can expect to receive after 35 years a pension on retirement of 46,600 marks a year (about £4,900). Adjusting the pension to increases in wages at the rate of 4–5% increase a year over 10 years raises it to 72,300 marks (£7,600). Such large amounts would require very high contributions and taxes, though whether they are paid depends on political promises rather than financial investment.

In the meantime, German pensions load industrial costs and living costs. Even more fundamentally, they probably distort the structure of German saving and property in favour of paper claims on *future* generations, who may not be prepared to accept obligations transferred to them from the past, and away from more tangible forms of ownership (such as homes) or claims on current production (stocks and shares) that create a more secure foundation for independence.

In 1911 Lloyd George almost slavishly copied Bismarck. Whom is Crossman copying?

Sweden

The consequences of accumulating contributions in excess of current pension disbursements is seen from the experience of Sweden, with which a British Labour Government may feel affinity.

2. "Provision for old age in Germany," *Progress,* No. 4, 1968–9. I am also indebted to Dr. Claussen for a talk in Paris, May, 1967.

Mr. Crossman says he has abandoned the 1957 notion of creating a National Pension Fund intended to earn the high returns earned by private investment funds, help modernise industry, and accelerate national economic growth (and, though this was not over-emphasised, give government a say in some major firms and industries). But in the early years of the 1972 scheme a surplus would develop because the contributions would be fixed high enough to cover increases in pensions. It could be about £250 million by 1978 if current forecasts and projections of contributions income and pension outgo, and earnings and numbers (partially) contracted out are not far wrong. How would it be invested?

If it were invested to serve the future pensioner it would be put into "growth" industries. But this would introduce political influence into industry. If it were used, like the National Insurance Fund, to buy gilt-edged stocks and other government securities it would ease the Government's management of money markets and the economy but give a low place to the interest of the future pensioner.

Whatever is decided by Mr. Crossman, or Mr. Roy Jenkins, or Mr. Harold Wilson in 1970 or 1971, they are not politically immortal. The men who come after them may think differently. The possibility that a sizeable superannuation surplus could be accumulated, at least for a period, remains. And it is all the stronger when flat-rate contributions are replaced by graduated contributions, for this reform replaces a floor by an unlimited ceiling. They may graduate contributions to only 50% over national average earnings in 1972, but that proportion is not sacrosanct. In West Germany it is 100%. It could be 100% in Britain in 1976 or 1984. And that would enlarge the coverage from 90 to perhaps 97 or 98% of employees.

Since other forms of political control over industry, not least conventional nationalisation, have fallen out of favour, the use of pension reserves cannot be dismissed; and assurances or disavowals by politicians in temporary power cannot be accepted because they do not bind their successors. Nor is it much comfort to the prospective pensioner to know that his contributions are put into government borrowing to bolster its weak creditworthiness resulting from inflation and the refusal of investors to put their savings into insecure government "securities."

Sweden shows the consequences when a government can lay hold of funds not immediately required to pay for current social services. In 1960 a new earnings-related pension, financed by contributions paid by employers (9.5 of earnings in 1969, higher in 1970) was introduced to supplement the flat-rate pension financed by general taxation. The purpose, as in the UK, was to cushion the fall in the standard of life when earnings cease at retirement (normally at 67 years, not 65).[3] For a lengthy number of years the incoming contributions were to exceed outgoing pension costs. By 1970 the fund was expected to reach 40 billion kronor, (nearly a third of the Gross National Product—132 billion kronor in 1968). Contribution income rose from 2,400 billion kronor in 1964 to an expected 6,500 billion in 1970, pension outgo from 100 billion to 900 billion. Interest on the fund is itself almost enough to pay current pensions.

The fund has become a dominant element in Swedish saving and investment; it is the largest savings institution and the largest supplier of credit. In 1970 it is expected to furnish 7,500 billion of (net) lending, as much as all other Swedish credit institutions put together. Private saving for life assurance has sagged, although other forms of private saving may have risen with rising incomes.

In the near future the National Pension Fund's assets will be as large as the commercial banks', and larger if contribution rates are raised. So far its investments and lending have been mainly in government securities and housing.

It is easy to see pressure mounting for some of the accumulated fund in the UK to be applied to housing if continuing rent restriction discourages private investment. In 1956 a Fabian Society pamphlet hopefully proposed:

> The money would be earmarked for . . . loans at low interest rates to the nationalised industries . . . and to local authorities for cheap housing.

A writer in *Co-operative News* in 1957 staked an uninhibited claim:

> A proper objective for national pension fund trustees might well include considerable commitment in the Co-ops. . . .

In Sweden the increasing supply of National Pension funds and channelling of private saving to the State and away from private pensions may impel the direction of National Pension funds to industry. Dr. Börje Kragh, Director of Konjunktur-institut in Stockholm,[4] has examined several methods of channelling National Pension funds to industry through the commercial banks with varying degrees of Government control, freedom to undertake risky investment, ability to reconcile profitability, risk and security,

3. The Swedish system is more civilised than ours. The pension may be drawn at 63 with a deduction of 0.6% for each month short of 67; and the converse with deferments.

4. "Sweden's National Pension Insurance Fund," *OECD Observer,* Organisation for European Co-operation and Development, April, 1968.

and susceptibility to pensioners' importunities. Some financial institutions would be less objectionable than others. The prospect of massive funds that could be used to bolster government securities, finance Council housing, support co-operative trading, invest in the governments of developing countries, or bolster emerging nations wooed by the Soviet Union would encourage and excite many well-intentioned, warm-hearted people in Britain. The prospect of a government-controlled investing agency channelling as much finance as all other British credit institutions put together, and replacing commercial competition by political dominance of saving and investment, should also alarm, dismay and arouse people to opposition.

What are the chances? The Parliament in Sweden has, after all, supported a government proposal for a government investment bank. The Parliament in Britain would have recurring opportunities and temptations to use "national superannuation" for political investment, and Mr. Crossman's disavowal of a surplus may, perhaps, not be accepted by future governments.

USA

Recent developments in American social insurance show that it has a propensity to grow for reasons that have little to do with human needs or compassion but much with sociological and political philosophy on the alleged virtue of universality, centralisation and the beneficence of government.

The national pension system, Old-Age, Survivors and Disability Insurance (OASDI), known generally as "social security," was introduced in 1937. It provides monthly pensions on retirement (or invalidity) to insured employees (or self-employed) and their surviving widows and other dependants. The pension is paid at 65 (or at reduced rates at 62) to pensioners, at 62 to wives (or dependant husbands), up to 21 to children at school, and to mothers of eligible children. The basic pension is related to the average monthly wage, calculated since 1950 up to the retirement age of 65 (men) or 62 (women), by a formula which provides 71% of the first 110 dollars of average monthly wages and 26% of the next 540 dollars, with a minimum of 55 dollars a month. Periodic increases in the basic pension have rather more than kept pace with prices.

Wives and children receive pensions of 50% of the basic pension, surviving children and their mothers 75%, widows 82½%.

The pensions are financed by equal contributions (described as payroll *taxes*) from employers and employees amounting to 8.4% (1969/70) on the first 7,800 dollars of average earnings. There is no "Exchequer Supplement" from the general taxpayer.

The system is thus earnings-related and "pay-as-you-go" without an invested fund, and in basic respects comparable to that proposed by Mr. Crossman. But it exhibits characteristics that are warnings of what to avoid rather than exemplars to emulate. If run by men who value checks to governmental authority, independent initiative and a private sector as a standard by which to judge the government sector, it might be run with responsible restraint. It would then be adapted to economic, social and demographic (population) change and individual circumstances; financed by methods that clarify costs, so that contributors discipline demands for higher benefits; and it would be arranged to provide pensions that left scope and incentive to earn and save to improve on them. That might be the system at its best run by politicians of stature, dedicated to the proposition that personal liberty should be cherished next to the relief of need.

So it might be. But it is not. For some months a senior civil servant, Robert J. Myers, the Chief Actuary to the Social Security Administration of the Department of Health, Education and Welfare in Washington has been warning that the system is in danger of being inflated to cover everybody. The rising pensions would be paid for increasingly out of general taxation, where the cost would be less immediately noticeable than if they were financed by higher contributions. The combined employer-employee's contribution is in any event designed to be raised from 8.4% of earnings in 1969–70 to 9.2% in 1971–2 and to 10% thereafter.

How much the basic (earnings-related) pension should be is a matter of judgement. It might be thought sufficient if only a small proportion of pensioners required to supplement it by what in the USA is still called public assistance. In 1969 this proportion was 7%. The solution might then appear to be to ensure adequate supplementation for the 7%.

This is not enough for "the expansionists." Like their opposite numbers in Britain, though with apparently much less cause, since about 30% of British pensioners receive supplementation, the American inflationist wants pensions raised for the 93% who do not require supplementation to ensure higher incomes for the 7% that do. This hardly makes sense, especially, says Mr. Myers, since the small minority contains pensioners whose earnings in the 1930s slump were much lower than those of pensioners who came later.

But, again as in Britain, "the expansionists" are using a dwindling minority to justify compulsory saving through the state for the growing majority who are becoming more affluent. If they get their way, says Mr. Myers in a recent Paper published in Britain,[5] they will establish government "social security" as a virtual monopoly and in time eliminate private pensions. Their methods are to proceed by degree to hitch federal pensions up all round: to raise the maximum earnings on which contributions ("payroll *taxes*") are based from 7,800 to 15,000 dollars and then jack it up with rising earnings, raise the pension by 100% or to begin with by 50% which would vary not merely with *prices* but with earnings (which even Mr. Crossman does not promise to do himself), and add a government contribution of, eventually, 50% of the employer-employee contribution.

The effects would be to reduce private pensions, private saving and investment funds for industry, and to increase government investment in industry, bringing political regulation, control and ownership. Evidently the dangers that few recognise in Britain are being emphasised in the USA.

There is also an ironic contrast. "The expansionists" in the USA want more general tax finance for the "insurance" pensions; in Britain they want more contributions—from the higher-paid wage-earner of today and tomorrow. In the USA it is plausible to propose higher taxes because taxation takes much less of the Gross National Product (30%) than in Britain (38%). Plausible, but not therefore more desirable. Mr. Myers emphasises that one reason why "the expansionists" are working for larger tax subsidies is the difficulty of raising employer-employee contributions, and another that an increase in general taxes might not be noticed so readily and therefore be resisted less. In Britain Mr. Crossman is driven to argue the opposite: that there is resistance to general taxation but that more revenue might perhaps be found from social insurance contributions by promising the *quid pro quo* of pensions in return. There seems to be a running battle of wits between the British "expansionists" and the reluctant taxpayer.

The opponents of taxation subsidies—among whom Mr. Myers openly ranges himself—say they would weaken the controls over pension costs because increases in pensions would be voted by politicians in the hope that no one would notice the larger subsidy from general government revenue. But, they argue, under the contribution system, the costs of higher pensions are soon noticed. Not even Labour Members agree with Mr. Crossman that the British worker will not notice higher contribution deductions from his pay packet.

The last Secretary of Health, Education and Welfare under President

5. *Expansionism in Social Insurance,* Occasional Paper 32, Institute of Economic Affairs, 1970. I am indebted to Mr. Myers for periodic exchanges of information and views since 1961, and in particular for a long discussion in Washington in May, 1968.

Johnson is quoted by Mr. Myers as saying that the expenditure on these services, presumably in the main by government, should rise from 19.8% of GNP in 1968 to 25% in 1976. Mr. Myers observes:

> . . . we might wonder whether 25% is to be the ultimate level desired by the expansionists. Why not 30%, or 50% or more?

The expansionist philosophy, he suggests, might go on to propose a public food service since some people, especially teenagers, do not eat the ideal food although they could afford to:

> . . . why not have the government tell each person what they should eat, then provide it, and see that they eat it?

It is easy to demonstrate the logical absurdity of "the expansionists" in the USA and their soulmates, the universalists, in Britain. The Chief Actuary of the USA Social Security Administration has not been known as a critic of social insurance *per se.* He is evidently now alarmed that it is being expanded too far. In Britain that danger would become more likely if national insurance is changed from flat-rate to earnings-related by the National Superannuation and Social Insurance Bill, 1969.

Proposals for the reform of American social security are also made by an economist, Professor Colin D. Campbell.

> If past experience is a guide, the Social Security Administration will probably continue to propagate the insurance analogy while in practice paying less and less attention to matters of individual equity. . . . Because of the recent increases in payroll taxes and benefit levels, taxpayers and beneficiaries may become more concerned with matters of individual equity than in the past. Also, as the social security program departs further from the insurance analogy, its inaccuracy as a description may become better-known and it will no longer be acceptable. If so, the need for a more accurate rationale for the program will become more urgent, and social security will probably be headed towards a period of reform.[6]

Australia

Australia is rarely if ever quoted by the advocates of increasing governmental control of pensions. Yet in economic structure and social fabric she

6. "Social Insurance in the United States: A Program in Search of an Explanation." The passage is quoted from a typescript of the article, subsequently published in the *Journal of Law and Economics,* University of Chicago Press, October, 1969.

has more in common with Britain than other countries offered as models to emulate.

Australia has no national insurance. The "National Welfare Fund," at one time allotted a part of personal income tax as a social services "contribution," is now not a fund with independent, segregated income but a reservoir filled from general revenue. The old-age pensions (posted fortnightly by cheque) paid at 65 for men and 60 for women, are 26.5 dollars a week for a man and wife (about £12) and 14 dollars for a man or woman (£6 10s), and based on a means test. Of approximately a million people of pensionable age, rather over half (55% in 1968) have received pensions and rather under half have been excluded by the possession of sizeable income and/or capital. The recipients receive more than they would if pensions were paid universally without regard for income or capital. In addition pensioners receive medical services without payment, and other concessions in transport, rates, etc., worth on average over 5 dollars (£2 5s) a week.

A distinguishing feature of Australian social policy has been the periodic refinement of the means test to conserve resources for pensioners with least means and to avoid discouragement to self-provision. Since 1961 the separate means tests applied to income and property have been fused into a "merged means test" in which property exceeding 800 dollars has been valued as yielding a notional income of 10%. For some years, until 1968, the means test allowed a married couple of pensioners to own a house, its contents, a motorcar, 800 dollars in cash or other property, and weekly superannuation or other income up to 17 dollars (that is, the property equivalent of 8,840 dollars) and draw the pension in full. The capital value of income and property disregarded could amount to 30,000 or 40,000 dollars (£14,000 or £18,000), and the couple could receive tax-free income of 42 dollars a week (25 dollars pension, 17 dollars disregarded income), or about £20. A married couple could draw part pensions (and the associated "fringe benefits") if they owned 24,200 dollars of property as well as income from property (interest, dividends, rent on a second house). Contrary to a common impression in Britain the means-tested pension does not seem to damage private saving.

The view of Mr. T. H. Kewley, of the University of Sydney,[7] a close observer of social security in Australia, is that the use of means test for cash benefits may be one reason why "Australia has made comparatively good progress

7. Based on his book *Social Security in Australia,* University of Sydney Press, 1965, discussions in Canberra, August, 1968, and his monograph *Social Services in Australia,* Australian Institute of Political Science, 1969.

towards eliminating poverty." He explains the fairly general acceptance of means tests in Australia, despite criticism mainly from people excluded from the pension and its fringe benefits, by the absence of social stigma (evidenced by the anxiety of people excluded to qualify), the liberal exemptions and the incentives to add supplementary private provision.

In 1969 the pension means test was "tapered" by reducing the amount of pension withheld for each dollar of earnings (above 10 for a single person, 17 for a couple) from one dollar to half a dollar. The intention was to increase the incentive to supplement the pension by earning or saving, and in general, as put by the Prime Minister in the budget debate, "to encourage thrift and self-help."[8] The 100% "tax" on earnings over the disregarded amounts was thus reduced to 50%.

In Australia pensioners are treated more humanely and more generously than in many other Western countries despite the absence of national insurance and, I would argue, because of the use of means tests. It has not entangled itself in the questionable practice of raising revenue by describing it as an insurance "contribution." It has not had to confront the balancing act of raising enough revenue to pay the pensions but not too much to accumulate a fund, or, having generated a fund, of having to decide to invest it in unprofitable government securities or in politically-charged industrial shares. It has not loaded employers with wage-costs. It has not had to raise taxes for universal cash benefits. It has not had to provide for its pensioners by roseate promises of bounteous pensions in the distant future.

In 1968 the Governor-General of Australia announced a departure—or a development—in social policy:

> My Government will review the field of social policy welfare with the object of assisting those in most need while at the same time not discouraging thrift, self-help and self-reliance.

A Cabinet Committee on Welfare was created under the Minister for Health and included the Ministers of Social Services, Housing, Repatriation (for ex-service benefits) and a Minister representing the Treasury. Before it could present its long-term recommendations, the General Election of 1969 supervened. The Government's policy on welfare was a main issue. The Opposition offered comprehensive, universal and generally free welfare. In spite of support from the Australian press and vocal academics, it did not defeat the Government after 20 years of office.

8. *Hansard*, House of Representatives, 21 August, 1969, Col. 584.

The high rate of Australian economic improvement in living standards, about 6% a year, may help to make it easier to dispense with universal policies of government welfare because buoyant incomes facilitate independence. But the policy of concentrating government aid on the 5% poor in the population and encouraging the 95% to provide for themselves, and the general philosophy that good living standards come from self-help rather than from government, also stimulate the economic improvement.

CHAPTER XIV

What Now?

The National Superannuation and Social Insurance Bill is presented as proposing an important advance in British social policy, a measure of humanitarian compassion for the aged. Let us not be deceived. Its immediate primary aim is to raise money by a new device which, Mr. Crossman hopes, will be less intensely disliked, less strenuously opposed and less harmful than taxation openly proposed and faithfully described. Its more general purpose is to find one more means of redistributing income from the well-off to the worse-off (in which it would partly fail).[1] Its ultimate effect would be to transfer vast sums unnecessarily from private decision to government expenditure.

At the NALGO meeting on 25 November, 1969, when he addressed people whom he thought he could regard as fundamentally friendly, he spoke more freely. In addition to the by now familiar disarming disclaimers and disavowals of evil intent towards the NALGO and other public sector pension schemes (which he nevertheless had earlier in a letter conceded would have to be "reviewed"—a euphemism for cut down), he repeatedly said that there was no alternative to "national superannuation" since present pensioners could not be provided for out of increased taxation. He explained he was at his wits' end to know how to pay for improvements in the National Health Service, education and other expanding services.

> . . . Competition for finance for welfare is intense; the N.H.S., education and the rest are already fighting for funds.

He claimed that the pensioners could not be helped by higher taxation because "you really will be crushed by taxation." *So that is the real aim:* money for present pensioners from future pensioners.

1. In assuring contracted out employees that they would not be subsidising those left wholly in the State scheme, Mr. Crossman has been led to concede that the subsidy would be "at the expense of the pockets of workers left in the scheme."

Two subsidiary aims, or justifications, were thrown in: that taxation would put pensioners at the mercy of the Chancellor, and that the flat-rate pension had limited contributions to what the lowest-paid worker could afford and consequently had brought pensions below the Supplementary Benefit level.

Earnings-related "national superannuation" was, therefore, the best available policy. There was no way of making employers bear the cost: in France, Italy, Sweden, Czechoslovakia employers paid about 70% of the cost but these four countries had among the highest living costs. (Mr. Crossman did not add that employees' contributions could also be passed on—*inter alia* to their wives as shoppers.)

In any case no one thought that state pensions alone should *not* be related to earnings, when state sickness and unemployment benefit were related (but should *they* be?); and occupational pensions were also related to pay (but by choice).

Occupational schemes, of course, were not always good. Some paid only £3 a week or less, and did not provide for preservation or dynamism. As a dialectician of no mean skill Mr. Crossman will not expect the non sequitur to carry conviction. The £3 schemes would in time be paying £5, £7, £9 and £11 *if he did not prevent them.* And incomplete, imperfect private pensions for some are no excuse for compulsory, growing state pensions for almost all.

What emerges from all this talk about wits' ends, fighting for funds, and being crushed by taxation is hardly a grand design for accumulating income for retirement but a harassed Minister scouting round for money and settling on a lesser evil that would attract less notice, opposition or unpopularity, and sugaring the pill with a *potpourri* of seasoning sauces that have nothing to do with the objectionable ingredient. Earnings-related pensions are being sold by unrelated tit-bits.

O, what a fall was there, my countrymen!

The high principle of 1957 has degenerated into the convenient expedient of 1970. The ground has shifted: national suprannuation is being enacted not so much because it is good in itself as because other methods (of financing existing pensions) are worse.

Then what are the other methods? Mr. Crossman can think of only one: higher taxation, which he says, rightly but very belatedly, would be "crushing." But who has made taxation as high as it is? Not the people. If they were asked they would prefer lower to higher taxation. Here Mr. Crossman enters a contorted argument. He says the people want more welfare—better education, medical care, housing, pensions, and so on, but are not prepared to pay more in taxes for them. Are politicians incapable of seeing the difference between paying higher taxes for state welfare, in which they have little say, and keeping their money and paying for better education, better medical care, better housing, better pensions in which they have much say? The hope for improved welfare is that people will wish to spend more on it voluntarily because they come to regard it as personal, consumer or household expenditure out of income. They will never see taxes—or social insurance contributions—as payment for welfare.

It is not the people but the politicians—of all parties—who have made taxation "crushing." And this because they never or rarely think of giving tax money back to the people to spend themselves. The hilarious alibi is that government has to provide free services because people cannot pay for them. Which people? Most people could pay; only a small minority—5% or 10%—could not (and even they could be enabled to pay). The majority of 90% or 95% is rendered unable to pay by the very taxes taken from them to provide them with free services. Thus runs the hysterical logic of politics.

Mr. Crossman is doing no more than quoting politicians' failings of the past to justify one more failing in the future. He sees no other way out except higher government revenue because he sees no other way of financing existing pensions except by promising future pensions. At this rate we shall commit future generations to parting with larger proportions of their incomes to the State in the hope of ever-larger pensions. This is an incongruous procedure for a civilised society. It should not take more than moderate intelligence to enable politicians to see that as incomes rise people can cope for themselves, and will want to.

There will never be an escape from this impasse except by separating (*a*) the financing of present pensions from (*b*) the financing of future pensions. (*a*) Present pensions could easily be financed out of taxation if increases were limited to retired people without considerable other means and if taxation were returned so that in time people were increasingly allowed to buy welfare where they chose. Of the national income of £35,000 million, some £8,000–£9,000 million are taken in taxes (including rates and social insurance) to pay for welfare. *But most of it goes back to the people and the families and the households from whence it came.* To suppose that the present volume of taxation is sacrosanct and cannot be reduced is to suppose that everything the government now does is wise, or that the people willingly part with their money and prefer to have it spent for them by public officials. Mr. Crossman and his friends should have more respect for the common people.

(*b*) Future pensions would then be freed to be accumulated in any way that employees, employers, and self-employed preferred—through the State, or in industry, by personal pensions, or by any other method of saving. It would be desirable to remove obstacles in the way of occupational and personal pensions, and to make competition more vigorous between the organisations that devise, install and administer them. The Inland Revenue would have to be shorn of its power to delay or inhibit occupational pensions. And government would have to do better at resisting inflation, or enable industry to under-write, and individuals to insure, against it.

It is to these more fundamental reforms of British social policy, public finance and the institutional framework for private pensions that we must look for the ultimate escape from the intensifying vortex of pension finance that plagues Britain—and almost every Western country.

There would be no hesitation by the public. If the politicians doubt that, let them ask the people. Let them, if they dare, inform the electorate of *all* the possible alternative policies, and then conduct a referendum on (*a*) compulsory national superannuation, (*b*) voluntary national superannuation, (*c*) encouragement for occupational, private and personal superannuation. If they shrink from finding what "the people" want, let them at least not claim to know without asking.

Fundamental reform would take time? It might take 5, 10, 15 years to straighten out the tangled skein of taxes and social benefits in which the mass of the people pay for welfare through the State and have their authority over it taken away from them into the bargain. But Mr. Crossman is asking for 20 years to create a new method of financing pensions. Why should we not spend as long—or less time—strengthening the individual against the State rather than the State against the individual?

It is essential to prevent the imposition in Britain of this new inflated form of taxation because it would enable politicians to escape from the task of explaining and justifying the taxation they levy now. On the contrary, they must be required by public opinion to explain why they tax people in order to supply them with services they could provide themselves. And they would have to do so if they were denied resort to "national superannuation" to escape a duty they have shirked for too long.

The strongest case, superficially, for national superannuation is that it is the quickest way of giving retired people more help by the politically smarter way of raising funds without calling them taxes. This is not a masterly act of statecraft, except on the lowest plane in which deception can be admired for its technical agility, but a confession of failure by politicians who prefer to govern by half-truths rather than by unpalatable whole truths that cannot be denied for ever. But even if no other method of raising the required funds in the short term were available, the good would be far exceeded by the economic, social and political damage done to parliamentary democracy and the free society. To deal with the acknowledged claims to more generous treatment of two or three million people who will mostly have passed on by 1992, national superannuation would fasten on all earners and future pensioners a new compulsory system of saving through the State that might last 50 years or more. In this act of political abdication there is no statesmanship.

The full majesty of British parliamentary institutions has been exploited to conceal a political charade. It would do nothing for the existing pensioner, the widow, the married woman, the disabled person, that could not be done better in other ways. It would unnecessarily restrict the freedom of nine-tenths of the people to save for retirement. It would confuse the contract of employment between employer and employee in the labour market by impeding the natural spread of pensions from salaried to wage-paid employees. It would load industry with costs that would have to be passed on to the consumer and the housewife. It would burden the middle-paid employees who would be left to subsidise the lower-paid, and generate friction between them. It would unnecessarily embroil government in insurance, saving and investment. It would further damage the respect for British politicians and political institutions: *Perfidious Albion* does not refer to exporters, merchants, bankers, shippers or private insurers. It would distract government from tasks that only government can perform. It would further aggrandize the State.

None of this can be welcomed by politicians in any party who care for people as individuals, for the resilience of the economy, for personal liberty or for political integrity.

For Britain in the last third of the twentieth century national superannuation would be national retrogression. To copy other countries confronting confusion, embarrassment and uncontrollable inflation in "earnings-relation" is to confound common sense. This is not the way forward for a humane, liberal, increasingly opulent society in which opportunity for the rising masses, which social policy could enlarge, would tragically be constricted. Let democrats—Conservative, Liberal, Socialist and unaffiliated—recall John Stuart Mill:

> Among the works of man which human life is rightly employed in perfecting and beautifying, the first in importance surely is man himself.

Envoi

The main lesson of this book is that the longer the radical solution of British pension policy—paying adequate incomes to pensioners in need out of taxation and building future pensions by funding—is delayed, the more difficult it will be to solve and the more damage will be done to British society, economy and polity.

Mr. Crossman has inherited a heavy enough task, and can partly blame other post-war politicians for its magnitude. It could have been foreseen by his predecessors as Ministers of Pensions and their colleagues in both parties. All have shrunk (as have many Ministers and governments overseas) from finding ways of supporting current pensioners in need out of current taxation without embroiling current saving for future retirement.

To acts of omission have been added acts of commission. The proposed 1972 earnings-related pension, like the 1961 graduated pension, is another political effort to escape responsibilities rather than honour them.

If Mr. Crossman cannot be blamed for its magnitude, the task may not be unwelcome to him as the pretext for expanding state pensions that he has long favoured on general philosophic grounds.

The duty remains for democratic politicians of all parties. The Crossman scheme is one more effort to pass the buck to the future. It is incongruous for an opulent society to have its retirement income generated increasingly through the State; undignified for self-respecting men and women to be dependent on unknown politicians and taxpayers of 1982, 1992 and 2002. Although it is too late to suppress private saving through occupational pension schemes, an extension of state pensions would repress their spread down the income scale to the mass of wage-earners who, into the bargain, would be forcibly relieved of earnings they could have saved with choice.

Sooner or later the inherited problem of untangling the finance of past pensions from that of future pensions must be faced. How far it requires a reconstruction of state pensions and welfare, a reform of taxation and public finance, a revised institutional framework for private saving by pensions and other methods are for statesmanship in the 1970s to decide. A necessary precondition is for the Crossman Bill to be rejected, or, if enacted, repealed.

APPENDIX A

Reprinted from The Policy Holder, *4 April, 1969*

It is time the pensions industry's candid friends spoke out about its questionable judgment in public policy and its failure in commercial enterprise. My argument is that the pensions industry—as a whole: consultants, brokers, and underwriters, but chiefly the life offices—have paid too much attention to government and too little to its customers: past, present and future.

It is proper for commercial enterprise and technical experts to be consulted by government, but not to the point at which they lose the power of independent appraisal and criticism. In their relationship with the government over the Crossman White Paper, the insurance companies have weakened their capacity to speak for their customers so much that there has been almost no criticism of the proposals. Does the LOA speak for all the life offices? I know it does not. But those who are disconcerted and dismayed have failed to speak up. I praise them for seeing that the LOA is going wrong, but condemn them for remaining silent.

The notion of "partnership" between the government and the life offices is politically questionable. In a democracy it is a dereliction of government to share its authority with industry; and it is arrogant of industry to indulge pretensions of sharing power with government. Moreover, in its economic aspect, the notion of partnership is a dangerous half-truth. It has some sense if it means that government, out of taxation, provides pensions for people who cannot be covered by private insurance, and the pensions industry covers the rest. But it is idle to be blind to the consequence of a *growing* state sector—that the relationship then becomes *competitive.* If the government provides pensions for a wide range of incomes, and over this range the average pension is 50 per cent of income; and if 9 out of 10 people are caught in the net, the state becomes a powerful competitor for employers' and employees' moneys. It is foolish for the life offices to welcome increasing state pensions that they can provide themselves.

This is the tragic *opposite* of what should take place as incomes rise towards the end of the century. Government should become a gradually shrinking junior "partner." Instead, the life offices are acquiescing in a growth in state pensions. They have lacked faith in themselves; they have misjudged the changing aspirations of the common people; they have lacked vision in seeing the consequences of spreading opulence.

In their anxiety to partner the state, the life offices have failed to point to the fallacies in the notion of graduating pensions with warnings under a state scheme: that it is not insurance but disguised taxation; that people who earn more can save more; that if they will not save more, they do not have to be compelled to do so through the state; that if people had a choice they would prefer private to state pensions.

Why is the LOA silent? Is it serving its member life offices? Itself? The state? The ultimate customer? For whom *does* it speak?

The life offices do not seem to understand that what politicians are ultimately concerned with is not pensions but power. LOA spokesmen, whatever they may believe, are not engaged in long-term actuarial calculations but are embroiled in short-term political calculation. Mr. Crossman would not be inviting the advice of the life offices except to help him devise a scheme that would win votes for the government.

The life offices have been just as naïve in dealing with Mr. Crossman as they were in dealing with Mr. Boyd-Carpenter. In 1959–60 Mr. Crossman called Mr. Boyd-Carpenter's scheme a swindle; a few Thursdays ago Mr. Boyd-Carpenter called Mr. Crossman's scheme an even bigger swindle. That is the maelstrom of party politics the life offices have got caught up in. That is the reality, not the subtle niceties of the innocent actuary. So much for keeping pensions out of politics, the hope of the actuaries back in 1959 expressed in their statement *Appeal to Statesmanship.*

Of course, the life offices hope for something—perhaps to salvage what they can of the occupational pension schemes. The only card they hold is their contribution to savings. But do you suppose that Mr. Crossman will put that before the prospect of appearing as a saviour of the government? With a plan that offers security to the electorate, young and old, rich and poor, male and female, in good health and bad?

Life office actuaries are contending with a political tactician, a master of propaganda against the Germans—one of his wartime jobs. Do you think those gentle gentlemen from the City are any match for a politician with much more at stake than their special concerns? Mr. Crossman has outmanoeuvred the life offices to such an extent that he now quotes them as his authority for the technical soundness of his scheme. And the director of public relations of the LOA writes a newspaper article which comes perilously near to defending the government. It is a short, slippery slope from consultation to unintentional, unconscious, collusion.

And all this without knowing the terms on which the government will graciously allow the life offices to continue occupational pensions. The LOA is now quoted by the government for the view that contracting-out in its attenuated form of abatement is "technically feasible." That is meaningless mumbo-jumbo. It is "technically feasible" to grow bananas in Scotland. It is "technically feasible" for the population of Britain to crowd into the Isle of Wight. What matters in the world of decision making is not technical feasibility but economic price. The LOA have approved the government scheme in principle, *in vacuo,* without knowing its price.

If contracting-out is made too easy—to save the occupational schemes' private saving—the state scheme will have to be bolstered by high contributions from people not contracted-out or by taxation. That will not make the government popular. And if in consequence contracting-out is made costly or complex, the LOA will have prejudiced the whole future of the occupational schemes, the pensions business of the insurance companies, the pension brokers, and the consulting actuaries.

The LOA has put the interests of its policy-holders, past and future, at risk. The life offices were naïve and defeatist to associate themselves with this scheme before knowing its terms. They should not defend it, even in principle. They should withdraw from it without further temporising or equivocation. Instead, they should put their trust in the customer and in their skills in meeting his requirements.

Mr. Crossman says the life offices do not or cannot (*a*) preserve pensions on a change of job, (*b*) raise pensions with prices or incomes after retirement, (*c*) give widows pensions, (*d*) give dependent wives pensions.

Do the life offices really believe this? There is nothing here that the private market cannot provide, if not in precisely the same form, comparable in effect. If the LOA and the National Association of Pension Funds spent as much time and ingenuity on these problems as they have done in helping Mr. Crossman with his, they would have solved them long ago. What has stopped them is lack of commercial spirit and lack of competitive drive.

Nor need private pensions be supplied to every firm or individual in order to resist the political charge that the life offices have failed and that the state must take over. If small firms, or firms with high labour turnovers, cannot be served by federal schemes, they can pay their employees enough to buy personal pensions. And there are many ways to supplement a pension.

And so I say to the pensions industry, put not your trust in politicians: no-one knows who will be in power in 1972. Study your customer: he prefers *you* to the state; he will see through the false prospectus of national superannuation.

APPENDIX B

A Note on Sour/Sentimental Sociology

One of the civilised scientific sociologists, Professor D. G. MacRae, has made a persuasive case for "sociology" in a defensive article "Is Sociology Necessary?" in *New Society,* 18 December, 1969, the home of both civilised/scientific and sour/sentimental sociology. He refers to "a feeling that sociology is something dissolutive of society and yet not so firmly based, positive and powerfully generalising as to be a real science," and affirms that "the majority of people paid to be sociologists in British society are . . . malcontented and liverish critics."

Daniel P. Moynihan, formerly Professor of Education and Urban Politics at Harvard, Assistant Secretary of Labor for Policy Planning and Research under Presidents Kennedy and Johnson, and now Assistant to President Nixon for Urban Affairs, said in a recent book on America's welfare programmes: ". . . social scientists tend to be politically liberal [in the American sense of collectivist] or left, especially when they are young. Economists would seem to be rather an exception: as the discipline gets "softer," the radicalism grows more pronounced." He adds: "Social scientists love poor people. They also get along fine with rich people. (Not a few are wealthy themselves, or married to heiresses . . .). But, alas, they do not have much time for the people in between."[1] Irving Kristol has also referred to the sociologists' "initial animus against the status quo."[2]

Much the same is true of many British sociologists and people interested in social affairs and welfare policy in education, medical care and housing. Some, on the right as well as on the left, often with public school education, suffer from a sense of guilt they try to exorcise by advocating a society in which uniformity will suppress the inherited differentials from which they are trying to escape, and which they would deny to merit as well as to inherited wealth.

1. *Maximum Feasible Misunderstanding,* The Free Press, New York, Collier-Macmillan, London, 1969.

2. *The Public Interest,* Spring, 1968.

APPENDIX C

"The existing State pension is the same for everyone. But, it is said, pensions should vary with earnings.

"Is this good enough reason for the new scheme?

"Does a £12-a-week man need more coal or calories to sustain him in old age than a £11-a-week man?

"If he thinks he does, he is able to save more voluntarily.

"And, if he does not, should a state scheme force him?

"The scheme is said to be essential to raise more revenue with which to pay the existing basic pension. . . .

"Of the six reasons given for it at various times by the Government, the political parties, the insurance companies, or other interested organisations . . . this, I think, is the real reason."

From "The Social, Economic and Political Implications of the State Graduated Pension Scheme." One-day Conference on Government Pension Scheme 1961. British Institute of Management, 24 May, 1960.

WITHER THE WELFARE STATE

PREFACE

As part of the Institute's educational purpose in explaining the light economic analysis can shed on public policy, the *Occasional Papers* were created to bring outstanding essays and lectures to wider audiences than those to which they were originally addressed.

Occasional Paper 60 is an extensively amplified version of material assembled for the Opening Address to The International University of the Open Society Conference at Cambridge on 3 July 1981. It has a neglected theme on which the author, Arthur Seldon, has spent as much of the time as he could find overflowing from his work for the IEA since 1957 and as Editorial Director from 1959 to 1981.

Throughout this period he has never wavered in arguing that the ambition of politicians to confine their voters to "free" state welfare would founder on the rocks of mounting cost and denial of choice. When the party men have tried to discount argument and even evidence of failure, it was Mr. Seldon who devised the idea of going over their heads by attempting to discover the individual preferences of the British people in the light of priced alternatives. The result was a series of pioneering field studies from 1963 to 1978, whose findings we reported in *Over-Ruled on Welfare,* published in 1979. It found that the politicians were wrong in supposing people would go on paying more taxes for services that gave them no choice.

In this *Occasional Paper* Arthur Seldon tries to take further what some may regard as unconventional and hazardous thinking on the way in which the welfare state may be expected to develop in the remaining years of the twentieth century. Many will find his judgements stimulating, others startling, and some merely speculative. Sceptics would do well to understand that his speculations are based on sober economic analysis projected as trends into the next two decades.

What can hardly be contested is his argument that the welfare state has suppressed the emergence of the developing welfare services that were growing before it was promulgated in the unnatural collectivism of war nearly 40 years ago. Undoubtedly those diverse services would have developed more vigorously if policy had been shaped to encourage rather than supersede the blend of voluntary, commercial, co-operative and charitable endeavour more congenial to a free society.

From this further example of the failure of political conceptions founded on little more than hopes and short-term electoral opportunism, a lesson stands out for students of economics. It is that they should, like Arthur Seldon, follow Sir Dennis Robertson and "stick to their last" in stubbornly analysing the interaction between the supply of and demand for scarce resources which politicians of all parties prefer to regard as inexhaustible. The message for the authors and readers of party manifestos is that the fundamental laws of economics cannot in the end be suspended by political edicts, however impressively embodied in Acts of Parliament.

August 1981 *Ralph Harris*

FOREWORD

Is the welfare state likely to remain unaffected in the next two decades of national and international economic change? Government policy in the short run may appear to be bounded by administrative practicabilities, occupational pressures, public opinion as swayed by spectacular events or disclosures—like the maltreatment of mentally ill patients in National Health Service hospitals—or calculation of electoral gain or loss, especially at a time of the first major political realignment for 50 years.

Below the surface of these more evident influences, less obtrusive widening opportunities for improvement and reform are being made possible by rising incomes and by continual advances in technique. Moreover, these and other changes in the underlying conditions of supply and demand make new forms of welfare—in education, medical care, housing, pensions and lesser services—desirable as well as feasible. Yet they cannot easily be accommodated within the centralised decision-making, based on the centralised financing, of state institutions, even where authority is formally delegated to regional or local agencies.

This *Occasional Paper* speculates on the changes that could be expected in the welfare state in the coming 10 years or more despite zealous doctrinal blessing by academia and the church or stubborn political defence by politicians and administrators. It emphasises two arguments rarely encountered in public—or academic—debate. The first is that the welfare state will meet increasing strain in the attempt to perpetuate itself in the face of market forces that conflict with it. Here the question is not whether it *should* continue into the twenty-first century but whether it *can*—at least within the settled assumptions of British free institutions and personal discretion in family life. I think it cannot.

The second neglected argument is that the true cost of the welfare state to set against its supposed achievements is the array of welfare services it prevented from developing. I argue from the evidence of history, the experience of other countries, and the expectations indicated by economic analysis that this cost far outweighs the benefits, and that the welfare state has been a grievous *cul-de-sac.*

The possibilities or probabilities of alternative welfare developments are less apparent to the politician and the official, the doctor or teacher, preoccupied with the day-to-day task of stretching meagre resources to meet elastic requirements, than to the outside observer sensitive to the tug-of-war between the artificial government-created institutions in welfare and the continual shifts, sometimes imperceptible, sometimes swift, in supply and demand. These market forces can be suppressed for a time, but only at the price of increasing tension and eventually irresistible conflict with the underlying reality of the technical potential and the human aspirations denied.

These speculations on the withering welfare state, and what better services could emerge to replace it, are not remote from reality. The trends compel daily attention. Although market forces can too easily, and for a time, be ignored by government with four- or five-year horizons, we have seen again and again that they have an immediate impact by limiting the scope for short-term and often short-sighted policies. And they indicate the tensions and conflicts that would be postponed to the coming generation if they are persistently ignored.

These tendencies are presented here in the form of an analysis of the continuing reconstruction of welfare that government of any Party or coalition likely in the coming years, whether Conservative or Social Democrat–Liberal, will find increasingly difficult to resist.

August 1981 *Arthur Seldon*

ACKNOWLEDGEMENTS

I should like to thank Gerald Frost, Chairman of the International University of the Open Society, for providing the occasion for these reflections, Ralph Harris for pointed suggestions on a draft, Robert Miller for assistance in assembling the Tables, and Ruth Croxford for easing my work by her exemplary loyal efficiency.

A.S.

I. The Argument: Four Propositions

The main theme of this *Paper* is based on four propositions.

1. The proposition from economic analysis is that the welfare state is withering away because it is being undermined by market forces in changing conditions of supply and demand for education, medicine, housing, pensions and lesser components of "welfare."

2. A proposition from everyday empirical observation is that consumers are increasingly able to pay for, and will therefore demand, better education, medicine, housing and pensions than the state supplies, and that suppliers are increasingly able to provide private alternatives in the market.

3. A proposition from logic is that, if it is to continue, the welfare state will have to resort increasingly to coercion of consumers and of suppliers by repression or suppression of private services.

4. A proposition from political judgement, with support from history, is that the British will not tolerate the required degree of coercion and will devise expedients to escape it, so that the state institutions will wither away.

The secondary theme, though even more important for public policy, is that, as the welfare state recedes, the more variegated and more responsive spontaneous welfare services that have been repressed for 50 years or more will re-emerge in much advanced form.

II. The Changing Market Forces of Supply and Demand

The transition from the welfare state to welfare with individual choice in the market will not be as difficult as politicians, government administrators, academics and journalistic observers suppose. Market forces will prove stronger than political power for ten main reasons, four on the side of demand, six on the side of supply.

First, as incomes rise—despite the high taxation required by the welfare state—more people down the income scale will want differentiated and more personally responsive education, medicine, housing and pensions than the state aims (but fails) to supply equally out of taxation.

Parents will want and be able to pay for more individual schooling. Patients—and their employers—will want prompter medical treatment. The children of council house tenants will want to own their homes (Table I). Everyone will want pensions more suited to his personal requirements.

The only convincing evidence of public preferences—that based on knowledge of the relative *prices* of state and private welfare assembled systematically since 1963[1]—has been ignored by Conservative and Labour Governments. The belated recognition by Messrs. Carlisle and Jenkin, the Ministers in charge, of the desire for choice in education and medicine is a condemnation of Conservative politics—that it has trailed, not anticipated, market forces which facilitate policies they are supposed to further.

Second, the family will increasingly assert the affection of blood relationship and resist incursion of the state by contracting out, even without the advantage of a return of taxes for state services not used (below, pp. 244–45, 260).

Third, the emancipation of women who, more than men, know the advantage of competition from their daily experience in household shopping, will strengthen the family rejection of monopoly in state welfare.

Fourth, the growing realisation that the welfare state is inherently inequitable because the exercise of "voice" in national or local government services is unavoidably unequal (pp. 254–55) will intensify the demand for

Table I. The Post-War Trend in Home Ownership and Council Tenantry

	Private				Government	
	Owner-occupation		Private renting		Council tenantry	
	million	%	million	%	million	%
1951	3.9	31	6.4	52	2.2	17
1971	8.9	52	3.5	18	6.0	31
1976	11.0	53	3.1	15	6.6	32
1980	11.9	55	2.8	13	6.8	32

Source: Nationwide Building Society.

1. Analysed in Ralph Harris and Arthur Seldon, *Over-ruled on Welfare,* Hobart Paperback 13, Institute of Economic Affairs, 1979.

the right to "exit,"[2] to make voice more likely to be heeded and thus to equalise the influence of the politically adroit and the politically maladroit.

Fifth, technical innovation will multiply the private substitutes for state services. Computerised commercial courses on home television, video "books," etc., will supplement formal state schooling. Over-the-counter self-medication, radio services, etc., will replace indifferent, inattentive, tardy state doctoring. Scanners and audio-visual aids will enable private hospitals to supplant state hospitals. Air transport will enable the chronic and acutely ill to receive prompter or more specialised treatment overseas.

Sixth, local units run by local suppliers—doctors, teachers—will be found better than units run by remote officials for the responsive services that the public will want.

Seventh, small units will be found better than large units to generate co-operativeness between managers and staffs.

Eighth, regional, sectarian, racial and other groups will reject standardised state-politicised services. More independent schools will be established by minority non-conformists of teachers and/or parents, more hospitals by locally-oriented doctors and industry, more responsive preventive screening by industry and trade unions through insurance.

Ninth, widening markets will make national welfare states more difficult to segregate. More patients and doctors will move to the EEC for items of medical attention, or permanently. More children will be sent to schools in Scotland, if it wins home rule, Eire, or Europe. "*State*" education, a "*national*" health service, *local* government housing, "*state*" pensions will suffer by international comparison with private alternatives.

Tenth, increasing tax rejection by avoidance, evasion or "avoision"[3] (an amalgam of avoidance and evasion) will undermine the financing of the welfare state. Tax evasion, officially estimated at 7½ per cent of earnings, unofficially (by Professor Edgar Feige[4]) at 15 per cent or more, but conceivably nearer 25 per cent, is a measure of rejection of the welfare state in particular as well as of intrusive over-government in general.

I anticipate that the welfare state will be increasingly replaced by local, voluntary services that develop organically in response to changing circum-

2. Professor A. O. Hirschman analysed these methods of influencing or controlling government suppliers of services in *Exit, Voice, and Loyalty,* Harvard University Press, 1970.

3. *Tax Avoision,* essays by economists, sociologists, Inland Revenue Staff Federation officials (past and present), IEA Readings 22, 1979.

4. "The UK's Unobserved Economy: A Preliminary Assessment," *The Journal of Economic Affairs,* July 1981.

stances of preference or technique in the coming 10 to 20 years. I doubt whether the National Health Service will survive to the end of the century as a comprehensive structure. I expect 40 per cent of the people to be covered by private health insurance and 25 per cent of children to be in private schools by 1995. People in occupational pension schemes will rise from 11½ to 15 million or more. And despite council house subsidies I expect the percentage of owner-occupiers to rise from 55 per cent to near the 80 per cent of New Zealand (the Commonwealth country most like Britain) by 2000, and much sooner if council homes are sold with fewer restrictions on re-sale, and with the prospect of other owner-occupiers rather than tenants as neighbours.

III. False Claims and True Costs

These trends will be reinforced and accelerated as the "welfare" state, which has for too long escaped the critical analysis that all institutions should receive in a free society, comes to be judged by its failures rather than by its claims.

Its escape derives from its name, a model of disarming, mischievous political labelling. Like other question-begging terms that have confused public discussion in Britain, "welfare" implies beneficence in the *motives* of policy-makers that distracts attention from the *consequences* of their policies. "Social" insurance, "national" health service, "public" education, "state" pensions, local "community" housing: all these good words have been employed to insinuate the claim that services provided by the state, or its regional organs, or by local government, are necessarily or essentially for the general good, the common weal, the national interest.

Yet the "welfare" state is not intrinsically different from any other kind of "state"—the nationalised fuel state, or the socialised transport state, or the regional water authority, or the local fire-fighting, refuse-collecting or sewage-disposal authority. They are all run by fallible men spending other people's money in supplying them with services they may not want or that could be supplied better in the market. Politicians and bureaucrats and other government employees are not a breed of men (or women) different from the rest of us who work in the open market. Their motives—a mixture of self-interest and selflessness—are similar. But their exposure to the temptation to benefit themselves at the public expense is even larger.[5] They may be

5. Discussed further below, pp. 256–57.

rewarded for success less than the rest of us, though security and honours may mean more than money, but they are also penalised less for failure. That is why they are *less* responsive and *less* accountable to those they are supposed to serve than are the rest of us who have to sell our services in the competitive market.

It is time the "welfare" state was dissected as sharply as we have long examined the state itself, and as critically as we have examined business activity in the market. And the verdict must be based not only on the evidence produced by the state to describe or defend its activities, for its evidence is necessarily biased—the truth, possibly the whole truth, but weighted and coloured by self-interest. We must interpret its evidence in the light of what *realistic* assumptions about human nature and political institutions—supposedly "representative" government—would lead us to expect. And if the evidence conflicts with what experience and logic suggest, we must discard it even if we have no evidence to the contrary. I contend that the onus of evidence is on the state to demonstrate its superiority over alternatives it obstructs or suppresses, not for its critics to establish its inferiority.[6]

The Real Cost of the Welfare State

Nor can we judge the welfare state by its real or supposed performance. We must judge it by its opportunity cost—*the voluntary, private, organic welfare institutions that the state supplanted and suppressed.* That is a more difficult but a more historical and more pertinent contrast than a comparison between the welfare state as it has developed and the voluntary welfare institutions that had emerged decades earlier under very different economic, social and political conditions.

How voluntary welfare *would* have developed in the market is not how it *had* developed at the stage when each segment of state welfare was introduced by Act of Parliament. Yet this is what the defenders of the welfare state would have us believe. "Look," they say, "how crude education (etc.) was before the welfare state." It is, of course, unhistorical to contrast welfare in the welfare state with the early, immature, partial forms of welfare as they had grown spontaneously a quarter, a half, or a whole century earlier. Real incomes have more than trebled or quadrupled. Individual and family atti-

6. Dr. Digby Anderson, Director of the newly-created Social Affairs Unit, has, with his colleagues, impressively developed the argument that the state has abused its monopoly of rhetoric as well as of money to conceal its deficiencies. (*Breaking the Spell of the Welfare State*, SAU, 1981, *passim.*)

tudes to self-dependence would have matured. The market institutions—charitable, voluntary, occupational, commercial, political—would have multiplied and have been refined, as they have been in Europe, North America and Australasia, and as they are developing in the market oases of Asia—Singapore, Hong Kong and Taiwan. Welfare as it *would* have developed without the welfare state would have been very different from welfare as it *was* in 1870, 1919 or 1946 before the welfare state. The question is whether by now voluntary welfare institutions would have been better or worse. But that is the question to which the defenders of the welfare state never address themselves. I here argue that they would by now have far outshone the standardised, unresponsive, conservative, costly, politically-distorted institutions of the welfare state.

Not least, since all systems are imperfect, we must require the state to demonstrate that it can more readily purge its imperfections than the market can. I will argue that the state loses on this decisive test. Market failure is essentially corrigible. Government failure is incorrigible.

IV. A Century of the Welfare State, 1881–1981

Although there were earlier origins in Britain, the welfare state can be regarded as beginning in Germany, with Kaiser Wilhelm's and Bismarck's introduction of social insurance in 1881. And the very earliest phase revealed the twin motivations of its founders and of its sponsors, managers and employees in the following century. The Kaiser and the Reichskanzler were concerned to remove or alleviate the anxiety of the German worker incapacitated by accident or age in order to outflank the opposition parties. The day-to-day reality of the welfare state has ever since been "compassion" concealing power-seeking, selflessness as a cloak for self-interest, God inscribed on the banner of Mammon. The reality is concealed maltreatment of the aged, open strikes against children in hospital, the cutting of school lunches rather than superfluous staff.

But in the past century God has increasingly been used to serve Mammon as the welfare state changed fundamentally from establishing *minimum* income during the emergencies of ill-health, unemployment and old age to the imposition of *maximum* standards in education, medicine, housing, pensions and other services. The change was fundamental, because maintaining minimum income is not incompatible with free institutions, but imposing maximum standards is. The reason is clear. *Minimum* income does not preclude individual effort to rise above the minimum. *Maximum* standards

A—The Developing Working-Class
Education Repressed by the Welfare State

For many decades, since the early 1800s and even earlier, education had been spreading without government organisation or collective payment by taxes. The first state subsidy to (*private*) education came in 1833. Even from what we should now regard as tiny incomes, parents were finding the few pennies a week to send children to "voluntary" schools (as parents are now doing in low-income developing countries in Africa and Asia). The schools expanded from rather under half a million children in 1818, not long after the Napoleonic wars, to over one and a quarter million in 1834, and they could not all have been the children of the rich. Parents were helped to pay the fees by church and lay organisations. . . . In 1965 an economist turned historian, Professor E. G. West, in a book at first regarded as notorious but now seen as a classic, *Education and the State,* questioned the conventional reading of history . . .

. . . even by 1851 two out of three million working-class children were receiving some kind of daily instruction. It was, of course, short and inadequate by our present-day standards—only four, five or six years, ending around the age of ten. But it was spreading, and by 1870 more children were at school for more years than earlier, and were increasingly leaving later. Moreover, this schooling was entirely voluntary and almost entirely paid for by fees. Even where there was assistance from other sources (private, church or state grants) parents provided most of the money.

Are we surprised? Commonsense and an elementary understanding of human nature should have made us doubt the view that it was not till Forster's Act created "board schools" that "a national system of education" (the supposed purpose of the 1870 Act) was developing . . . too much attention was paid to the spectacular writings of the social novelists such as Dickens, Mrs. Gaskell and Disraeli who attracted attention by reporting and dramatising the exceptional rather than the general . . . Dotheboys Hall was a fictional creation based on a visit to a Yorkshire school in a cold winter in the late 1830s. Dickens, aged twenty-five or twenty-six, went with a false name and wrote up the school in *Nicholas Nickleby* in 1838.

. . . Professor Mark Blaug has found that, at least until very recently, conventional British histories of education largely ignored the evidence on the spread of literacy in the nineteenth century before the coming of state education in 1870. Yet school attendance and literacy in 1850 in England, *almost wholly privately-financed,* exceeded that in the world as a whole a century later.

Charge, pp. 63–4

require state suppression of effort to rise above the maximum. The purpose of the welfare state in day-to-day reality has changed from the prevention of inadequacy to the pretence of equality. And since the effort to create and enforce equality—however unsuccessful—requires the suppression of differences, the welfare state has come into conflict with the free society.

Equality by Coercion: The Misuse of the Welfare State

The British welfare state has logically and ineluctably become the main instrument in the creation of equality by coercion. Its misuse is seen most recently and graphically in the two main benefits in kind that the state provides largely out of taxation—education and medicine. The comprehensive school is the politician's, the bureaucrat's and the social engineer's tool for equalising education. The NHS is his tool for equalising medical care. And he pursues equality regardless of the cost. Moreover, equality in education is pursued at the cost not only of the ability of the family to educate its children as it prefers, but also of the freedom of the innovator to devise new forms of education to improve on the known, the conventional, the established. Yet freedom requires the ability to experiment with the unknown, the nonconformist, the heterodox—to push out ahead of the herd to discover whether the new is *better* than the old. But equality requires that none shall forge ahead unless all can advance equally at the same pace. And that is inimical to freedom—and, of course, in the end, to advance itself.

How far the attempt to create equality has almost destroyed freedom for consumers and suppliers is indicated by its virtual suppression of the growth in independent education. Few people in Britain would suppose that education can be supplied in any other way than by the state. This is the assumption rarely questioned by anyone. Yet how many know that most working-class children were at school, and that their parents were paying fees, long before the beginnings of state education in 1870? (Box A, opposite.)

No wonder the welfare state is stagnant relatively to less centralised, more flexible systems of welfare where change is welcomed and rewarded. No wonder that, while the British NHS is slow to innovate in methods of organisation and financing, or even to emulate the pioneering advances in other countries, medical care in the USA displays the widest variety and the most advanced innovations in financing and organising medical service—in health maintenance organisations, pre-paid group practices, and other experimental techniques unknown in Britain because they would disturb the smooth running of the centralised NHS.

The irony is that equality could have been approached much more securely, even if less dramatically, by encouraging innovation free of state control and allowing people to learn from personal, local experience in the market which techniques to employ and which to discard. Apart from the spectacular exceptions, grotesquely inflated by the critics, there is more rapidly developing equality in access to medical care of a high and rising quality in the USA than there is to the mediocre medical care of the British National Health Service. The incidence of bankruptcy to pay "catastrophic" medical bills has been wildly distorted. The poor and the aged have been provided for by Medicaid and Medicare, though not too wisely. The troughs of American medicine have been caricatured by supposedly responsible British observers but the peaks have been irresponsibly suppressed.

The higher expenditure, as a proportion of GNP, in countries with more scope for private insurance than in Britain (Table II), indicates the readiness to pay more in premiums for services that are linked more or less to the quantity or quality of medical care received than in taxes where, by definition, no such link is permitted since, as in the NHS, it would violate the principle that medical care received should bear no link with payment (by taxes) at all.

The lower figure for Britain is sometimes quoted as evidence that the NHS is more effective in avoiding waste than are other financing systems. I very much doubt that inference. Costs tend to become inflated whenever payment is by third parties outside the doctor and patient, that is, by an insurance organisation or by the state. Clearly where "someone else" is paying, doctors and patients can indulge in conscious or unconscious collusion in a longer stay in hospital, a more renowned surgeon, a more expensive drug, an unnecessary "frill." But third party payment—by the state—takes place in the NHS where it is the very essence, the pride and joy, of the system.

There is no comparison between the two systems. In the NHS, however high collusion sends costs escalating, the patient does not have to pay in higher taxes. But in insurance financing the patient with persistently high bills is much more easily noticed, and can be made to pay higher premiums to discourage collusion. And in other countries, not least the USA, there is a constant search for methods of avoiding inflated costs by co-insurance and other refinements.

Nor is the associated argument, that the state in the NHS keeps costs down better than insurance systems, much more convincing or decisive. That the state *can* keep costs down because it controls the purse-strings is a truism. It keeps an eye, for example, on exceptionally high prescribing costs. It does not follow that it *will* keep costs down by avoiding the escalation

Table II. International Comparison of Expenditure on Medical Care (per cent of GNP)

	Hauser and Koch[a]				EEC Report[b]			
Countries	1965	1970	1975	1977	1966	1970	1975	OECD Study[c]
Belgium			8.4				6.2	5.4[d]
Denmark					3.8	4.6	6.1	6.5[d]
Federal Republic of Germany		5.9	8.8		4.8	5.2	8.0	7.0[d]
Finland	5.0	5.8	6.7	7.4				6.4[e]
France					5.1	5.5	6.7	7.1[d]
Great Britain	4.1	4.7	5.7	5.8	4.3	4.6	5.4	5.5[e]
Italy					3.2	3.9	5.2	6.1[d]
The Netherlands		7.1[g]	8.2	8.4		6.3	8.4	7.6[g]
Switzerland		5.1[f]	6.9	7.9				5.5[f]
United States	5.9	7.2	8.6	8.8				7.5[d]

[a] Institute of Public Finance and Fiscal Law, Saint Gall, Switzerland.

[b] Current costs only (public and private). B. Abel-Smith and A. Maynard, *The Organisation, Financing and Cost of Health Care in the European Community,* Social Politic Series No. 36, Commission of the European Communities, Brussels, 1979.

[c] *Public Expenditure on Health,* OECD Studies on Resource Allocation, No. 4, July 1977, pp. 10 and 26.

[d] 1974. [e] 1975. [f] 1973. [g] 1972.

Source: A. Brandt, B. Horisberger and W. P. von Wartburg (eds.), *Cost-Sharing in Health Care,* Proceedings of the International Seminar on Sharing of Health Care Costs (Wolfsberg, Switzerland, March 1979), Springer-Verlag, Berlin, Heidelberg, New York, 1980.

caused through collusion and confining costs to the ideal amounts. That inference would require the unrealistic assumption that politicians are philosopher kings and officials omniscient bureaucrats. Since both are ordinary fallible humans concerned about their votes, their jobs and their incomes; since, moreover, they have "monopsony" power as virtually sole buyers of doctors' services, medical appliances and prescriptions, the likelihood is that they will depress costs *too* far and push them *below* the ideal amount as determined by doctors' advice and patients' preference. And that is the essential explanation of the relatively low figure for Britain.

Political, Medical and Economic Ideals

Moreover, although it cannot be claimed that expenditure under insurance is ideal, since patients may be guided by doctors who advise medically unnecessary treatments, there is even more uncertainty about expenditure under taxation. The only judgement that can safely be made about the UK's 5.5 to 6.0 per cent of GNP is that it is the *politically* ideal proportion. It is decided by politicians actuated by short-term motivations of election or re-election. It has only an uncertain and remote link with the *medically* ideal expenditure, as doctors would like, and even more remote with the *economically* ideal expenditure as the public would wish, and as it subconsciously influences by its awareness of "opportunity costs," since money can also be spent on education, housing, or anything else.

Not least, the power of doctors as "agents" of patients to mislead them into unnecessary expenditure is overdone. Patients are not at the mercy of mercenary medicine men, except *in extremis,* emergency or crisis; even then their families may be available to speak for them. On other occasions, which are many, possibly a majority, patients and their families can make choices between alternative treatments, comprising not only physical elements (the surgeon's skill, etc.) but also psychic aspects that may be decisive in survival and recovery (timing, links with family, etc.).

What is true is that the NHS has virtually destroyed awareness of the possibility of choice, both within the NHS and between it and private medicine. And that is the essence of the subservience of the patient to the doctor. It resides not in the professional or technical supremacy of the doctor but in the inability of the patient to escape from the occasional rogue elephant who may exploit "the agency relationship."

That is why, although all systems are vulnerable to abuse, the patient's best defence lies in a multiplicity of exits that can be built into health insurance

Table III. Medical Care, UK and USA: Doctors, Nurses, etc. Available for Each Daily Staffed Bed

	UK (NHS)	USA (All Systems)
1948	—	0.67
1950	0.52	0.73
1955	0.53	0.81
1960	0.66	0.96
1965	0.72	1.15
1970	0.77	1.57
1975	?	2.06
1980	?	?

Source: C. M. Lindsay, *National Health Issues: The British Experience,* Roche, New Jersey, 1980.

Note: British observers usually contrast the NHS with medical care in the USA, which they claim has horrors (bankruptcies to pay medical bills, neglect after accidents until proof of insurance cover is produced, etc.). These extremes are exaggerated—they are good "copy" for zealous missionaries. The *trend* in the common standard generally available in the USA is rarely emphasised. It is much better than in the UK. The *absolute* difference may be due partly to differences in income, though even that cannot be wholly allowed since the lower income in the UK is partly the result of the higher taxes made necessary by the very NHS. But the *trend* abstracts from this difference in absolute income. Even then this Table shows that one indicator of quality of service—the number of doctors, etc., per hospital patient—is far superior in the USA. In the NHS it rose by less than 50 per cent from 1950 to 1970: in the USA by 1975 it almost trebled, so that the rate of increase was three times as fast.

and not in the Hippocratic oath or other vain devices for ensuring "professional conduct" or in the power of the state, as in the NHS, to discipline offenders by controlling standards or numbers, the worst system of all.

The choice is thus not between the over-spending of insurance (Europe, North America, Australia) and the optimal spending in tax systems (UK). It is between *over*-spending and *under*-spending. Who shall decide? Politicians, public officials, or people? An indication of the difference is in Table III, which shows that there are now probably twice as many doctors, dentists, midwives and nurses per hospital patient in the USA as in the UK. Is that what the British people want?

V. Voluntary Welfare Would Have Developed Better Than the State

Britain could by now have developed welfare services with no avoidable infringement of individual, family or innovator freedom if it had allowed supply to respond more freely to demand, and if demand had been allowed and encouraged to bid for new, untried forms of supply—as it has been in Australia and elsewhere. The market is often very imperfect, but perfection is approached by continual refinement. It is part of the case for freedom to choose between alternative competing sources of welfare that the process is the chicken-and-egg without conscious beginning or end but evolving organically in response to unforeseeable change in the conditions of supply and demand.

If the state had not been misused to provide education, medicine, housing and pensions, they would have evolved in response to changing individual requirements and technical possibilities—demand and supply—as in other personal, family and housing requirements: books, over-the-counter medicaments, house furnishings, and a multitude of channels for saving. The state would have had two main functions. It would have had to provide the "public goods" element which cannot be provided by the interplay of supply and demand because people who would refuse to pay for their share in the hope of a "free ride" cannot be refused by exclusion or because the cost of making them pay exceeds the revenue. The familiar examples are the environmental and preventive health services, which the state was beginning to develop in the 1840s and 1850s long before the welfare state was fabricated. And the state would have had to re-circulate income to enable all to pay in the market for the goods or services considered minimal. This again is what it began to do with grants for education in 1833 and old-age pensions in 1908. The state encouraged re-circulation of income in the family by tax concessions in covenants and in private efforts by concessions to charities, but it could have gone much further without socialising income through the state.

What Should Have Been Done: Income Redistribution (Cash/Vouchers, Means Tests, Charges)

In retrospect we can now see what should have been done in the past 50 years to anticipate the argument for a welfare state to supply massive services in kind. For this is where the most damage has been done. It is the services in kind—education and medical care—that are the fount of its objectionable elements of political influence, bureaucracy, paternalism, and not least its destruction of choice in markets, which other English-speaking countries have preserved, in addition to treating their poor better than we do.

First, the state should much sooner on a larger scale have redistributed income in the form of purchasing power—generalised in cash or earmarked by voucher. The case for redistribution by social benefits in kind would not have gathered force even in the opportunistic democracy developed by the widening franchise. And the conflict between welfare and freedom could have been largely avoided.

Second, all social benefits should have been related closely to individual circumstances, not least the capacity to earn and the amount of earnings. But instead of the sensitive, humane refinement of means tests as measures of entitlement to social benefits, the welfare state has developed benefits distributed universally irrespective of circumstances, requirements or preferences—all in the name of equality. The massive superiority of selective benefits is an intellectual battle that has now been won, but the victory came too late to prevent the creation of monstrous universal benefits that will require grievous effort to repeal.

Third, insofar as the state, for administrative convenience or economies in large-scale supply, provided services in kind, it should have financed them not by taxation from non-users as well as from users, but by charges from all users according to the extent of their use, with low incomes "topped up" to enable the relatively poor to pay. Instead, the welfare state has grown without the information on cost that could have been created by pricing, and without the variation in use according to individual circumstances and preferences that would have distributed resources most effectively with the minimum of avoidable coals to Newcastle in the elaborate structure of cancelling benefits and taxes.

How far welfare benefits are cancelled by taxes and in reality are paid for by the recipients ("beneficiaries") is rarely analysed by welfare state advocates. The best available figures, assembled by government in annual surveys of household expenditure, suggest that most families pay for most or all of their "free" (or subsidised) benefits in cash or kind. The average British family comprises two adults and two to three children. In a recent year (1977) their average original gross income was £5,083. Their cash benefits and the value of the NHS, state education and welfare foods they were calculated as receiving (on average) came to £1,171. Their taxes, direct (mostly on income) and indirect (on purchases, etc.), amounted to £1,797. Thus they ended £626 *worse* off at £4,457, their final income (Table IV).

This was the family with average income. But the welfare state is supposed to redistribute income to the poor. Ten per cent of families had gross incomes of £2,923, much lower than the average. Their benefits looked large—£1,194. But that gingerbread had most of its gilt knocked off by taxes—£887, leaving only £307 to add to the final income. Still worse, a household with

Table IV. Tax-Benefit Balance-Sheet in 1977:
Households of 2 Adults and 1–4 Children

	(Based on a sample of 1,924 households)		
	Average	2nd decile	3rd decile
Original Income	**£5,083**	**£2,923**	**£3,551**
Add Benefits			
Cash	283	321	190
Education	507	481	413
NHS	326	338	332
Welfare Foods	55	54	41
	+1,171	+1,194	+ 976
Less Taxes			
Direct	994	328	597
Indirect (net)	803	559	682
	– 1,797	– 887	– 1,279
Net Gain/Loss	– 626	+ 307	– 303
Final Income	**£4,457**	**£3,230**	**£3,248**

Source: "The Effects of Taxes and Benefits on Household Income, 1977," in *Economic Trends,* HMSO, January 1979.

gross income not so much higher at £3,551, still a long way below the average, had £976 added in benefits but had to pay £1,279 for the welfare state (and other) benefits, leaving it £303 *worse* off. (Figures for other households are discussed in the IEA book that reviews the Harris and Seldon field studies going back to 1963.[7])

The importance of the Harris/Seldon researches is that, by introducing price for the first time to my knowledge in such field studies, they establish a trend even where the enquiries were incomplete or defective because they were the first of their kind. The response by people in all socio-economic sub-groups showed a fluctuating but steady increase in the desire for a choice in education and medical care by the recipients to the offer of a

7. *Over-ruled on Welfare,* Hobart Paperback No. 13, IEA, 1980.

voucher worth a portion of the cost of private education or of insurance for private medicine. The demand for a choice in education, measured by acceptance of a voucher worth two-thirds of day school fees and requiring the recipient to add the last third, rose from 30 per cent in 1965 to 51 per cent in 1978. At this rate it would rise to 66 per cent by 1988. The demand for a choice in medical care, measured by acceptance of a voucher worth two-thirds of the cost of private insurance, rose from 30 per cent to 57 per cent in this period and at this rate would reach 77 per cent in 1988.

Two observations remain. The figures do not cover all benefits or taxes, and they are a "still" rather than a moving picture over the family lifetime. The remedy is for government to assemble more complete statistics to cover all possible aspects. But however complete the statistics, they will overstate the extent to which the welfare state redistributes income because it fails to ensure equal access to people with varying cultural bargaining power.[8] The statistics also therefore understate the extent to which people with lower incomes pay for their "free" benefits.

Even the degree of equality it may appear to have achieved on paper is measured by measurable *quantitative* indicators, like the average value of state education or the NHS that an individual can be calculated as having derived in a year. But the statistics do not assess the *qualitative* aspects (waiting, queuing, choice of school or doctor, personal attention, timing, and so on, p. 252) that statistics cannot measure.

What Stopped the Classical Market Economy in Welfare?

Why were these reforms not introduced in the last 50 to 100 years? I put this proposition to a distinguished historian of economic thought, Professor T. W. Hutchison, not so long ago. He put these intriguing but neglected questions to himself:

- "Could . . . additional tax-revenue have been elicited from the taxpayers of the day to finance freedom of choice in health and education . . . ?
- "Could voucher schemes have been used to 'induce our future masters to learn their letters'? [The answer is yes, they almost were—below, p. 247]

8. Discussed below, pp. 255–56.

- "... Would the climate of influential opinion at that time have excluded such a latter-day, libertarian idea as, then, politically unrealistic?"[9]

And, although not unsympathetic to the approach to welfare through freedom, he concluded:

> ... It may be indulging in a kind of rather pretentious, hindsighted over-optimism to suppose that, in the climate of the day, the rates of taxation and the freedoms of the pre-1867[10] classical market economy could have been preserved.

The decisive question for our times is whether the welfare state was *inevitable.* Was it the *only* way to deal with insecurity of income in emergencies or with lack of access to welfare services?

But the answer is not elusive. If the consequences of the welfare state had been foreseen, if the price it demanded in massive taxation, oppressive bureaucracies, the suppression of individual choice, the invasion of the family, the consolidation of monopoly "public sector" trade unions, and the restrictions on innovation had been foreseen, would even the beneficiaries have preferred the state to provide welfare out of taxation rather than keep their earnings and pay for welfare that responded to their requirements—because they could escape from suppliers who failed to satisfy? Above all, would the welfare state have been preferred if it had been foreseen that, once established, it would resist unforeseen changing conditions and would require an administrative earthquake to dislodge?

Classical Economists Warned the Politicians

It is now forgotten that some far-sighted men saw the dangers and warned the politicians against easy but short-sighted solutions. The economists Nassau Senior, John Stuart Mill (despite his socialist aberration a priest of liberty), Alfred Marshall and others were better counsellors to the Victorians than the politicians.

> We may look forward to the time when the labouring population may be safely entrusted with the education of their children; ... the assistance and

9. Professor T. W. Hutchison, "The Changing Intellectual Climate in Economics," in *The Emerging Consensus . . . ?*, Hobart Paperback No. 14, Institute of Economic Affairs, 1981, p. 36.

10. The year of the widening of the British franchise under the second Reform Act.

superintendence . . . of the Government for that purpose . . . [is] . . . only a means of preparing the labouring classes for a better, but remote state of things . . . in the latter part of the twentieth century . . . when that assistance and superintendence shall no longer be necessary.

Nassau Senior, 1861

. . . the mode in which the government can most surely demonstrate the sincerity by which it intends the greatest good of its subjects is by doing the things which are made incumbent upon it by the helplessness of the public, in such a manner as shall tend not to increase and perpetuate but to correct that helplessness . . .

. . . government aid . . . should be so given as to be as far as possible a course of education for the people in the art of accomplishing great objects by individual energy and voluntary co-operation.

John Stuart Mill, 1848.

. . . universal pensions . . . do not contain . . . the seeds of their own disappearance. I am afraid that, if started, they would tend to become perpetual.

I regard poverty as a passing evil in the progress of man; and I should not like any institution started which did not contain in itself the causes which would make it shrivel up as the causes of poverty shrivelled up.

Alfred Marshall, 1893

But the politicians were not all myopic. Even the superiority of topping-up low incomes over services in kind to all and sundry was known to them. W. E. Forster, Gladstone's Minister of Education, knew about vouchers though his 1870 Bill called them "tickets."[11]

The results of the welfare state were not foreseen by the politicians 50 or 100 years ago, when they could have been avoided. But they are evident today, when the desire to reform the welfare state is increasingly strong, but the administrative inclination to reform it is weak.[12]

In 1981 the question is: now that these results are increasingly self-evident, how much more rapidly could the welfare state yield to market forces that

11. Professor E. G. West recounts, in *Education and the State,* 2 ed., 1971, introductory essay, pp. xvii–xix, the opposition to the idea enshrined in the Bill's first draft that poor parents should pay money for their children's education in the form of a "ticket" (voucher).

12. The built-in resistances to reform have developed despite the general absence of evidence for the efficacy of state welfare discussed by Dr. Digby Anderson and others in *The Ignorance of Social Intervention,* Croom Helm, 1980.

would reform it to meet consumer preference and to make better use of technical advance?

VI. The Wrong Turnings

To see what must now be done to enable the welfare services to respond more promptly to change, we have to see where the wrong turnings were taken.

. . . in Education, 1870

In 1870, despite spontaneous development in voluntary schooling that served three-quarters of all children, the Gladstone Government took a wrong turning by filling in the gaps not by supplying purchasing power to enable the families of the remaining quarter to pay for schooling but by introducing a framework in which it was eventually provided "free" for all, and, of course, taxing them to pay for it. From that wrong turning we have arrived at state education that can be used to create an exclusive state monopoly in which 95 per cent of the children are virtually locked in because the cost of choice in schooling has been put beyond them by the compulsion to pay taxes for schooling they may not prefer. What began as a minimum is developing into a maximum. What began plausibly as social justice for the poor has degenerated into coercion more of the poor than of the rich.

. . . in Housing, 1919

In 1919 Parliament required local authorities to build housing to let at rents subsidised by taxes because the spontaneous growth in home ownership and renting since the nineteenth century (Table V, Box B) had been reduced to a trickle by the 1914–18 wartime rent controls which discouraged post-war investment in home-building. Instead of removing the rent restrictions, which would have restored private home-building to sell or let, the Lloyd George Coalition Government took a wrong turning which has in our day led to one family in three, 6½ out of 18½ million, occupying local government-owned housing that has virtually destroyed their inclination to choose their homes, to move to better jobs, to improve their condition. And no government of any party to this day has had the wit either to remove rent restrictions or to make rent subsidies portable[13] so that at least people are

13. This original proposal was examined by the late Professor F. G. Pennance in *Choice in Housing*, IEA, 1968.

Table V. Private Housing for the Poor, 1875–1910
(Homes and residential shops under £20 in annual value, Great Britain, in thousands)

	Total	Five-year increases
1875	3,922	—
1880	4,271	349
1885	4,589	318
1890	4,891	302
1895	5,126	235
1900	5,510	384
1905	5,935	425
1910	6,368	433

Source: Abstract of British Historical Statistics.

Note: This rate of expansion can be contrasted historically with Mr. Harold Macmillan's claim to a Conservative conference in the 1950s to build 300,000 houses in a year, council and private.

not discouraged from moving in response to industrial change, even if to another government-owned home. What began as wartime alleviation of housing costs to avoid inflationary wage demands has become a grievous peacetime drag on the economy. And the present Government's half-hearted efforts in selling council homes will take a century to dispose of them.[14]

. . . in Pensions, 1925

Since 1925, Conservative and Labour Governments have drawn every man and woman in employment into accumulating a pension with the state in "social insurance" to provide income in retirement. Yet on each occasion it could instead have encouraged the spontaneous development of pension saving through friendly societies, trade unions, provident non-profit organisations or insurance companies that had been growing for 60 years (Table VI).[15] The freedom of 100 per cent of the British working people to save and invest for old age in the ways they prefer, much more suited to their requirements, has been unnecessarily restricted by government. What began as apparent collective forethought has become collective conformity and individ-

14. Some 90,000 out of the 6 million were sold in the first 1½ years to the end of 1980.

15. Dr. Charles Hanson outlines the now-too-often forgotten growth in voluntary insurance that was all but suppressed by state ("social") insurance in the welfare state ("Welfare Before the Welfare State," in *The Long Debate on Poverty,* IEA, 2nd edition, 1974).

B—Working-Class Home Ownership in the Nineteenth Century

The spread of home ownership among the working classes, like their urge to send their children to school, or to insure for sickness or old age, began before the mid-nineteenth century. It was, by late twentieth-century standards, on a very small scale, though it is not recorded as prominently as the poor conditions from which the social novelists drew material for their dramatic fictions. Yet it was more important than the poor conditions that were gradually improved, because it was a pointer to what developed later in home ownership and private personal or occupational pension saving, though not in education and medical care where the state repressed further development.

Government inquiries, some of whose members were sceptics, "were given figures of home ownership which clearly surprised some," says a University of Hull historian.[16] In 1871 the Royal Commission on Friendly and Benefit Building Societies was told that 13,000 Birmingham working men owned their homes and were buying them out of average wages of some £1 10s. a week. In 1884 the Royal Commission on Housing was told that the Leeds Permanent Benefit Building Society had enabled 7,000 working men to buy their homes.

In 1873 Thomas Wright wrote in *Our New Masters* (a reference to the newly enfranchised working men):

> The aim of the great majority of the best members of the working classes—the cleverest, most energetic, and persevering men—is to raise themselves out of those classes. Numbers of them succeed in this aim,

ual frustration, accepted as inevitable because the alternatives have been forgotten. Even the great Churchill was misled. He described national insurance as "bringing the *magic* of averages to the rescue of millions." The tragic truth revealed by experience is that the *fetish* of averages has been used by the state to plague the untypical individual. And we are all increasingly untypical. (Box C.)

. . . and in Medicine, 1948

In 1948, in an act of political "vandalism," aided and abetted by senior doctors, the state almost destroyed the developing varied structure of spon-

16. David Rubinstein, *Victorian Homes*, David & Charles, 1974, pp. 215 *et seq.*, from which these references are quoted.

> become in a greater or lesser degree capitalists, or get into positions in which their interests are identified with those of capital rather than those of labour. Still larger numbers—numbers so large that they form a considerable section of the working classes—though they do not rise out of their class, become in their endeavour to do so, comparatively rich men—have money in banks, and shares in co-operative and building societies, and are as watchful against and strongly opposed to anything that is alleged will tend to interfere with "the sacredness of private property" or lessen dividends, as are any of the great capitalists.

Two years later Samuel Smiles, who it may be said looked for such evidence of self-help, wrote in *Thrift:*

> There are also exceptional towns and villages in Lancashire where large sums of money have been saved by the operatives for buying or building comfortable cottage dwellings. Last year Padiham saved about fifteen thousand pounds for this purpose, although its population is only about 8,000. Burnley has also been very successful. The Building Society there has 6,600 investors, who saved last year £160,000 or an average of twenty four pounds for each investor. The members consist principally of mill operatives, miners, mechanics, engineers, carpenters, stonemasons, and labourers. They also include women, both married and unmarried. Our informant states that "great numbers of the working classes have purchased houses in which to live. They have likewise bought houses as a means of investment . . ."

taneous medical activity from voluntary hospitals to Friendly Society health insurance that had grown up in response to personal, industrial and local circumstances, requirements and preferences, and replaced it by a bureaucratic, monopolistic monolith dignified by the familiar euphemism—the "national" health service. The voluntary structure was, of course, imperfect, untidy, uneven, and costly, but it had been growing up in response to the circumstances of patients and employers and the capabilities of local doctors and nurses from *below.* The state imposed a strait-jacket from the centre devised by politicians, bureaucrats and suppliers from *above.* It made the same mistake as in education, housing and pensions: instead of filling in the gaps it all but destroyed the developing organic growth and replaced an imperfect but gradually improving structure by an even more imperfect "service" that lacks the built-in improvement mechanism of competition yet resists reform. What began plausibly as mercy for the sick has degenerated into mer-

Table VI. The Growth in Nineteenth-Century Self-Help Private Saving

	Friendly Societies[1]		Societies and Savings Banks[2] (£ million)	Life Assurance Companies[3] (£ million)
	Members (million)	Funds (£ million)		
1891	4.2	22.7	213	180
1899	5.2	32.7	340	257
1909	6.2	48.2	460	379

Source: C. G. Hanson, "Welfare Before the Welfare State," *op. cit.*
[1] Registered in Great Britain and Ireland.
[2] Figures assembled by the Registrar of Friendly Societies.
[3] Life and annuity funds of Ordinary and Industrial Life Companies, UK.

cenary militancy by the unions of medical suppliers, from doctors to doormen. What began as justice for the underdog is dissolving into the hindmost for the old and the mentally ill who cannot attend conferences, move resolutions or horse-trade in smoke-filled rooms in Blackpool or Brighton.

VII. The Flaws of the Welfare State Are the Flaws of the Political State

These wrong turnings have created the welfare state that now has all the vices of the state itself. The political state has seven deadly sins, and the welfare state displays all of them.

First, it is based on ignorance of the preferences of consumers—parents, patients, home-occupiers, pensioners—because it has no machinery for gathering information from individuals. In the NHS the so-called "representative" structure the state has created in local, area and regional councils, boards and authorities is a charade. In practice they are run by political ideologues, medical activists, trade union manipulators and occupational lobbyists, who are good at committee management and behind-the-scenes bargaining.

Second, ignorance provokes inefficiency. Health indicators may seem to show that the NHS does not perform worse than other more varied health systems overseas. But they measure only the measurable. They do not reflect the immeasurable elements that count with the patient: the waiting and queueing, the choice of doctor or hospital, or the timing of treatment, the responsiveness of doctors and nurses. Because the NHS can be judged only by

C—Developing Private Pensions and Their Repression by the Welfare State

If it had been known around 1900 that incomes would treble in half a century, other arrangements might have been devised for helping people who had not been able to save for their old age. It is now debatable whether state pensions were the best way of helping needy old people, or whether they are suited to a system of representative institutions . . . their history shows that . . . they have brought disadvantages that were not foreseen when they were introduced. These defects require urgent scrutiny before we embark on another 50 years of pensioneering.

State pensions provided wholly by the taxpayer were followed in 1925 by the system that began as subsidised compulsory national insurance for retirement but has degenerated into another system of universal state benefit financed almost wholly by the taxpayer. That because of rising incomes he is increasingly subsidising himself is an added irony.

The discussion of pensions in Britain has been overlaid by political propaganda, sociological subtlety and actuarial expertise. It is time to go back to first principles. In a society which values personal liberty, which increasingly yields incomes high enough to permit saving for retirement, and in which people are capable of apportioning income between working life and retirement, arrangements will as far as possible be left to individuals. A man will be free to decide whether to spend most of his income on himself or his family while young enough to enjoy it and leave the future to take care of itself, or to live modestly while he earns and look forward to years of carefree ease when he retires. This is an intimate, elemental, personal decision, and a free society will not lightly tamper with it.

. . . formal pension schemes, based on funds built up from employees' and/or employers' contributions, . . . spread slowly after the 1914–18 war. The first large scheme insured with a life (assurance) office was installed by the Gramophone Co. (now Electrical & Musical Industries) in 1930; it was administered by the Legal and General Assurance Society. Yet by 1936 only 1.8 million people had been covered. After the war high taxation of profits, the tax concessions on contributions to pension schemes, and high labour turnover combined to produce much faster growth. By 1951 6.3 million and by 1958 8.75 million people were covered. The figure now is probably not far short of 10 million, comprising about 8 million men (out of 16 million employed) and 2 million women (out of 8 million), more than half in life office schemes.

Pensions for Prosperity, 1960

quantitative indicators, it puts quantity before quality.[17] In this sense the NHS is the worst medical system in the world outside the Communist/Socialist countries.

Third, the welfare state replaced choice for consumers between competing suppliers by monopoly from which there is no escape, except at a cost that the rich can bear better than the poor. Indeed, its logic, as Mr. Neil Kinnock for Labour and Mrs. Shirley Williams (though not for the Social Democrats) consistently demonstrate in education, is to close, bolt and bar all exits.

Fourth, the welfare state, contrary to the claims of its sponsors, becomes unjust, inequitable, unrepresentative, unaccountable and inegalitarian. For "voices" are innately unequal because they derive from accent, temperament, character, cultural background, social origins, occupational links, political skills, individual adroitness and influence. And all these inherited or acquired qualities are virtually impossible to equalise. They are clearly more difficult to even up than are the differences in income or wealth that determine access in the market. The result in the NHS is indicated in Table VII.

Fifth, the welfare state creates social conflict because the distribution of its benefits is decided by activists elected by majorities—or even minorities—in both national and local government. The schools, the health services and the housing of London's citizens are decided by a small *coterie* of activists in the Greater London Council. The welfare services of the minority of Roman Catholics in Northern Ireland are decided by the majority of Protestants. The family lives of the Scots and Welsh are decided by the English. And there is other subjection by sex, occupation, race.[18] Social conflict is intensified by the welfare state because it uses the political process to decide the use of resources, through "representative institutions" that are in practice controlled by *un*representatives who happen to be politically endowed, dexterous or cunning. Mrs. Williams entitled her political testament *Politics Is for People.*[19] She may wish to "involve" all the people to "participate" in "democratic" decision-making, but her title omits the key word that explains the *failure* of the welfare state—"politics is for *political* people." Par-

17. This familiar flaw of state institutions is demonstrated mathematically for the NHS by Professor C. M. Lindsay in *National Health Issues: The British Experience,* Hoffmann–La Roche, Nutley, New Jersey, USA, 1980.

18. A. Seldon, "Change by Degree or by Convulsion," in *The Coming Confrontation,* Hobart Paperback 12, IEA, 1978.

19. Penguin, 1981.

Table VII. "Equality" of Access to Medical Care in the NHS

Socio-economic group		Ratio of expenditure per person reporting ill (V and VI = 1.00)
I and II:	Professionals, employers and managers	1.41
III:	Intermediate and junior non-manual	1.33
IV:	Skilled manual and own account non-professional	1.13
V and VI:	Semi- and unskilled manual	1.00

Source: Julian LeGrand, "The Distribution of Public Expenditure: The Case of Health Care," *Economica*, 1978.

Note: The calculations presented in this Table by an economist at the University of Sussex suggest the differences in cultural power that determine access to medical care. The text in this IEA *Paper* argues that they are more difficult to remove than differences in income would be as the market in medical care developed in Britain. Professionals, employers and managers were found by Professor LeGrand to have almost half as much again spent on them on average than was spent (in 1972) on semi-skilled and manual workers. In spite of the efforts to redistribute central expenditure from the richer to the poorer regions through the resources allocation working party (RAWP) and other devices, I doubt whether these cultural differences have been much reduced. If these methods to equalise expenditure do succeed, new ways will be found to restore the differences.

ties are organised, managed and directed by the politically inclined, the politically active, the politically adroit, the politically artful. But most people are not, least of all the ordinary people, the working classes. In the state they lose to the few who are, who can argue their way into, or buy homes near, the best state schools. In the market the ordinary people are, or can be made, equal in status as consumers.

"Representative" Government Does Not Represent the Individual

The notion that representative government and parliamentary democracy represent, or can represent, the widely diverging opinions of the public in general, and can therefore be made accountable to it, is most simply reflected in the argument of Mr. Anthony Wedgwood Benn and his associates who, it seems, are taking increasing control of the Labour Party. It is difficult to believe that they do not know of the arguments of sympathetic sociologists like Professor Brian Abel-Smith and others who have long argued that the middle classes were doing better out of the welfare state than the working classes. This is one of the few aspects of the working of the NHS on which

I have agreed with Professor Abel-Smith, and I must accept that he was among the first to draw the attention of others to it. But it is now common ground between both academic defenders and critics of the NHS. And it must be evident that the same inequality is revealed in access to state education and to council housing and, I would argue, to virtually every other government service, national or local, to which access is obtained by argument, influence or by buying into it indirectly (as in buying houses near the best state schools). It therefore cannot be long before it must also be recognised and accepted by politicians. And those who do not recognise it, and who go on pretending that equal access can be ensured by "representatives" or by officials or by their own sort, will before long discover that the members of the public who have experience of the differences in access will remind them of it at the polling booths.

This is the flaw in the very conception of the "representative" government and "democratic" institutions of the Western world, the very reason why "politics" should *not* be used except where it is unavoidable, in "public goods" (where it is very defective). The "politics-is-for-people" approach leads directly to the argument of Mr. Ian Mikardo that the politically active *should* have more influence than the inactive. In other words, if the machinery is not suited to most of the people, too bad. "One man, one vote" is right for democracy, but not for the welfare state. The "inactive" will form the new underlings with one vote apiece, but one "active" man, two (or nine, or ninety) votes. This is the two nations of the welfare state that its progenitors did not tell its beneficiaries, or perhaps failed to see (or failed to look?).

Sixth, the welfare state rests on coercion. It empowers majorities to coerce minorities, groups and individuals. It even empowers minorities to coerce majorities. Thus, by a shift of several per cent of votes in the local London elections last April, the intimate, daily, personal, family lives of millions have been invaded by a handful of ideologues. That is an unfailing recipe for discord and rejection.

Abuse and Corruption

Seventh, the disarming description "welfare" must not be allowed to conceal the truth that the welfare state harbours the same opportunities and incitements to abuse and even corruption as the non-welfare state in fuel or transport, or as local government in all its rag-bag of activities. A man or woman does not become a saint by being appointed a "public" official, nor by being moved from the Ministry of Defence to the Department of Education and Science, the Department of Health and Social Security, or the Department of the Environment. It is unrealistic to suppose that men of middling income but with the power to dispense massive contracts that can mean profit or loss, economic life or death, will always resolutely resist the temptation that disfigures all economic systems where decisions are made by officials. If the inescapable conclusion that the welfare state, national and local, must be tainted or riddled with corruption is denied, it is for the Departments of State to lay the evidence before vigilantes of probity in public life manned not merely by independents but by sceptics who suspect from first principles that it is.

The power-hungry, the bureaucrat, the technocrat, the ideologue and the autocrat find openings in all systems. That system is best, which roots them out soonest. The openings are most common, and last longest (because the inducements to close them are weakest) in the state, not least in welfare.

Architects were given their heads in council high-rise blocks more than they would have been in private home-building.

Medical technocrats, like the Northern surgeon who preached 1,000-bed or even 5,000-bed hospitals, have been allowed to try out their notions at the expense of patients more in the NHS than they would be in private hospital building, charitable or commercial.

Educational sociologists have been allowed to lord it over children in 1,500- or 2,000-place comprehensive schools because the state system could ignore the demonstration by the market, in the form of fee-paid schools, that the optimum number was nearer 650 to 850.

And the academic zealot has been taken more notice of by politicians in state pension schemes than he would have been by competing private insurers.

The agency relationship is nowhere more rampant than in the NHS (p. 240). And bribery and jobbery have more scope in the state because they operate under the guise of "public service."

The state thus exposes the public to depredation because escape from it is more difficult. In the market the abuses are worst where there is monopoly. But monopoly in the market is not endemic: it can be disciplined by changes in supply and demand, or limited by law. In the state, monopoly is the very essence.

Eighth,—a bonus to the seven deadly sins—the welfare state will use secrecy to avoid being judged. For its operators are judges and juries in their own cause. When, many moons ago,[20] I was asked to meet officials to discuss the scope for pricing health prescriptions, they replied, in the hearing of the Minister, that high charges would disrupt household budgeting and low charges would not be worth collecting. They won the tactical argument because there was no way to question their strategic suppositions or statistics except by local experimentation. And that was excluded as impracticable.

VIII. The Road Back—Or Forward

The eight deadly sins indicate the obstacles on the road back—or rather forward—in the way of resuming the developing structure of welfare services that was emerging for 50 years spontaneously in response to personal, local and industrial circumstances and preferences.

I. Recognition of the Error of Statism—and Its Replacement

The first obstacle is the whole body of thought that has looked to the state to cure almost every ill—from unemployment and inflation to poverty and inequality. That intellectual error can be countered only by a body of thought that is better rooted in realistic assumptions on the aspirations and limitations of human nature and the day-to-day working of political institutions that are tested by experience in history. This International University and the Institute where I have worked are parts of that intellectual counter-revolution. But much more has to be done, not least by the re-emerging private services to demonstrate from their day-to-day activities that they can better the state. And their demonstration will have to be supplemented by devising techniques for enabling *all* the people, not only the moneyed or the higher-paid worker, to pay. The ability to pay is the key to the development of private services in all forms. The IEA is setting in train a 3-year study that merits wide support to examine the scope for reconstructing the edifice of state benefits to this end. Such devices—reverse taxes, tax credits, vouchers, etc.—must precede, or at least run in parallel with, expansion in the scope for private entrepreneurship in education, medical supplies and financing, housing, possibly pensions, and a host of smaller services. There would then be faster growth in life assurance for school fees, BUPA-type and HSA-type health insurance, saving for house purchase, and insured pension schemes

20. The incident is recounted in *Pricing or Taxing?*, Hobart Paper 71, 1976.

and annuities. Table VIII shows the increase in post-war health insurance, but there is enormous scope for expansion.

II. The Vested Interests

The second obstacle is the political, bureaucratic and occupational vested interests that have coagulated in the welfare state and will resist reform whatever the evidence that it has failed, and whatever the wish of the people that new forms of welfare be at least tested by experiment. Here much more fundamental re-thinking, and much more radical measures, will be required than the timid attempts we have seen so far. There can be no reform without disturbance to expectations (of jobs or income), cherished convictions (usually absorbed uncritically) or institutions thought to be untouchable. The biggest change is that many or most people in the public service will learn the exhilarating experience of turning 180° from looking to politicians for their budgets to facing their customers and taking money—the most democratic passport man has evolved—in payment. That transformation will put doctors, teachers, nurses and university staffs into the category of customer-oriented producer that teaches humility as well as efficiency.

(a) The political vested interest will have to be undermined by constitutional limitation on the powers of government to yield to the pressure of vested interests to continue outdated or unwanted welfare services.

(b) The bureaucratic vested interest will have to be motivated to wind up state welfare by bonuses, prizes[21] or honours. They may have to be bought out by early pensioning over 50, removal to industry between 40 and 50, and dismissal under 40. ("Natural wastage" is politically easiest but it will not suffice because it will be too slow.) Most fundamentally, the bureaucracy must be regarded, like the railways, as a declining industry, with exceptions for specialists, and the general rate of remuneration lowered continuously until individual officials decide to move so that total numbers are reduced, eventually to perhaps a third.

21. The work of the American "Public Choice" economists on the failure of bureaucracy, Professors J. M. Buchanan, W. A. Niskanen, Gordon Tullock and others, has been virtually ignored by politicians in Britain. (Buchanan *et al., The Economics of Politics,* IEA Readings No. 18, 1978; Tullock, *The Vote Motive,* Hobart Paperback 9, IEA, 1976; Niskanen, *Bureaucracy: Servant or Master?,* Hobart Paperback 5, IEA, 1973.)

Table VIII. The Tenacity and Growth in Private Health Insurance, 1950–1980*

Year	Number Insured (thousand)	Number of Subscribers (thousand)	Annual Net Change in Subscribers (thousand)	Subscriptions £m	Benefits £m
1950	120	56	7	0.22	0.14
1955	585	274	52	1.83	1.54
1956	680	318	44	2.26	1.92
1957	755	354	36	2.76	2.32
1958	825	387	33	3.28	2.76
1959	895	419	32	3.85	3.24
1960	995	467	48	4.47	3.76
1961	1070	504	37	5.19	4.36
1962	1165	546	42	6.00	5.22
1963	1250	587	41	6.97	6.23
1964	1345	632	45	7.99	7.13
1965	1445	680	48	9.12	8.02
1966	1565	735	55	10.68	9.35
1967	1670	784	49	12.52	10.86
1968	1770	831	47	14.45	12.22
1969	1887	886	55	17.34	14.86
1970	1982	930	44	20.35	16.89
1971	2102	986	56	23.79	19.74
1972	2176	1021	35	28.90	24.49
1973	2265	1064	43	36.24	29.24
1974	2334	1096	32	45.20	36.24
1975	2315	1087	9	54.92	45.59
1976	2251	1057	-30	70.57	53.15
1977	2254	1057	0	90.72	64.68
1978	2388	1118	61	105.06	67.68
1979	2765	1292	174	122.06	83.96
1980	3577	1647	355	154.34	127.61

Source: UK Private Medical Care, Provident Scheme Statistics, 1980, Lee Donaldson, 1981.

*Figures are totals for the three main "provident" schemes: British United Provident Association (BUPA), Private Patients Plan (PPP), and Western Provident Association (WPA). Several small schemes operate mainly locally. The "contributory" schemes—Hospital Saving Association (HSA) and others—have around four million members.

(c) The trade union vested interest will have to be resisted by large-scale retraining of men and women or by transfer to the new private management of schools, hospitals, housing estates and pension schemes. But, more radically, it will have to be disciplined by repealing the immunities granted by short-sighted laws. And if some in the unions urge resistance to legal reform by disrupting industry, the response must be to expedite reform, for continuing deferment provokes and risks intensified disruption.

III. Buying out the Middle Class

The third obstacle, the articulate middle class or newly affluent beneficiaries of state welfare, will have to be bought out by countervailing benefits in reduced taxation to encourage payment for private education, medicine, housing and pensions in the market.

Envoi
The Welfare State and Market Forces

Time is on the side of freedom because, in the end, market forces are irresistible. Yet politicians who favour freedom can ease their path.

In a world in which Russian Communism will have disintegrated by the end of the century, China is going capitalist, Poland, Yugoslavia and other Communist countries have to use markets to sustain their economies, and the market oases of Asia and Africa offer undeniable examples to their continents, it is unthinkable that the British will prefer an enforced and chimerical equality to strenuous but spontaneous liberty. The Labour Party will not rule again because it is now seen to put the pretence of equality first, even by increasing coercion. The welfare state will wither away because it will be increasingly difficult to attempt equality when supply and demand facilitate diversity.

The Prospect

The unthinkable has happened. Five years ago the welfare state was not only morally sacrosanct but politically impregnable. It was thought a masterpiece of institutional design that enshrined man's humanity to man. Its critics, not least scholars with reasoned analyses in IEA *Papers,* were rejected as unrealistic visionaries out of sympathy with the moral spirit of the age. The welfare state was, with Marshall Aid, the most unsordid act in history.

What has happened in five short years is that politicians have caught up with public opinion that was nearer to, and increasingly reflecting, market forces.

The political climacteric of 1981, long delayed by the built-in political conservatism that induces politicians to cling to outworn institutions and parties, is that the party which was most doctrinally identified with the welfare state is being abandoned by the social class—"the workers"—that was supposed to be its biggest beneficiary. The social democrats, its evident natural inheritors, may continue to pay lip-service to the ideals of the welfare state still savoured by its intellectuals, but it will have to spurn them and follow its followers, whose aspirations the intellectuals ignore.

The historically unprecedented intellectual migration of our times from collectivism to liberalism continues even among intellectuals reluctant to change party. *The Political Quarterly,* for long the organ of the intelligentsia that held the welfare state sacred as creating inalienable rights to the best education, medical care, housing and pensions for everyone evermore, has bravely broken the tablets in an editorial on the party re-alignment (the editors are David Watt, Director of the Royal Institute of International Affairs and Professor Rudolf Klein of the University of Bath):

> . . . a centre movement (unlike the Labour Party) would not be a preservation society for the existing institutions of the welfare state or the existing distribution of industrial activity in the country. A commitment to equity is consistent with experimentation and flexibility in the design of policies: with exploring the potential of the private sector, of producer co-operatives responsible for the delivery of education or health services, and ways of enhancing consumer choice by the use of vouchers [*sic*—voucher advocates in Britain, though not in the USA, were once regarded as either the blackest of reactionaries or figures of fun]. The criterion for judging such policy options should be whether or not they enhance the life-chances of the worst-off, not whether they conform to the traditional ideology of the welfare state or the self-interests of those now employed in the welfare state.[22]

22. *Political Quarterly,* April–June 1981, in an editorial headed "Commentary: Towards a New Centre Party."

This is a revolutionary, historic statement. It indicates as much political re-thinking among welfare state advocates as political re-alignment from Labour to Social Democrat.

The significance of the appearance of the Social Democrats is that they are nearer to the beneficiaries of the welfare state that want to dislodge themselves from it. The new party will attract activists who think the welfare state can simply be purged of its defects by being liberated from centralised political control by the state. The leaders will find that de-centralised but still political control will not satisfy their working-class followers, who will want to be allowed to escape from the welfare state by choices *outside* it for the first time in their lives. It is not only Mrs. Williams who misinterprets the revolution in working-class expectations.

When the Social Democrats understand the army they will lead, they could go further than the Conservatives in loosening state welfare so that it rests on preference rather than compulsion. They may promise less than the Conservatives but accomplish more, because working-class support would enable them to thaw out the frozen state without losing popular political trust. The Conservatives, still reflecting middle-income people who run the welfare state, not least in local government, who find lucrative employment in it, or whose superior cultural power ensure they are at the upper end of its wide range of quality (equality is a figment of doctrinaire wishful thinking), will have to compete for working-class allegiance or see the Social Democrats rule from 1988 until the end of the century. But, whichever party rules, it will have to reflect the resistance to monopoly in state welfare (and everywhere else except in public goods).

Yet we cannot depend on a government of any party to liquidate the welfare state as an act of patriotism or in response to public preferences. In the end it will be market forces that will make the welfare state yield to private choice and technical advance.

READING LIST

Anderson, Digby, Lait, June, and Marsland, David, *Breaking the Spell of the Welfare State,* Social Affairs Unit, 1981.

Goodman, John C., *National Health Care in Great Britain: Lessons for the USA,* Fisher Institute, Dallas, Texas, 1980.

Hanson, C. G., "Welfare Before the Welfare State" in *The Long Debate on Poverty,* Readings 9, 2nd edition, IEA, 1974.

Harris, Ralph, and Seldon, Arthur, *Over-ruled on Welfare,* Hobart Paperback 13, IEA, 1979.

Harris, Ralph, *The End of Government . . . ?,* Occasional Paper 58, IEA, 1980.

Lindsay, C. M., *National Health Issues: The British Experience,* Hoffman–La Roche, 1980.

Pennance, F. G., and Gray, Hamish, *Choice in Housing,* Research Report, IEA, 1968 (out of print).

Seldon, Arthur, *Pensions in a Free Society,* IEA, 1957 (out of print).

———, *Pensions for Prosperity,* Hobart Paper 4, IEA, 1960 (out of print).

———, *Taxation and Welfare,* Research Monograph 14, IEA, 1967.

———, *After the NHS,* Occasional Paper 21, IEA, 1968 (out of print).

———, *The Great Pensions "Swindle,"* Tom Stacey, 1970.

———, "Who Will Rid Us of This Tyrannical Paternalism?" in *1985: An Escape from Orwell's 1984,* Churchill Press, 1975.

———, *Charge,* Maurice Temple Smith, 1977.

———, "Change by Degree or by Convulsion" in *The Coming Confrontation,* IEA, 1978.

———, "Individual Liberty, Public Goods and Representative Democracy" in F. A. Hayek Festschrift, *ORDO,* Vol. 30, Gustav Fischer Verlag, Stuttgart and New York, 1979.

———, "Disciplining the State by Pricing" in *The Taming of Government,* Readings 21, IEA, 1979.

———, "Why the NHS Must Fail" in *The Litmus Papers,* Centre for Policy Studies, 1980.

———, "The Next Thirty Years" in Lindsay, *op. cit.*

———, *Corrigible Capitalism, Incorrigible Socialism,* Occasional Paper 57, IEA, 1980.

West, E. G., *Education and the State,* IEA, 2nd edition, 1971.

PENSIONS WITHOUT THE STATE

Pensions Without the State

In 1957 the institute's first paper on provision for life-time contingencies—loss of income in ill-health, interruptions in employment and retirement—questioned the *rationale* of the expansion since 1925 in state pensions financed by compulsory "National" Insurance contributions. Since then state pensions, financed less by contributions but instead increasingly by taxes, have become one of the four main components of the political creation romanticised into the "welfare" state. The others are education, medical care and housing.

Richly varied methods of saving have long been used voluntarily by the British people to prepare for the uncertainties of life. Although many in the 1870s (and earlier) earned low incomes, they had sacrificed current consumption to prepare for future risks to help themselves and their families.

In 1957, only nine years after the establishment of the post-war welfare state, it was timely to assert that ". . . rights to pensions are not the only supports to which people can look forward in their old age." Private saving in many forms had created large reserves of

> private property, which offers a more certain basis for security in old age than the State and its pensions. They comprise a large accumulation of wealth out of which provision for retirement can be made. And more and more people are accumulating wealth in these forms.[1]

The Early Growth of Private Saving

This voluntary saving originated in the decisions of individuals of all income-groups, including many with low earnings, in the 70 years and more

1. A. Seldon, *Pensions in a Free Society,* London: Institute of Economic Affairs, 1957, pp. 5, 67 (Table II, including the notes).

since the middle-late nineteenth century. It revealed widespread providence, often in association with other people in the same occupations or other like circumstances, assertion of the dignity and pride of independence, concern for family.

The estimates of private saving in the 1950s were derived from compilations from the most reliable information available, by academic researchers, savings organisations and government departments. They found that millions of people were saving, some or possibly many in several ways, and had accumulated private property, in both financial instruments like savings accounts, insurance policies and stocks and shares ("liquid assets") and in real estate like homes and other property ("non-liquid assets") of roughly £34–35,000 million. (The Gross National Product in 1950–1955 was around £15,000 million.) There were multiple holdings in more than one kind of saving and sometimes several accounts opened by individual owners. The number of owners was known fairly precisely in some categories, like the 4.6 million owners of the homes they occupied, but less in others, like the owners of multiple savings accounts.

In all, the estimates indicated 23 million Post Office Savings Bank Accounts, eight million Trustee Savings Bank Accounts, millions of Defence Bonds, National Savings Certificates and Premium Savings Bonds to a total value of around £4,500 million. There were evidently around 3.5 million holdings of Building Society Shares and Deposits, some 14 million accounts with Industrial and Provident Societies, including Co-operative Societies, and over eight million accounts with Friendly Societies.

£2,000 million to £2,500 million were held in bank deposits, between £10,500 and £11,000 million in stocks and shares, and £3,000 million to £3,500 million in Government securities apart from Defence Bonds and National Savings Certificates (above).

Over 4.5 million homes (housing perhaps 10 million people) worth £6,500 million were owned by the occupiers. Land valued at £1,000 million was owned privately.

Not least, there were large holdings of assurance policies and annuities. Over 88 million industrial assurance policies and annuities worth nearly £900 million were held with assurance companies and 33 million worth nearly £250 million with Collecting Societies. A further nine million policies and annuities worth £2,275 million were held with life assurance companies. And savings of some £2,000 million were held in the form of household goods, business assets and other property.

Some of these figures were more or less precise, others were the then most available estimates. They seem to have been the best approximations to private saving a few years after the post-war expansion in the welfare state. Of the total population of 50 million, many with lower incomes, several million were evidently saving and accumulating property to meet the risks of loss of earnings.

There had also been expansion, mainly since the 1930s, in the number of men and women covered in pension schemes for retirement organised by their employers (though their cost could partly be passed on to other producers and consumers) as part of their working arrangements called "occupational" pensions. In 1951 they covered two and a third million employed by government and nearly four million by private industry, a total of 6¼ million, nearly five million men and 1.3 million women.[2]

These pensions in private industry had generally begun in the 1930s, mostly among people paid by salary, but during the 1950s and 1960s they spread fairly far down the income scale to employees paid by wages. In recent years occupational pensions have covered in all around a half of the work-force of some 25 million. Saving by pensions came later than by the other methods listed above, but it embraced people with lower as well as higher incomes.

The Politics of Pensions

It must have been clear to students of the subject in the early 1950s, as well as to politicians and their civil service advisers responsible for extending the state pensions that would affect families for 20, 30, 40 or more years ahead, that most people in all income groups were accumulating savings and property available to provide income in their retirement, directly by pensions or annuities and indirectly by savings and private property.

Only a few years earlier, in 1948, the post-war Labour Government must have known of these voluntary private alternatives to compulsory state pensions, especially the Prime Minister, (Major) Clement Attlee, the middle-class social worker at Toynbee Hall in the East End of London, and his Ministers of working-class origin like Ernest Bevin and Aneurin Bevan who had benefited from them in their family lives. Yet they ignored the genesis of this saving: the fundamental trait in the British character of independence and

2. Ibid., p. 4 (Table I).

self-respect and the instinct to combine in communities with common interests such as Friendly Societies to safeguard their families. Instead, the Government enlarged the original 1908 "Old-Age" tax-financed pension and the 1925 National Insurance pension into the 1948 Retirement Pension that was to be financed by National Insurance contributions but has ended in being paid for increasingly out of taxation.

The 1948 extension of the state pension originated what became perhaps the most damaging conflict in post-war British society between the political process and the growing saving habits of the people. All employers and employees were required to pay "National Insurance" contributions. This technical term concealed what was revealed in the end as a fundamentally fraudulent description for the tax that government in later years was induced to raise successively to help avoid openly described taxation, direct on incomes and indirect on purchases, and the borrowing required to pay for rising government expenditures, not least on other state welfare services, especially medical care and education.

The Classical Warning

Almost exactly a hundred years ago, in 1893, Alfred Marshall, the Cambridge economist who taught classical truths before his University succumbed to the political expedient of Keynesian full employment at all costs, told the Royal Commission on the Aged Poor to resist the "universal pensions" advised by the Fabians, Sidney and Beatrice Webb. He warned they "do not contain . . . the seeds of their own disappearance. I am afraid that, if started, they would tend to become perpetual."

He has been proved right. Even as upright an economist-turned-politician as Hugh Gaitskell could not resist misusing Beveridge's dangerous toy, the higher National Insurance pension, for political purposes by starting it almost from the first year rather than waiting until the National Insurance Fund had been built up over 20 years, as Beveridge had earlier advised (and as a private pension fund would have had to accumulate). The excuse, that the pensioners could not wait years for higher incomes, was unconvincing since people in most need could have been assisted from general taxes without encumbering the National Insurance Fund with uninsured liabilities and expenditures.

It was an unfortunate precedent, and it contributed substantially to the financial deterioration in National Insurance. Later Ministers of Pensions or Social Security faced acute embarrassment. Another academic-turned-politician, Richard Crossman, exchanged the accusation of "swindling"[3] with John Boyd Carpenter, his political opposite number, when in the 1960s both turned to graduating contributions in the vain effort to save the National Insurance Fund from becoming what it had been for some years—not a fund but a tank, emptied almost as soon as it was refilled.

Financial deregulation has enabled employers and employees to change from occupational to personal pensions, with advantages to both but also predictable abuses that accompany innovations where "amateur" buyers are initially less informed than "professional" sellers. To judge these abuses, the market "imperfections," which are coming to light after a few short years, have to be set beside the government "imperfections"—the wastes, inflexibility, inflation and deception in state pensions which have taken decades to be discovered and will take more decades to remove.

State Pensions Are Out of Date

The longer the basic state pension takes to be run down as more flexible private pensions and other forms of saving are preferred, the earlier the process should begin. The beginning has been urged since 1957.[4] The Government recently announced the beginning to start 60 years later in AD 2017. Such is the inflexibility of the state, which arouses expectations and produces governments tempted to take the short view about the dates of general elections, and puts the long view a poor second.

Whether private saving would have continued to expand if the state had not introduced its pensions in 1908, 1925, and 1948 is properly debatable. Nor can it be said with certainty that the increase would have been enough to dispense with the pensions introduced by the state. It is arguable that the less provident would not have saved in the expectation that a compassionate society would support them in impecunious old age, or that their more affluent children would pay for their homes and living costs. We shall never know because the necessity to save was lessened by the state pension system.

Yet it is implausible to suppose that the saving institutions formed from the 1870s and earlier, based on the habits of thrift, providence, family solidarity, and self-respect, would have weakened or died out.

3. A. Seldon, *The Great Pensions "Swindle,"* London: Tom Stacey, 1970 [reprinted in this volume].

4. A. Seldon, *The State Is Rolling Back,* London: E. & L. Books in association with the IEA, 1994.

Towards the Future

The history of what happened does not throw conclusive light on what would have happened to private provision for retirement if conditions had become more favourable to voluntary saving by the earlier winding-up of compulsory saving through the state. Yet rising real incomes, the unprecedented advance in living standards, the accelerated leisure pursuits, lengthening life-expectancy and the advancing years of working life beyond the artificial retirement ages of state schemes—all these perhaps unexpected trends point to the most supportable conclusion: that private saving and assurance through the long-established mutual and profit-oriented institutions, investment through unit and investment trusts, deposits in building societies and banks, private property in homes and newer ways of saving would have continued to expand in the last 60 years.

Not least, the more the market was allowed to devise new methods of preparing for comfortable retirement, the more competition in a free market would have invigorated the traditional institutions to modernise their methods and marketing. And the more the difficulty of governments in maintaining their pensions for growing numbers of state pensioners, the more the nation will have lost in repressing the varied vehicles of private saving, and the more we should now welcome their rebirth and recovery.

The governments of the main European countries are gradually and painfully accepting that they will be unable to provide the state pensions they have long promised their people.

In Britain, it is only since the 1970s that both major parties have attempted to extract more money in graduated insurance contributions in exchange for equal pensions. Both were at pains to find new justifications for this misuse of the national "insurance" system to justify redistributive taxation. Yet doubts were surfacing earlier in the 1960s. Ministers of both political parties showed anxiety. After several *Hobart* and other IEA papers in its early years on pensions, Margaret Herbison, Labour Secretary of State, and John Boyd-Carpenter, the Conservative Minister, asked the author for talks. Both seemed uneasy, but the time for courageous reform was apparently not yet. It would have required the "appalling candour" that Baldwin had to confess in the 1930s when he had failed to reveal that his party had not taken the public into its confidence on rearmament in the face of the Hitler threat of war in Europe.

But in 1996 the time for appalling candour has arrived. The people are having to be told that they would be wise to begin saving privately in their middle working years for their retirement 15 or 20 years later at age 65. And the system of national insurance for pensions income in retirement is belatedly drawing to its close. But its lesson must be learned: pensions cannot be left to the political process with its short time-horizons and its temptation to tax or borrow to disguise its inability to create the welfare services the people would prefer.

Not least, if they had been left to develop their private saving they could now look forward to more secure years of retirement.

THE VERDICT OF HISTORY

The Verdict of History

The welfare state is essentially a political artefact. Its origins lie in the party politics of the Victorian era. It was presented by the competing Liberals and Conservatives as an act of communal compassion in alleviating the condition of the poor, especially the enfranchised working classes. The state was not the only source of welfare and it had obvious defects. But from its symbolic beginning with the Education Act of 1870 to "fill the gaps" left in some towns by the growing private schools, it has been extended over the past century to provide medical care, housing (for several millions), pensions, insurance for unemployment, and much else for everyman and his wife and children. The implicit political judgement on everyman today is that he is less competent, less responsible and less provident than his great-grandfather who managed on a tithe of his earnings.

The purpose of this collection of essays is to attempt the rare exercise of judging the benefits of the welfare state by counting its costs. Macroeconomic financial cost conveys little of its real-life cost in the sacrifice of the varied systems that would have developed in the open market from the mid-nineteenth century.

The "counter-factual" applies historical judgement to assess the alternatives that the chance confluence of circumstance, the "accidents" of history, displaced. There is much unquestioning approval of the benefits of the welfare state: its compassion for the poor, the homeless, the sick, the indigent in old age. Yet its contribution to civilised living cannot be judged solely by its achievements. They were made with massive resources that could have been used in other ways that even scholarly histories often ignore and imply would not have emerged or been developed to suit the changing times.

Historians conventionally study "history," understood generally as the developments that took place. Dynastic, constitutional, political, military histories are often qualified by judgements on the better decisions the chief players *might better have made,* the mishaps avoided, the happier results that might have followed. Yet "social" histories rarely pause to count the opportunity cost of the welfare state in the better welfare it suppressed.

Their judgements would have been more productive if they had studied rather less the decisions of political power in government and rather more the *potential* economic power of the common people. The majority decisions of the political process usually submerge minorities and individuals who would be heeded more effectively in the market. The power of government is constrained and, in the end, it can be overridden by the market, as the welfare state is being replaced by more responsive competitive services in the approach to the twenty-first century.

Historical Evidence

Three other historical approaches are irrelevant or inconclusive: comparison, or rather contrast, with the embryo private alternatives emerging in the mid-nineteenth century, with the mature but government-restricted alternatives in the late-twentieth century, or with the younger societies of the former British Dominions. The most relevant material available to objective scholars for historical judgement is the ample evidence presented in this book on the early services and institutions most likely to have expanded if they had not been repressed.

First, recent researches into the early history of education, medical care, housing, saving for old age and retirement, reveal the voluntary early efforts of families to provide themselves with all the main elements of the welfare state.

Second, the very large expansion in incomes since the 1860s would have been available to pay in the market if people had been free to continue and develop their responses to the private (often church) schools, medical benefit insurers, and, later, homes for sale and personal pensions.

Third, rising discretionary expenditures on the improving quality and widening range of food and clothing, amenities and luxuries were available more readily and earlier to the wealthier who could pay both the taxes and the prices for education and medical care still now largely denied to the working classes by compulsory state welfare that is more responsive to the better-connected middle classes.

Fourth, the welfare state was inflated by its controllers and staffs. The economics of politics, inspired by the Scottish and English classical liberal philosophers, and refined by the American school of public choice, clearly points to its micro-economic political temptations. Politicians acquired widening power. The bureaucracy inflated its growing empire. The professional associations of doctors, teachers, nurses, public administrators, and trade unions of clerical and manual workers found easier "rent-seeking" from government monopolies spending taxpayers' money than from competing mutual fraternities spending their members' money or from profit-earning suppliers and insurers risking their shareholders' money.

Scholars are here in the realm of exchanging reasoned judgement. There can be no confident exclusion of the probability that the welfare state has entailed horrendous "cost" in the lost services that would have grown to serve the mass of the people. There is no convincing or decisive reason to suppose that they would have ceased to develop more responsive private education, medical care, housing, saving, pensions, insurance for unemployment and much else "tailored" for individuals, trades, professions, communities.

The balance of probability points to their expansion under the influence of innovators and entrepreneurs tested in competition and then trusted by people who knew their local society and branch managers. Such local associations and communities rested on fraternal understanding and sympathy based on loyalties of neighbourhood, district and religion foreign to the best intentions of the state. This was the spontaneous evolution of community that grew from the bottom rather than the spurious communitarian imposition by political coercion from the state at the top.

Members of mutual organisations would then have remained until today "brothers." Or they would have emerged as sovereign consumers—"customers" who could escape from inadequate suppliers. Instead they are "beneficiaries"—state school "parents," NHS "patients," council "tenants," state "pensioners" without individual power to bargain or escape, and, if working class, often supplicants.

British Rail has replaced direct-paying (though often taxpayer-subsidised) "passengers" by "customers." The welfare state fights shy of "customers" who pay indirectly by taxes. The anxious reasoning of its managers is understandable. "Customers" would not have accepted "national curricula" framed by far-off civil servants little concerned about family instinct and affection. "Customers" would have resented long waiting for hospitals run by administrators answerable to government or professional associations. "Customers" would not have tolerated council housing or tower blocks controlled by councillors sensitive to trade unions. "Customers" would hardly have accepted state pensions manipulated by Westminster politicians for party advantage.

Welfare State Is Socially Divisive

The welfare state has intensified the divide between the middle classes who pay for what they choose and the working classes who mostly have to content themselves with what they are given by the state. It has retarded the social merging evident in more mobile Western societies undivided by the British "national" health and other "public" services.

Both government and the market are prone to "failures." The market, as Professor Jackson illustrates, has had three main "problems" of adverse selection, moral hazard and agency. The crucial and debatable question for historians is whether or how far the market would have discovered its characteristic solutions.

Economists have been devising methods of removing market "imperfections." And governments in some countries have increasingly adopted their thinking, replacing state by private services, partly for political motives though probably more for economic reasons. State services have been found unpopular because tax rejection has reduced government funds and lowered quality.

Even with the lower incomes in the developing countries Dr. Gabriel Roth, in a research study for the World Bank, found that they had been evolving private innovations in the supply of "public" services.[1] They were able to overcome the "public goods" and "free rider" obstacles, once considered inherent barriers to the market supply of education, medical care, water and sewerage, and communication services. And they have found ways to meet the exceptional circumstances of people with the lowest incomes. More recently Dr. Fred Foldvary, for the American Locke Institute, has developed methods of competitive supply of "public" goods in advanced countries.[2]

And Chile, a country that has faced the acute problems of encouraging economic growth in a developing country, is teaching lessons to the developed West by demonstrating new devices for privatising erstwhile state welfare services in social security, medical care, higher education, local government, and communications.[3]

1. G. Roth, *The Private Provision of Public Services*, Oxford: Oxford University Press, 1987.

2. Fred Foldvary, *Public Goods and Private Communities: The Market Provision of Social Services*, Aldershot: Edward Elgar Publishing, 1994.

3. Cristián Larroulet (ed.), *Private Solutions to Public Problems: The Chilean Experience*, Santiago: Libertad y Desarrollo, 1993.

Government or Market? Choice or Restriction

An analysis of the relative achievements and failures of collective (government) and individual (market) choice leads Professor Richard Wagner of George Mason University in Virginia, writing in the methodology of "public choice" (better described as the economics of politics), to oppose "the welfare state" against "the general welfare."[4] He emphasises the constitutional difference between limited ("contractarian") government, in which the legislators cannot suppress the scope for the market to produce welfare, and "unlimited" ("majoritarian") government in which voter majorities are able to suppress minority or independent initiatives.

It would seem that the argument rests with the open, if less tidy, system that allows experimentation rather than with the tidier but restrictive system that excludes or inhibits it by demanding political conformity. It has, as a major example, long been considered that insurance against the risks of unemployment is a case for state organisation on the apparently clear ground that the decision to be "unemployed" is subject to moral hazard because the individual can, for physical and even more subjective psychological reasons, reject offers of employment and claim the insured sums of money. In this book Professor Beenstock demonstrates the principles on which moral hazard could be tested by objective experience such as seasonal trends in unemployment and insurance offered in the market by competing insurers.

On comparable grounds, it is plausible to argue that all state welfare services could be open to constant comparison with possible private alternatives to decide which is the better for the public. Not least, state education could be under constant test to ensure that it meets the preferences of parents.

Further alternatives, such as delivering monopoly state services by competing private suppliers, or financing them by prices rather than taxes, have been explored in recent years.[5] The obstacle is essentially that government can protect its services from open comparison. Experiments in the voucher system were suppressed by the Conservative Government in 1983 largely

4. Richard Wagner, *To Promote the General Welfare,* San Francisco: Pacific Research Institute for Public Policy, 1989.

5. Vincent and Elinor Ostrom, "Public Goods and Public Choices," in E. S. Savas (ed.), *Alternatives for Delivering Public Services,* Boulder, Colorado: Westview Press, 1977. The advantages of direct charging by prices in place of indirect financing by taxes are discussed in A. Seldon, *Charge,* London: Maurice Temple Smith, 1977, and in Richard Wagner (ed.), *Charging for Government,* London: Routledge, 1991.

because it was opposed by vested interests, mainly in the teacher trade unions, that preferred to be employed (ultimately) and their remuneration decided nationally by the state rather than by parents with bargaining power based on the payment of school fees. It is difficult to argue that parents, especially those with the lower incomes, have gained from the suppression of the opportunity to compare schools and move freely between them.

The crucial weakness is not so much in the market as in the political process. The most intractable obstruction to reform is not so much moral as political. The failures of government that must be set against the failures of the market are considerable. The test of the relative significance of government and market "failures" is less in their frequency than in the ease with which they can be escaped. The natural recuperative powers of the market induce competing private suppliers to find ways to reduce their defects earlier than the state monopoly. The market discovers the "scoundrels" sooner.

The state has suppressed the price mechanism in schooling and medicine without creating a better method of valuing resources. It has weakened the family by usurping the rôle of parents in schooling, medical care, and, still in the 1990s for millions, in housing. The state has based its welfare policies on their income-effect and neglected their price-effect on incentives to make the most of natural or acquired abilities. The financial differences that decide access in the market have been replaced by cultural differences of personal accent and social connections that are more difficult to offset in deciding access to the state. It has distorted individual life-patterns by responding to immediate personal producer interests at the expense of long-term personal consumer interests.

Conclusions: State Imperfections and Future Demands and Innovations

The imperfections of the state have remained concealed for decades up to and exceeding half a century. The state prevents the market from discovering the imperfections of the welfare state and the remedies. To prove itself, state welfare must be open to competing methods of production. In the last resort it must return its taxes for dissatisfied consumers to spend as they wish on private services at home or overseas.

The decisive probabilities are three:

First, as incomes rise, more people are being enabled to escape from the welfare monopolies both at home and, for medical care and saving, increasingly overseas to the single market in Europe and to the world market enlarged by the World Trade Organisation. The finally emerging working classes are growing impatient with their relatively poor state schooling and medical care.

Second, accelerating innovation will supply new methods of producing consumer-oriented welfare services beyond the capacity of centralised, standardised, bureaucratised government. Education and medical care no longer require universally large buildings called schools and hospitals that the state will preserve too long.

Third, both supply and demand will be reinforced by the state itself, which induces more people to reject the offensive taxation it demands to pay for unsatisfactory services. Conventional tax rejection is being increasingly supplemented by the barter that eludes official measurement even more than tax avoidance and evasion.

The case for continuing or expanding the national welfare state is weakened by its incapacity to determine the decisions of people who can escape to international markets. If the political process cannot produce modernised welfare services because it is prevented by ideological faith in the state, by bureaucracy, and by vested interests, the market process will replace it because its remaining defects will become more remediable or loom less large than its suitability for the twenty-first century. Then the British will be one nation of consumers in buyers' markets in welfare. That, in the end, would seem the verdict of history.

THE RETREAT OF THE STATE IN SOCIAL WELFARE

The Retreat of the State in Social Welfare

The Nature of the State

We live in a decisive stage in the history of the functions of government, in the liberties of the people, and in the nature of our democracy. All three are involved in the belated but growing acceptance in all schools of thought that the state must retreat from the over-expansion of government. Accelerating scientific and technological advances are more far-reaching in their economic and political repercussions than any since the Industrial Revolution of two centuries ago. They require us to question the powers of government and the political process that elects it. Not least must we consider that the state *should* do, but more what it now *can* do (and therefore what it *cannot* do) because of fundamental changes in everyday life. Here is the missing link in the efforts and failure of recent governments to adjust their welfare policies to changing conditions in society, conditions which are enhancing the power of the people to choose the lives they would like to, and now increasingly can, live.

The state is reluctant to accept both the weakening of its powers and the realization of its defects. In spite of its claims to do for the people better than they can do for themselves, the state is not all-seeing, impartial between supplicants for its favours, and efficient in the use of its revenue or borrowings. Furthermore it is not always just: it is tempted to yield to the strongest importunists, and not to the most deserving causes. It yields to people organized as producers much more than to the same people unorganized as consumers. It distorts their preferences by encouraging them to put their immediate short-term interests before their underlying long-term futures. In 1986, while on a visit to the site of the Battle of Gettysburg, in company with one American and one British economist working on the nature of democracy, we stood near the spot where in 1863 Abraham Lincoln promised government of, by, and for the people. Sadly the democratic state has emerged very differently from what Lincoln promised. In real life it has produced government "of" the politically active, "by" the political managers, "for" the political importunists. In plain English, this is government of the busy, by the bossy, for the bully.

These excesses of the democratic state have provoked even more fundamental reactions from the people. It is the people who can now, and will increasingly in the coming years, limit the state's powers. The most recent developments in the distribution of power between government and governed are even more fundamental than Lincoln could have foreseen. In our times, today and tomorrow, and even more in the days and months and years after tomorrow, the state will gradually lose its powers. It has no magic wand. It cannot do what its wisest counsellors advise by passing laws, announcing rules, and proclaiming regulations. It has new and advancing competitors for its services, and they have been expanding and advancing to the point at which they are increasingly preferred. The waning power of the state, too long misunderstood by historians, is now more manifest, and especially in the realm of social welfare. The state has retuned its engines of expansion into state education, state medicine, state housing (through local government), state pensions, and state "social" insurance since the Second World War and earlier. Indeed it has been better at tuning engines for advance than for the more relevant and more urgently needed tuning of engines for retreat.

The state is now in no man's land. It has advanced too far and cannot easily retreat in good order because it simultaneously risks unpopularity from the customary beneficiaries of its "free" services, and growing reluctance to supply the resources for the people who want, and can find, better services elsewhere. In recent years democratic government has been intensively analysed by new schools of social scientists who reveal the decisions of the people's "representatives" in government to be very different from those of the people themselves. This was true in the creation and post-war expansion of the welfare state, and now still more true in the failure to adapt the welfare state to a changing world. After a century or more of advance the state is facing unexpected obstacles to retreat. It is having to accept that its government is not sovereign or as final as it thought. Its overexpanding laws, rules and regulations can increasingly be escaped by the people.

Government has been slow to learn that the changing nature of economic life has increasingly put the preferences of the people beyond its own power to suppress those same preferences. And its statistics are misleading because more economic life lies beyond its reach; statistics of national production and incomes are inaccurate. They understate the total production of goods and services and overstate the degrees of poverty, inequality, and unemployment. All these historic trends underlie the unavoidably accelerating retreat of the state from social welfare that will continue to accelerate in the twenty-first century.

The explanations of the imperative task to adjust the domain of government to the increasing power of the people are economic, political, and technological. Above all they are economic, because the science of economics provides the unique indicator—costs and prices—of the most dispensable alternatives in deciding the best use of scarce resources. The welfare state has suffered from the crucial weakness that it has deprived itself of this instrument. Its claim to provide welfare "free" was never well founded. Yet this truth was rarely questioned because, from the earliest days in the late nineteenth century, most people have paid for "free" social welfare indirectly through taxes on purchases or earnings. Oscar Wilde's taunt in *Lady Windermere's Fan* that people who know the price of everything know the value of nothing was the opposite of the truth. It is still exploited by influential people who claim the common people's money to pay for their favoured causes—in the arts, heritage, environment and elsewhere. Their claim that the money they exact from government will do untold good is shallow. The so-called cultural "values" of the cognoscenti are the preferences or prejudices of the few hundreds with influence in government; the people's money is questionably commandeered and misused by government. Lloyd George was condemned for "raiding the Road Fund" for other purposes urgently required by government; the Lottery Fund is now being "raided" for purposes not preferred by the people who risk their weekly pounds.

Only the "empowerment" of the people by returning their purchasing power and through the freeing of prices will reveal the true preferences on which they would wish to spend their money. History suggests that they would be spending more on education, medical care, housing, and insurance and saving for the years after work than the state can now raise in taxes to spend *for them.* The concealing of these costs underlies the confused thinking in the retreat from social welfare. In its latest efforts to withdraw from some forms of social welfare the state confronts a new dilemma which stands midway between overexpansion and inability to retreat.[1]

Democracy has expanded all its four main functions: in social welfare, in the supply of the "public" goods of law and order once thought the necessary function of government, in the public "utilities" of fuel and transport, and

1. A. Seldon, *The Dilemma of Democracy: the Political Economics of Over-Government,* Hobart Paper 136, London, Institute of Economic Affairs, 1998.

in local government services (from providing literature for the working man to improve himself, to the tennis courts, swimming pools and golf courses—subsidized but not widely used by people too old to swim, too slow for tennis or too frail for golf). In all four functions, government has expanded too far into overgovernment. Its resources fall short of its capacity to supply the people with social services—in education, medical care, and housing; these same people increasingly obtain them from elsewhere at lower cost and higher quality. If government does not withdraw, that is, retreat unilaterally, it will lose both its authority to influence the pace of withdrawal and, even more fundamentally, weaken its repute within Lincolnian democracy as answerable to the people.

The Social Welfare Services Ripe for Withdrawal

The main elements of state welfare and its defective financing fall into three groups:

- *education and medical care* universally supplied and largely "free" of direct payment at the time of service, but paid for indirectly by taxes;
- *housing* for five million families subsidized by low rents, and *minimum incomes* for all in sickness, unemployment or old age, and subsidized by disguised National Insurance costs;
- *discretionary "charitable" assistance* supplied by general tax-paid subsidies.

The conventional historians of the social services assess the strengths and weakness of past government policies but draw unfounded conclusions which argue for further state activity to remove blunders or to extend measures that earlier proved ineffective. To such academics the costs of the social services to the nation are seen only as the financial outlays required for improvements. That approach is not sufficient to decide the best possible services for the people. The economist uses the "counterfactual" approach which considers what other methods of organizing social welfare might historically have replaced the failed constructions of the state. These are the alternative forms of welfare that might have been organized in other ways than by government (central or local) but which have been lost for decades. This more revealing approach issued from the teaching of "opportunity costs" by the Austrian School of Economics, led by Frederick Hayek who brought it to the London School of Economics in the 1930s. This school taught that the real "costs" of the state, not least in welfare, were the alternatives that might have developed had they not been discouraged or suppressed by the state. This vital missing link in its social welfare policies has long been neglected by the British state. What the state should have discovered after the Second World War, or before it, were the alternatives lost for far too long, the opportunities forgone by the persistence of the state in suppressing services that had long before emerged spontaneously in the early, mid- or late nineteenth century. These lost alternatives emerged from the natural growing instinct of people in families to take care of their own, throughout all the vicissitudes of life.

But instead the British family has been weakened because the state has usurped the authority of parents. Few children, especially in the lower-income families, have looked to their parents to provide their schooling, their medical care, or even their homes. They have had to look to the political authorities, the politicians and their "public" servants, who have widened their powers to invade family bonds. The "opportunity cost" approach reveals the long-ignored loss of another virtue of the people. In the perspective of history it is now clear that the state discouraged or suppressed spontaneous assistance to friends, neighbours and strangers by the personal charity that would have developed through the churches or through local groups of citizens; this is the selfless humanity that has long grown on a much larger scale in that other England that developed in the United States of America. It is not surprising that economists rather than sociologists, impressed by the powers of the state, have argued that the church encourages good relationships with non-churchgoers as well as churchgoers; in this they have followed their founder, Adam Smith. An economist in the USA has recently discovered[2] that, where state subsidies ceased, church membership and the demand for preachers rose markedly. Churches prospered when church leaders had to appeal to individual worshippers for encouragement and support rather than to legislators in government. Individual people as members of cohesive families were more sensitive to the condition of the less fortunate than they were as taxpayers.

As the state inevitably retreats in the twenty-first century we may expect the natural instinct of humanity, the urge to help the unfortunate, to expand with rising incomes. The efforts of the churches in founding schools for the young, supporting hospitals for all ages, building almshouses for the old,

2. Professor Kelly Olds, "Privatising the Church," *Journal of Political Economy* 102 (1994) 277–97.

and giving money and comfort to the poor will grow far beyond the capacity of the state to supply these things from taxes unwillingly paid. Small wonder that parents in all social classes have usually preferred their children to attend church schools, rather than secular schools subject to political control by local authorities; Mr. and Mrs. Blair typify many other British parents. The difference is that working-class parents anxious about lagging children do not have the cultural influence of middle-class people to make their case with head teachers, hospital officials, housing managers, or National Insurance officials for better or early consideration. They also lack the power to escape from lagging secular schools by using the voucher method, a system which the government has abandoned in Britain for nursery schools, but which is showing how it can widen choice for working-class families in several states of the USA, where it is welcomed by lower-income black parents.

The Rejection of State Welfare

The main reasons why individuals and families are now rejecting state welfare and withdrawing increasingly from state services are four-fold: first, rising incomes; second, technological advances; third, the reluctance to pay for state services through charges, insurance or taxes; and fourth, the widening number of escapes offered through informal employment, barter, electronic money, or by purchase from competing private suppliers at home and overseas.

Rising Incomes

Rising incomes are enabling more families across the income scale to pay for schooling by fees, for medical care by insurance, for housing by purchase, and for pensions and loss of income in sickness and unemployment again by insurance and saving in various forms.

Technological Advances

Personal and family withdrawal from state services is expedited by the technological advances that enable industry to produce "bespoke" goods and services tailored for individual and family requirements in place of standardized state service "off the peg." It must have been apparent to the well-intentioned supporters of "social" welfare (especially after the Second

World War) that the standardized state services would before long be rejected. They mostly provide "straightjacket" schooling and medicine, standardized homes and uniform pensions. Yet millions of people of all ages and incomes increasingly cook (or buy) individually created meals, wear individually tailored clothes, live in homes built in varying shapes and sizes, filled with the latest labour-saving devices (and leisure amenities for discriminating homeowners) and accumulate pensions for people retiring not at the state's artificial ages of 60 or 65 but at varying ages from 55 to 75—or even 85.

Reluctance to Pay for State Services

The retreat by the people, if not by the state, from social welfare is increasingly stimulated by the reluctance of the beneficiaries to pay for it in the only ways they can—by charges, insurance or taxes. The increasing resistance to higher taxes takes the form of both legal avoidance and illegal evasion. They are legally separate but functionally linked and morally difficult to distinguish between. They are linked because increasing experience of tax avoidance teaches new methods of tax evasion. They are legally separate but recent Chancellors of the Exchequer in 1997 and 1998 have revealed a reluctance or inability to separate the two. Their plight in financing government is indicated by the self-contradictory anxiety of successive Chancellors to penalize as illegal the tax avoidance that the law specifically allows as legal for the intention of earners of all kinds of income—wages, salaries, fees, commissions, "tips," and profits to minimize their loss of earnings by taxes by varying their working lives. This is evidence of the desperation and increasing hostility of an impecunious British government to its historically law-abiding citizens. Its excessive requirement for revenue to finance services that taxpayers are evidently reluctant to use and pay for is weakening the bonds of mutual trust that should underlie a democratic government which spends over 40 per cent of national income on such services.

The latest evidence of government desperation is the "psychological warfare" waged against the generality of the profession of accountants on whom the Inland Revenue depends to present taxpayers' accounts. There is here a new moral dilemma for government that will drive it to retreat further from social welfare and to leave taxpayers to pay for private services they prefer by methods they prefer. If the state is indeed driven to penalize taxpayers for acts that are legal it will further risk resistance to other laws, rules and regulations over the whole range of economic life. It is a long time since the peasants of Kent (where I live) rose in 1381 to rebel against their taxes. But now I hear the rumblings of rebellion in the most bourgeois of churchgoing Kentish homes. The question must now be faced: we need to decide where the essential blame lies—with the taxers who demand more in revenue than the people are readily prepared to pay—or with the taxpayers for rejecting taxes seen as impertinently invasive of family and working lives.

There is now increasing research by economists into the extent and likely reasons for the intertwined combination of avoidance and evasion that I have christened "tax avoision." It is no longer sufficient to continue with labels that beg the question of the relative moral responsibility of the citizen and the state implied by the old term "black market" or by the "underground" that echoes the wartime resistance of the French to oppression and tyranny. I use the morally neutral term "parallel economy" as the truest description of the loss of sympathy between government and people. And the avoidance of moral condemnation offers the best hope of returning harmony by arranging taxes that people will willingly pay for goods and services they cannot buy in open markets. The best researches of the extent and reasons for tax rejection have lately revealed that it is essentially the excesses of government that have depressed tax revenues.[3]

It is no longer true, as it may once have been in the days of the smugglers and lately of the drug peddlers (and is still stubbornly asserted by government spokesmen and civil servants), that the sole or main way to maintain tax revenue is to raise tax rates. The most refined researches, by Professor Friedrich Schneider of the Johannes Keppler University in Austria, reveal that tax revenues are depressed essentially by four causes: increases in direct taxes on incomes, indirect taxes on purchases, the complexities of the taxation structure as a whole, and the severity of the regulation of industry and economic life in general. What is true in Austria is probably true, partly or largely, of Britain. In its search for finance to pay for the social welfare system, remaining after a too reluctant retreat by the state, the British government now would be wise to conduct similar researches.

Methods of Avoidance

The fourth reason for government to retreat from social welfare comprises the increasing and developing escapes to new sources of goods and services from national and overseas suppliers brought to every private home

3. Professor Friedrich Schneider, "The Shadow Economies of Western Europe," *Economic Affairs*, 17, 3 (September 1997) 42–8.

by the Internet. There is much to be said about all the rapidly accelerating developments that ease "escapes" from government; I settle on barter as the most natural but most neglected escape. Barter can enable otherwise law-abiding citizens to exchange personal services produced by specialized skills. As such it is designed essentially to benefit friends, neighbours, members of clubs and other associations in widening circles by producing nonmonetary "incomes" nominally otherwise taxable. There are no official statistics or estimates of this return to natural exchange, but the informal evidence indicates substantial development in recent years. This is undoubtedly likely to form a rapidly increasing feature of British private and communal life. The quiet grassroots revolution in the form of local exchange and trading systems (LETS) has been recorded by the press over a period of several years. Most lately it has been documented by consistent research in England.[4] Such exchanges can be seen as a new form of spontaneous private welfare rescuing people with low incomes, or no incomes at all, from avoidable poverty. The latest development sees it lubricating barter exchange by forms of local "money." Simple barter is difficult to arrange because it requires a double coincidence of wants: individuals must want precisely what other individuals offer. This pure exchange of barter is eased by a new kind of "money" that satisfies its essential economic function as anything that is generally acceptable in exchange.

There was a time when barter meant the direct exchange of goods for other goods by specialists in complementary skills—for example, primitive farmers exchanging with hunters. In the 1990s or earlier, informal local currencies have been easing exchange between people of modest means through a modern form of what Samuel Smiles would have called "Self-Help" in local exchange and trading systems. In West Norfolk, the new money is called "shells." In Greenwich the name is "anchors," in Brixton "bricks," and in Manchester and no doubt other former textile areas of the North West "bobbins."

In parts of Yorkshire a new currency is being used, in effect "exchanged," for personal services—house maintenance, gardening, and childminding—and for everyday goods—food and (second-hand) clothing. Its use is being further extended to training or tuition in manual or artistic skills as in painting and cooking.

These are early forms of a new growth of informal exchanges in free markets that will liberate unused skills and create new forms of income. They il-

4. G. Seyfang and C. C. Williams, "Give DIY Economics a Break: Local Exchange and Trading Systems Are a Great Benefit to the Unemployed," *New Statesman*, 27 March 1998, 24.

lustrate the old truth, long forgotten, that the people have been misled to expect government to provide services they could better provide for themselves. In King's Lynn and West Norfolk the LETS have developed mutual aid by advice and assistance in everyday activities that encourage local communal life. The far-reaching potential of this spontaneous development is being harnessed by local authorities. The European Commission has incorporated the promotion of LETS into urban and regional development. The obstacle so far seems to be government in Whitehall. The uncertainty whether LETS earnings will count against social security benefits has discouraged participation by unemployed people. The Federal Government of Australia encourages such forms of exchange precisely as a new way to find work training and experience. The possibility of exonerating LETS from Whitehall rules might liberate many more people into dispensing with the state welfare for which they cannot or will not pay.

The Culpability of Overgovernment

The pioneering spirit of the English, which created the merchant venturers, the East India Company, and the entrepreneurial risk-taking spirit that prompted innovation in British industry, have not been conspicuous in the structures of the post-war government. These structures created the latest expansion in social services but there is now a reluctance to retreat in the face of economic change. The lack of a clear understanding of the imperatives of retreat is now revealed in the four divergent approaches to the belated reforms.

The Secretary of State for Education is at least willing to invite advice from people with experience of running the private schools that have transcended the defects of the state system and its schools: generally lower standards of performance, unruly behaviour including assault of teachers, and truancy. The difficulty remains of building advice services from private organizations. Moderate investors must be persuaded to risk their savings with schools sanctioned by central government and run by local officials with little knowledge of and less sympathy with the commercial skills required for the high efficiency demanded in competitive private schooling.

The Secretary of State for Health sees no flaws in a state system that has chronically failed to raise as much funding as healthcare systems in all other western countries in Europe, and even more in North America, where combinations of tax financing with optional private insurance raise far more—35 percent more in Europe, 50 per cent in Australasia, 60 per cent in the

USA—than in the British National Health Service (NHS). He is prepared to continue a fifty-year-old system unchanged on the same principles—no knowledge of costs—for a further fifty years. A century of the NHS which learns nothing from other countries would look sadly out of place in the likely world of the twenty-first century.

The government has no fundamental solution for improving the conditions in which five million elderly couples live out their years in *council housing* or high-rise blocks. These long-outdated structures cannot be adapted to the much higher standards of private owners or tenants, not least among their own children. Government expedients include short-term increases in yet more subsidies to patch up council homes which will be of little interest to younger people as their new homes in 2010 or 2020; alongside this stands the latest drastic and desperate expedient of demolishing large numbers of council homes in the slums.

The fourth service, the unfunded "pay-as-you-go" *National Insurance pension,* has finally been acknowledged as a failure that will not produce the higher incomes in retirement that most people have come to expect. The new proposal for a compulsorily funded private pension paid by insurance and invested to yield the income to pay the pensions is a confession of failure of statesmanship. It comes too late to save enough for the incomes that will be required in old age by those already over the age of fifty-five.

All these state services are destined to be perpetually short of the tax funds necessary to raise their standards. The only long-term solution is to recognize that they were created when tax revenue seemed secure. The ultimate solution in the twenty-first century is for the state to accept the necessity to retreat in good order by returning taxes to the parents, patients, tenants and pensioners to enable them to buy schools, hospitals, homes and pensions of their own choice on the open market. The sooner this ultimate retreat is arranged the more the state can help it to be orderly. If not, democracy will be seen to have no policies for an advancing society. Much of current revenue is required to repair existing social welfare buildings—schools, hospitals, housing, and offices. The essential flaw of contemporary democratic government is that it requires frequent but increasingly reluctant voter approval to maintain the good order of structures inherited from the past. Much the same is true of schools and hospitals, social "homes" for the unruly young and the uncomfortable old, and the clerical offices that disfigure our towns, not least when they are newly built for the thousands of public officials who may not require them for much longer.

Most of these structures were built by government in the twentieth century; they now plague the government of today. It need not have been the fate of our children, the sick, working-class families, or the ageing if government had retreated from social welfare in the last hundred years as people built preferred services by paying fees, charges or prices. That is what they had been doing since the early nineteenth century until well into the twentieth. Little of that is taught in our school history books or discussed currently by sociologists. In 1860, the Newcastle Commission reported that three out of four working-class children were at schools charging fees paid for by their parents, sometimes aided by charities or the church.[5] After the establishment by Gladstone of local board schools in 1870, direct spending by families was increasingly replaced by indirect spending by the same people in their taxes on their purchases, but with much less influence on their schools.

Towards the last third of the nineteenth century, working men were insuring privately for medical care with friendly societies and similar working-class organizations.[6] In 1911 when the Liberals, Lloyd George and Winston Churchill, introduced compulsory social insurance for 11.5 million male employees, no fewer than 9 million had been covered for some time by private insurance. Long before, in the 1870s and 1880s, working people in the industrial north were buying their homes with the help of the early building societies. And, in 1946 to 1948, when post-war Labour, sadly encumbered by prewar thinking, introduced the enlarged pensions schemes, Attlee and his colleagues must have known that the occupational pensions begun in the 1930s were spreading and would have spread further. This was a failure of democratic government, not least in its short-term myopia induced by the anxiety to win voter gratitude by dealing with urgent, pressing, short-term "problems" that build complex distortion of policies in the longer run. The social services demonstrate more than other policies the unsuitability of politics in education, medical care, housing, and much else that can damage family and private lives. With the best of intentions, but the worst of democratic foresight, governments down the decades have expanded social welfare too soon, too far, and too long, and their retreat is now too slow.

Admirers of Beveridge have persevered with the social schemes he out-

5. Professor E. G. West, *Education and the State: A Study in Political Economy,* London, Institute of Economic Affairs, 1965.

6. Dr. David Green, "Medical Care Without the State," in Arthur Seldon, ed., *Reprivatising Welfare: After the Lost Century,* IEA Readings 45, London, Institute of Economic Affairs, 1996, 21–37.

lined in 1942, some of which he had himself abandoned in his last years of disillusion with politicians. Meeting with him as early as 1947, as a fellow member of the Liberal Party, to discuss aspects of state pensions on which the Liberal Party had asked me to chair an enquiry, I found he was busy writing a book, *Voluntary Action.*[7] In this he warned uninformed enthusiasts that the "social welfare" being prepared by the politicians would endanger the very institutions that had been built by "the people," that is, by the lower-income working classes. In 1962, when two former Fabian economists, the renowned Colin Clark and the sage Graham Hutton, joined me and my Institute of Economic Affairs colleague, Ralph (later Lord) Harris, to dine with Beveridge at the Reform Club, he lamented the fate of his national pension scheme. His saddest regret seemed to be the failure of perhaps the most upright academic-politician of the day, Hugh Gaitskell, to follow his advice and build the National Insurance Fund over twenty years, before paying the new retirement pensions. The political excuse was that the higher benefit could not be paid to other beneficiaries without including pensioners—another excuse for a short-term expedient that created long-term tensions *après le déluge.* The National Insurance Fund was for only a few years a "Fund" invested to yield income for the pensioners. For most of the years since then it has been not a fund, but rather a tank with a pipe of National Insurance contributions *leading in* and a large pipe of pensions *leading out.* That is still true in 1998, with the added burden for people approaching pensionable age that they must—by government decree—personally accumulate a second pension. One other academically-responsible politician, Sir Keith Joseph, saw the coming dilemma in the 1970s, but his political friends did not share or support his anxious vision.

The Historic Delusion

Talk of "the retreat of the state" creates apprehension among the many who have regarded it as the saviour of the sick and the poor. A dominant anxiety is that democracy has taught the doctrine of Thomas Hobbes that its creation of "sovereignty" (government power over economic life) is essential for the maintenance of good order and civilized life. The alternative to the political state with the power to regulate economic life and to coerce the people to conform to it, warned Hobbes, was "a state of nature" that would

7. Sir William Beveridge, *Voluntary Action: A Report on Methods of Social Advance,* London, Allen and Unwin, 1948.

create perpetual "war of all against all" in which life would be "nasty, brutish and short." This dire prospect has habituated the Western world into accepting and tolerating the political state with its overgovernment. Yet from the start of the twentieth century or earlier overgovernment has been an obstruction to the liberties that democracy was supposed to protect.

Hobbes wrote in the seventeenth century. His warning has long been overtaken by the technological advances of the nineteenth century with its massive rises in living standards. A century after Hobbes, at the end of the eighteenth century, it was still plausible for Tom Paine to urge, in his classic *The Rights of Man*, an early structure of Beveridge Plan benefits from maternity grants through a form of cash school vouchers all the way to funeral expenses. In the introduction to the 1958 edition of *The Rights of Man* I wrote of Paine's proposals:

> In his day this was advanced thinking. In our day we have no sooner erected a structure of state provision for the needy than it has in some respects become out of date with rising personal incomes. The welfare state is, or in a free society should be, a passing phase; but there is a danger that it will be erected into a permanent appendage: the crutch will be beaten into a shackle.[8]

So it has been for forty years since 1958, and indeed for over a century and a half. The recent reforms in state welfare call out of us a reassessment of Hobbes' flawed warning. This was rejected by the inter-war Labour-inclined scholar, A. D. Lindsay, the Master of Balliol, in his introduction to Hobbes' *Leviathan:* he argued that law is not obeyed solely because it is created by the state; rather it is respected essentially because it is wanted by the people. This truth is still overlooked by the politicians of our day.

> . . . if Hobbes is right [said Lindsay] in maintaining that without some authority there can be no state . . . he forgets that the power of the sovereign, even though legally unlimited, depends upon the skill with which it gives expression to the general will; if it disregards the general will there will come a point at which no amount of legal or constitutional machinery will avert disaster.[9]

8. Arthur Seldon's Introduction in Thomas Paine, *The Rights of Man*, Everyman's Library 718, J. M. Dent, 1906, reprinted with a new introduction 1958, pp. v–xiii.

9. A. D. Lindsay's Introduction in Thomas Hobbes, *Leviathan*, Everyman's Library 691, J. M. Dent, 1924, pp. vii–xxiv.

The legal and constitutional machinery of the twentieth century has not prevented the emerging revolt of the masses or the remonstrances of the bourgeois.

Hobbes was earlier refuted by the seventeenth-century philosopher, Benedict de Spinoza, whose Portuguese family fled from persecution to Holland. Lindsay repeats Spinoza's magisterial dictum:

> A sovereign has right insofar as he has might, and he has might only insofar as he rules in such a way that his subjects regard rebellion as a greater evil than obedience.[10]

The sovereign state is now having to retreat from social welfare and other superfluous functions. But it is retreating too slowly. The subjects are rebelling. And they will continue to rebel until government retreats sufficiently to liberate the freedoms created by economic advance.

10. A. D. Lindsay in Thomas Hobbes, *Leviathan*, Everyman's Library 691, J. M. Dent, 1924, p. xxiv.

INDEX

The text for this book is set in Minion; the display type is Meta Plus Book. Both are relatively new faces, chosen to reflect Seldon's influence on and activity in contemporary social and economic thought. Minion was designed by Robert Slimbach for Adobe in 1990. In spirit and intent it derives from the Garamond tradition. Meta, designed by Erik Spiekermann in 1993, with open spacing for legibility at small sizes, has grown into an extended family and is now widely used.

Printed on paper that is acid-free and meets the requirements of the American National Standard for Permanence of Paper for Printed Library Materials, z39.48-1992. ♾

Book design by Barbara Williams, BW&A Books, Inc., Durham, North Carolina
Typography by Graphic Composition, Inc., Athens, Georgia
Printed and bound by Edwards Brothers, Inc., Ann Arbor, Michigan